COUP DE DÉS (COLLECTION)
Books and Ideas after Mallarmé

MICHALIS PICHLER (ED.)

COUP DE DÉS

COLLECTION

Books and Ideas after Mallarmé

with essays by Annette Gilbert, Craig Dworkin, Luc Boltanski, Arnaud Esquerre, Ryoko Sekiguchi, and Michalis Pichler

Spector Books Center for Book Arts

Table of Contents

Editorial note: All book covers and spreads within this publication are depicted at 1:5, 1:2, or 1:1 scale. Unless stated otherwise (below the lower-right corner of the image), they are depicted at 1:5 scale.

All book titles have been treated in a case sensitive manner and follow the use of capitalization as they appear on their respective covers.

Mallarmé's *UN COUP DE DÉS JAMAIS N'ABOLIRA LE HASARD* is spelled all capitalized, following the cover and title page of the 1914 edition. Its short version is *UN COUP DE DÉS*.

Foreword

I am delighted to present *Exposition littéraire autour de Mallarmé*, put together by Michalis Pichler, and this catalog featuring the outstanding, scholarly works of Luc Boltanski, Arnaud Esquerre, Craig Dworkin, Annette Gilbert, Ryoko Sekiguchi, and the artist himself.

The singularity around which this exhibition turns is Stéphane Mallarmé's avant-garde text *UN COUP DE DÉS JAMAIS N'ABOLIRA LE HASARD*, or *A throw of the dice will never abolish chance*. *UN COUP DE DÉS* was first published in *Cosmopolis* (May 1897), but this edition is not regarded as definitive. Beneath the innumerable interpretations of this text that have been produced over the last century lies Mallarmé's own: a handwritten treatment of the poem that ordained precisely how the work ought to be realized. Mallarmé died the following year, in 1898, at which time his vision existed only within an exacting, hand-drawn maquette that determined the typeface, size, and spacing prescribed for each line and word. In practice, for the typesetter, Mallarmé's facsimile amounts to more than a script of text to set: it contained directions for a performance to be staged on the page and, thereby, in voice.

Mallarmé was cognizant of the work's orchestral and sonic parallels, writing in his forword to the 1897 publication: "with its retreats, prolongations, and flights, *by reason of its very design*, for anyone wishing to read it aloud, results in a score." (translated by A. S. Kline, 2007; emphasis added). Mallarmé's instructions are to *UN COUP DE DÉS* what the phrase marks and cadence are to a work of music. The poetry is as much a product of the words as the space held between them, their relative scale, and their relationship to the book format. The title invokes the dualities of fate and randomness, certainty and uncertainty. Mallarmé's poem scatters across the page and lands not unlike dice thrown onto a felted table, with geometric and numeric conviction—perhaps pre-ordained. One is compelled to investigate the degree to which the world is destabilized by variables of chance, rendered stable with intent. At a glance, one's eyes travel between the range of typographical treatments, estranged from a linear reading. The poem emerges first as an image, then as language. The result: an eruption unto interpretation, just as a dice roll depends on the stakes, it depends on the context in which they are read.

UN COUP DE DÉS has inspired, directly and indirectly, a tremendous breadth of harmonic work—much of which is on display in this exhibition. The variable forms of these works and, moreover, of Mallarmé's text itself, further complicate the concept of authorship and what is deemed authoritative. Moreover, what implications might appropriation, alteration, interpretation, and *translation*—in every sense of the word—invite to the fore? Questions of this nature emerge often at Center for Book Arts and in the field of artists' books writ large, a discipline that regards, as Mallarmé might, a book's material presence and form as aspects inseparable from and in conversation with its content—*by reason of its very design*. Moreover, these essential questions underscore the exhibition and this catalog as a whole.

I wish to extend my deepest gratitude to Michalis Pichler for the expertise, vision, and labor that went into *Exposition littéraire autour de Mallarmé*. I wish to thank CBA's dedicated team of staff and volunteers, with special thanks to Camilo Otero, Slavko Djuric, Zoe Katz, and Allison Carter-Beaulé for their efforts toward realizing this exhibition and accompanying catalog.

Corina Reynolds
Executive Director, Center for Book Arts

Essays

Michalis Pichler
Books and Ideas after Mallarmé

By now, the appropriation of Stéphane Mallarmé, and in particular *UN COUP DE DÉS JAMAIS N'ABOLIRA LE HASARD*, constitutes a genre of its own. *COUP DE DÉS (COLLECTION)* is an attempt to gather, present and contextualize these editions, re-editions, and appropriations of Mallarmé's *UN COUP DE DÉS JAMAIS N'ABOLIRA LE HASARD*, those which are attributed to Mallarmé, as well as those attributed to and claimed by other authors in a post-naive maneuver (COUP), as their own. Moreover, the collection comprises publications that feature the word constellation "*COUP DE DÉS*" on their cover. As we will see, it is especially this last criterium that both holds the collection together and opens it up toward the direction of *hasard*, or chance in French. All of these continuous re-writings of the text(s) and book(s) make *UN COUP DE DÉS* an intertextual text *par excellence*.

COUP DE DÉS (COLLECTION) is a book about books and a bookwork in its own right.

The research is heavily informed and nurtured by visiting Art Book Fairs (since 2007 having attended approximately one hundred Art Book Fairs as an exhibitor) and organizing Miss Read: the Berlin Art Book Fair annually since 2009. It is further enhanced by online research and a network of peers: artists, poets, collectors, scholars, often "double agents."

In the following, this essay will explore how Mallarmé's *COUP* came about in the first place and how the absence of an authoritative edition contributed to keep it indeterminate. We will look at how *UN COUP DE DÉS* has become a reference piece that gets, increasingly, appropriated by contemporary artists and authors who often operate independently from the commercial gallery system and gather around the networks of Art Book Fairs within a field that has been subsumed under the umbrella term "publishing as artistic practice."

We will look at the various methods employed by artists who appropriate books in books and how these methods play into the realizations and materializations of the pieces gathered here. We will also explore the totalizing principles that hold together *COUP DE DÉS (COLLECTION)* and how they in turn generate the collection, which is comprised of the trinity of its pieces, the differences between the pieces, and the vacant spots that reside on both sides of the fringes of the collection.

Last but not least, we will look at concepts such as the New Art of Making Books, "Liberature," and *Materialzärtlichkeit*, which all question the notion of the publication as a neutral container for information and argue for a consideration of the physical shape and structure of text and of publications and their materialization.

Mallarmé's COUP(S)

UN COUP DE DÉS JAMAIS N'ABOLIRA LE HASARD was published in 1897, the year before Mallarmé died, on eleven pages in a magazine called *Cosmopolis: An International Monthly Review*, somewhere in the middle of the magazine. The cover did not feature the title of the poem. Mallarmé had actually composed the poem on eleven spreads, where many lines started on the left page and were continued on the opposite page, disregarding and crossing the abysmal spine. For the *Cosmopolis* edition, these spreads had all been reduced to single pages, much to Mallarmé's dismay. It was certainly not the first text that was visually composed on a printed page or a page meant to be printed, treating the page (and the spread, that is, opposing pages) as a spatial entity, but it turned out to be or grew into what was arguably one of the most influential "visually written" texts.

But Mallarmé, not too satisfied with the actual materialization of his *UN COUP DE DÉS* in the pages of *Cosmopolis*, left copious notes as to how it actually should be printed, before he died in 1898, almost as a testamentary poem that stretched the text over twenty-one pages—or actually twenty-four, if you count the blank pages. These blank pages have to be accounted for, as will be argued here.

It was not until sixteen years later that these instructions served as a blueprint for a second edition from 1914, this time a monographic edition, by Éditions de la Nouvelle Revue Française, or NRF. That post-mortem edition, itself being a second edition, then became the canonical edition everybody refers to today. Because Mallarmé's notes left space for interpretation, and since he was not able to oversee that edition due to his death, there can be no authoritative edition; the idea of the book is a radical indeterminacy. That, though, appears to be in line with Mallarmé's claim that equivalent to creating is "the notion of a thing that evades, that is missing."[1]

1 Stéphane Mallarmé, "I(1894)" in *Œuvres complètes*, vol. 2, ed. Bertrand Marchal (Paris: Gallimard, Bibliothèque de la Pléiade, 1998–2008), 68.

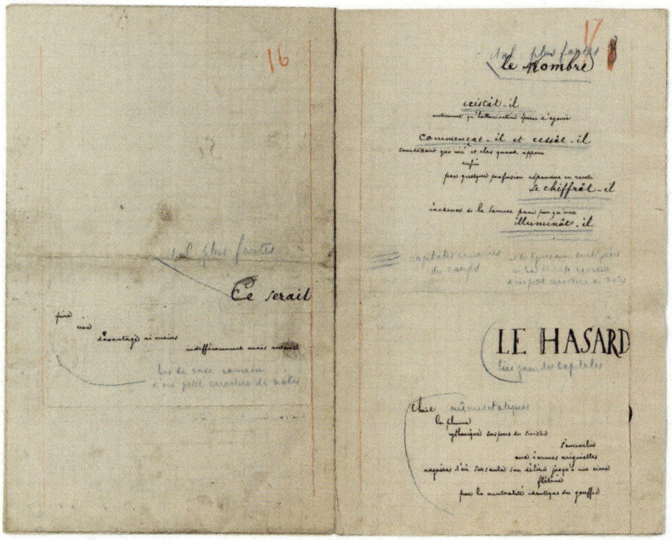

Fig. 1. Mallarmé's manuscript with meticulous notes for *UN COUP DE DÉS*, which served for the phantom edition of Ambroise Vollard, 1896.

This absence of an authoritative edition also somehow keeps the case open, forever unclosed. This opens up a space much like what poet Ryoko Sekiguchi explains as "*Nagori* (名残), where attachment, longing and temporalities interweave." She continues, writing that

> the etymology of the word is related to *nami-nokori* (波–残り), the 'remains of waves,' referring to the imprint left on the sand by waves as they retreat from the beach. The traces of waves, these ephemeral furrows drawn into the sand by them, and also the algae, shells, small driftwood and pebbles which have been washed ashore and remain there. There is neither sense nor reason in these sediments, but once they are there, they settle down for a short, transient time.[2]

According to Sekiguchi, the concept of nagori describes the after-season, or more precisely, "the longing for the season which has left us," and is related to the concepts of *hashiri* (走り) and *sakari* (盛り), which describe the "early-season" and the "main-season." *UN COUP DE DÉS*, though, never having reached sakari, forever oscillates between hashiri and nagori.

Therefore, *UN COUP DE DÉS JAMAIS N'ABOLIRA LE HASARD* must forever remain an infinite fragment, much like the Propylaia (Προπύλαια), the entrance building to the Acropolis in Athens, whose realization had to be interrupted due to the outbreak of the Peloponnesian War in 431 BC. A reduction of

2 Ryoko Sekiguchi, *Nagori. La nostalgie de la saison qui s'en va* (Paris: P.O.L. Éditeur, 2019), English translation by the editor and Misaki Kawabe, in this volume.

Fig. 2. Propylaia (west-wing and central hall, outside walls). Photo: Michalis Pichler, 1997.

Fig. 3. Lifting boss on the outside wall of the west-wing, Propylaia. Photo: Michalis Pichler, 1997.

the Propylaia's construction resources prohibiting completion was already anticipated in 434/433 BC, but in the intermediate years before the interruption, architects and craftsmen had begun to polish parts of the building in the inner part of the middle tract, thereby giving hints to the intention of its finished state. On the contrary, on the outer parts of the middle tract and the west wings, the walls were not polished, and some of the lifting bosses were not even removed. The interesting twist here is that, considering the usual building process of marble temples in the fifth century BCE Greece, the premature polishing of these walls and execution of the cannelures of the columns would not have made sense and would have even put these parts of the building at risk of damage if, at a later point, they would have attempted to finish the entire building. Therefore, it is fairly safe to assume that, from some point on, Propylaia were planned and conceptualized as a fragment and punctuated with "consciously placed quotations of completion."[3]

"To prove, through the realized parts, that it exists, and that I at least recognized that which I was not able to create,"[4] said Mallarmé about *Le Livre*, but it somehow suits UN COUP DE DÉS just as much. It is in this sense that Maurice Blanchot stated "the work is the expectance of the work," and that, "UN COUP DE DÉS is the book to come."[5]

3 Thanassis E. Kalpaxis, *Hemiteles* (Mainz: Philipp von Zabern, 1986), 128.
4 Stéphane Mallarmé, autobiographical letter to Verlaine, 1890.
5 Maurice Blanchot, "Das Kommende Buch" in *Der Gesang der Sirenen* (Frankfurt am Main; Berlin; Wien: Ullstein, 1982).

Appropriation of Books in Books

Since then, we have seen countless re-editions, both attributed to Mallarmé but also by and attributed to other authors and artists, who took Mallarmé's *UN COUP DE DÉS* as material for primary texts and artworks in their own right.

Over decades, *UN COUP DE DÉS JAMAIS N'ABOLIRA LE HASARD* has seen numerous editions, anthologized editions of his œuvre (which usually do not feature the title of the poem on their cover), monographic editions, bilingual editions, illustrated editions, all attributed to Mallarmé, while the illustrations have been attributed to other artists and were considered to run parallel to the text.

As early as 1931, though, something interesting happens, and the illustrations start to get integrated with the text, which in turn complicates the notion of authorship. The poet and physiologist Camille Soula's and Ernest Frankel's editions (from 1931 and 1960, respectively) are early manifestations, which still figure as hybrids, something between a text attributed to Mallarmé and something of their own, even though their interpretative drawings that go with the text are clearly primary information and engage in the writing of a palimpsest. Mario Diacono's and Marcel Broodthaers's editions (from 1968 and 1969, respectively) take it a step further by putting their own name on the cover or on the title page.This body of work is growing so rapidly that it is safe to claim that by now the appropriation of Mallarmé constitutes a genre of its own.

As was argued elsewhere,[6] there are varieties of strategies that are employed by these "post-naive" authors, who appropriate books in books:

1. the strategic use of found and pre-used material, be it image, object, sound, text, or thought
2. the use of an existing layout scheme or corporate identity (…)
3. the 1:1 use or paraphrase of a historic title, using the same or alluding words, syntax, or rhythm
4. the reenactment of an "old" concept with "new" material
5. the reenactment of "old" material with a "new" concept
6. the making available of (hard-to-find) material by providing a file or physical copy, be it authorized or not, be it with or without claims to second-order authorship
7. if a book paraphrases one explicit historical or contemporary predecessor in title, style and/or content, this technique is what i would call a "greatest hit."

In the last line, the term "greatest hit" is introduced to designate a *certain* kind of appropriation, one which makes a 1:1 reference to a specific predecessor.

6 The following list was first assembled in the essay "Appropriation" (2009), see https://www.printedmatter.org/programs/critical-essays/5-appropriation and elaborated in "Art History and Karaoke: Introducing Books and Ideas after Seth Siegelaub," in *BOOKS AND IDEAS AFTER SETH SIEGELAUB*, ed. Michalis Pichler (New York: Center for Book Arts / Berlin: Sternberg Press, 2016).

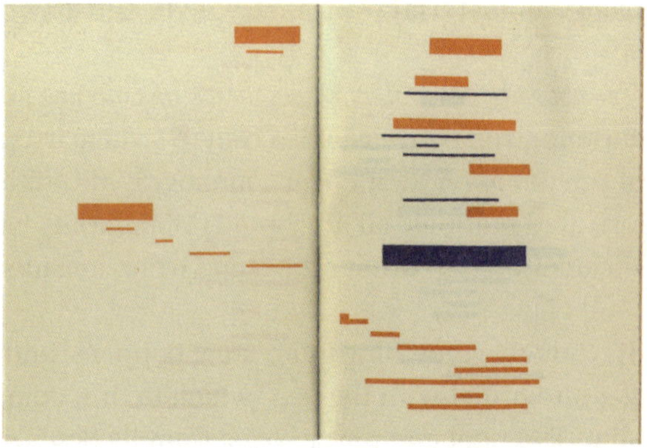

Fig. 4. Overprinting of the text with image/bars: Mario Diacono (1968).

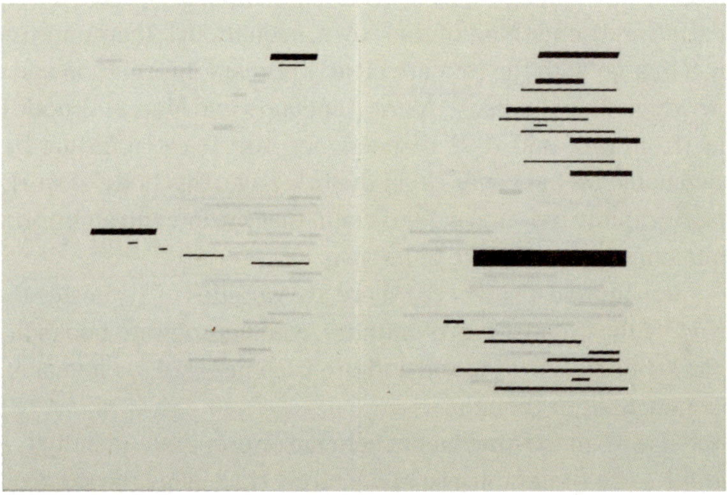

Fig. 5. Overprinting of the text with image/bars: Marcel Broodthaers (1969).

An interesting phenomenon is the fact that some of these appropriations tend to have been invented almost at the same time or shortly after one another. In 1969, Marcel Broodthaers overprinted *UN COUP DE DÉS* in a way that corresponded directly to the typographic layout used in the 1914 NRF edition and titled the book *UN COUP DE DÉS JAMAIS N'ABOLIRA LE HASARD (IMAGE)*. Much lesser known is the fact that a year before, in 1968, Mario Diacono had already produced a version in which Mallarmé's same lines were overprinted by rectangular stripes while italicized lines were overprinted using parallelograms, a feature that was also used by Broodthaers and later, by Guido Molinari and Michael Maranda.

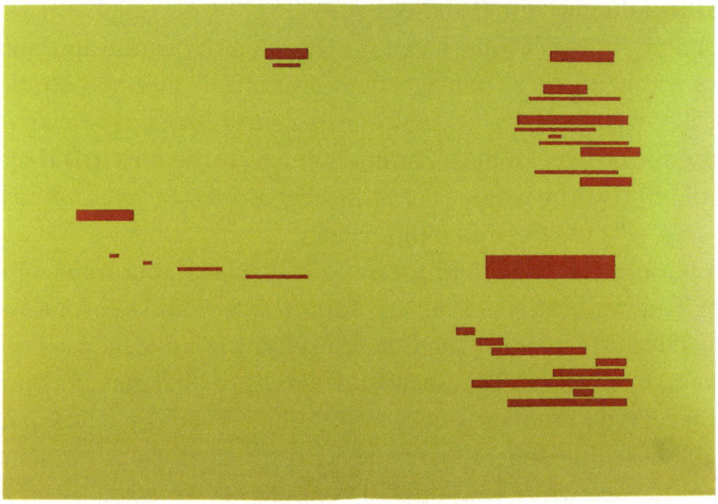

Fig. 6. Overprinting of the text with image/bars: Guido Molinari (1985).

Fig. 7. Overprinting of the text with image/bars: Michael Maranda (2008).

Decades later, some artists started cutting out or engraving these same stripes, publishing them as a book as well as creating a multiple as spatial installation (Pichler, 2008) or producing unique gallery wall pieces (Wyn Evans and Gericolais, 2009).

An exponential acceleration in the occurrence of these appropriations of Mallarmé's (and also Broodthaers's) UN COUP DE DÉS can be detected in the twenty-first century, and Annette Gilbert's anthology *Reprint / Appropriation (&) Literature* (Luxbooks, 2014) lists seven of these, or if accounting for *La Bibliothèque Pirate* by La Bibliothèque Fantastique, eight. Many of these oscillate in ambivalence between affirmation, repetition, and catechesis of the canon and its intertwining, renegotiating, and transformation.

Bibliophagia, not Homage

Unfortunately, it has become a comforting habit to dismiss appropriation of books within books as homage, fandom, and subaltern prostration to masters of—usually Euro- or Anglocentric—art history. However, nothing could interest us less. Homage, or not homage, is the fork in the road here, a point of bifurcation, where *COUP DE DÉS* becomes *COUP DE DENTS*,[7] a bite. It is time to counter homage with bibliophagia.

Bibliophagia "is not subjection (a catechesis), but transculturation, better: a 'transvaloration'. It is both appropriation and expropriation, de-hierarchization, deconstruction. Everything gone, which is not ours, deserves to be negated. That means: deserves to be eaten, devoured," wrote Haroldo de Campos (about anthropophagia).[8] We make many acquaintances, choosing but a few as favorite meal. We are polemists, but also anthologists: we devour only the opponents we consider courageous.

Melanie Strasser picks up de Campos's notion of cannibal translation and insists that cannibal translation beats the drum of liberation. The bibliophage breaks away from all forms of subservience to the original. He neither suffers from an inferiority complex nor does he know the nostalgia.[9]

Translation as a cultural metaphor and practice makes it possible to renew what is given, to read it again instead of negating it or merely imitating it, and thus, also to undermine the hierarchy between one's own and the foreign, identity and difference, original and translation. It becomes a starting point for a rethinking of the past, one's own tradition—ultimately for thinking of translation as a medium for the reappropriation of the European canon.[10] Reading, translating, is an act of critique, a reconstitution of history, tradition, and memory and also an act of self-positioning and relating oneself to it. Instead of monologue and monopoly, cannibalistic translation, in which transformation is inevitably inscribed, creates polyphony, achronology, the possibility of utopia. Translation is criticizing, analyzing, dissolving, transforming, and creating.[11]

The reading of bibliophagia is a roaming around, a permanent curvature, a circular movement, and it has nothing in common with the movement of progress. It is a reading of rubble and ruins, of garbage and leftovers, of the expelled and the lost. Bibliophagia draws a circular relationship between original and translation. The anthropophage cum bibliophage "is not just someone who fights, who kills and eats. He is ignited at the same time, he burns, is eaten by what he loves (…) Eating the other, speaking the other means exposing oneself to the risk of silence, the danger of being devoured by the other."[12]

7 *COUP DE DENTS* was coined by Haroldo de Campos in the footsteps of Oswald de Andrade's *Marxilar dialects*. Andrade signed articles in his *Revista de Antropofagia* (1928–9), with the pseudonym Marxilar, making a wordgame, by Marx with *maxilar* (the jawbone). Before de Campos, Helene Cixous had already said "Jamais un coup de dents n'abolira le hasard alors qu'il ne manquerait pas de faire couler le sang du Sujet." (A pair of teeth will never abolish chance, even though it will inevitably spill the subject's blood) in *Neutre* (1972).

8 Haroldo de Campos makes this point about anthropophagia, precisely not from the submissive and conciliatory perspective of the good savage, in "Da razao antropofagica," in *Latin American Literary Review* 14, no. 27, Brazilian Literature (Jan.–Jun., 1986): 42–60.

9 Melanie Strasser, "Kannibalogie," (Vienna: Turia + Kant, 2020), 77. Translations by the author.

10 Strasser, 40, 56.

11 Ibid., 71.

Bibliophagia "is characterized by a double dialectic of give and take. In a paradoxical movement, it affirms and denies the other and at the same time affirms and negates itself."[13]

As the age is miraculous, bibliophagia was born from the dynamic rotation of destructive factors:

Cutting, tearing out
Glueing in
Collage
Surgical interventions: *Penetrage*, recto-verso collage
Negative space: holes, cuts, cutting windows and tunnels
Lost situations
Objet perdu
The verso of fragments
Doppelgänger
Chamaeleons
Butterflies
Production mistakes
Shadows when turning the page
Pages glued together
Erasing, filtering, highlighting
Crossing
Queering
Blacking
Rebinding
Folding
Inserted pages
Cut-off spines
Invention, through copy and surprise.[14]

Collecting *UN COUP DE DÉS (COLLECTION)*

According to Luc Boltanski and Arnaud Esquerre, "a collection is an accumulation of entities, which in order to be collectable, have to physically materialize."[15] Boltanski and Esquerre also insist that "in order to be subsumable under a totalizing principle, every possible thing can become part of a collection." These totalizing principles (or the collection criteria), in turn, *generate* the collection, define its limits, borders, and its fringes, which reside around these borders, and define the phantasma of a complete collection. "A systematic collection is thus based on a premeditated repetition," and in our case, in a premeditated repetition of Mallarmé's poem, either under his or someone else's

12 Ibid., 67.
13 Melanie Strasser makes this point about anthropophagia. See "Kannibalogie," 91.
14 The latter paragraph and list is pulled from "Bibliophagia," first printed in Michalis Pichler, "Bibliophagia," in *Counter-Signals* 4, "Identity Is the Crisis" (2021), 184–85, 185, and also published online at *herri magazine* 7 (Stellenbosch, South Africa), 2021, https://herri.org.za/7/michalis-pichler/.
15 Luc Boltanski, Arnaud Esquerre. *Enrichment: A Critique of Commodities* (Cambridge: Polity, 2020).

Fig. 8. Georges Bielec, *LE DESTIN SUR UN COUP DE DÉS* (Paris: Éditions EVILFRANCE, 1982). 1:1

authorship, as well as, alternatively, any book that carries the phrase "COUP DE DÉS" on its cover. Through this third criterion, the collection opens up toward the world of books and creates a gateway (Propylaia) for coincidences (hasard) and for coincident but specific objects of printed matter, which then inscribe themselves into the collection. After Boltanski and Esquerre:

> A collection properly so called includes three sorts of entity. First of all, necessarily, there are things. But, secondly, there must be differences, and we can even go so far as to say that a collection is above all a collection of differences, even if those differences become pertinent only insofar as they are deposited in things.[16]

And finally, they introduce a third sort of entity, which they designate by the term *lack*: "to say that every collection is composed at once of things that bear differences and of lacks means that things that are missing are always present, at the heart of the collections, but precisely in the form of lacks."[17]

COUP DE DÉS (COLLECTION) is gathering mechanically reproduced material and is generated by the following governing principles:

1. Editions and re-editions of *UN COUP DE DÉS JAMAIS N'ABOLIRA LE HASARD* under Mallarmé's authorship, either as:
   – monographic
   – bilingual
   – anthologized/collected editions
   – an appendix to theory (but reproduced in full)
   – illustrated editions (where the illustrations are credited to an artist, but the text is credited to Mallarmé)
2. Editions of *UN COUP DE DÉS JAMAIS N'ABOLIRA LE HASARD*, or of texts, editions, or artworks that explicitly refer to it, under the authorship of other artists and authors:
   – hardcore 1:1 appropriations ("greatest hits")
   – softer appropriations that loosely refer to *UN COUP DE DÉS*, re-using text fragments or formal elements
3. Books that feature the phrase *COUP DE DÉS* on their cover (either referring to Mallarmé or not):
   – secondary literature, critical writing by writers and philosophers who discuss Mallarmé's *UN COUP DE DÉS*
   – books that only carry the phrase *COUP DE DÉS* on their cover without referring to Mallarmé (hasard section)
   – military books that use the phrase as a strategical term
   – game manuals that use the phrase
   – novelists who use the term, often in trivial literature (three-penny novels, also comics)
   – series that are titled after it.

16 Ibid.
17 Ibid.

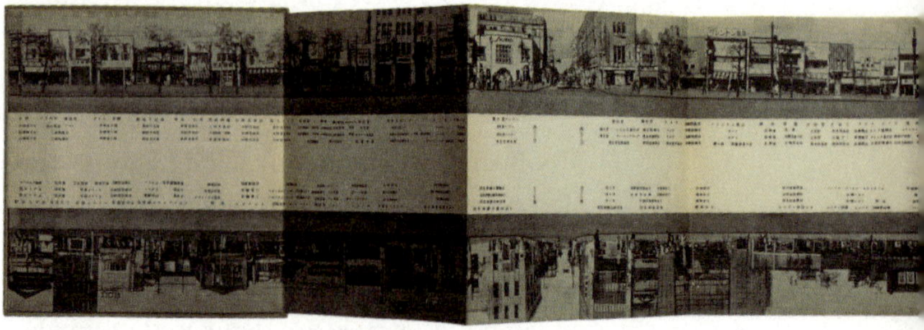

Fig. 9. 鈴木芳一 (Yoshikazu Suzuki), 銀座八丁 (Ginza Haccho), Tokyo, Toho-Shuppan, 1954.

Publishing as Artistic Practice

If the 1960s and 1970s were the heyday of *artists' books*, the 2010s (and 2020s) strike us as the heyday of *publishing as (artistic) practice*. Art Book Fairs are at the center of that. Most of the authors who have engaged in producing their versions of *UN COUP DE DÉS* have, sooner or later, showed up at Art Book Fairs and operate within the ecosystems that surround these events.

Other related collection areas of appropriations, or works that are created by means of applying the aforementioned methods of appropriation, uncreativity, and the post-naive, are, for instance:

1. Books and ideas after Edward Ruscha

The collection area of Books and ideas after Edward Ruscha is relatively differentiated and of vast occurrence. In the first place, artists Yann Serandour, Tom Sowden, Hermann Zschiegner, Jeffrey Brouws, myself, and also Ruscha have acted as collectors of the genre (as have, more recently, antiquarians like 6books).

These collections have generated group exhibitions such as *Follow(ed) After Hokusai* at Arnolfini, Winchester Gallery at the University of Southampton, and Gallery P74, and *Books & Co* at Gagosian New York, Paris, and the Brandhorst Museum, and have been catalogued in publications such as *SIX HANDS AND A CHEESE SANDWICH* (2011, "greatest hits" and Zavod P.A.R.A.S.I.T.E.) and *VARIOUS SMALL BOOKS* (2013, MIT Press).

2. Preceding Ruscha, books and ideas after Katsushika Hokusai

As a provisional starting point, the collection assembled by Tom Sowden and myself opened up to pre-Ruscha and post-Hokusai publications containing numerical titles with definite and indefinite enumerations of Hokusai's *Thirty-Six Views of Mount Fuji*, as well as *100 Views of Mount Fuji*.

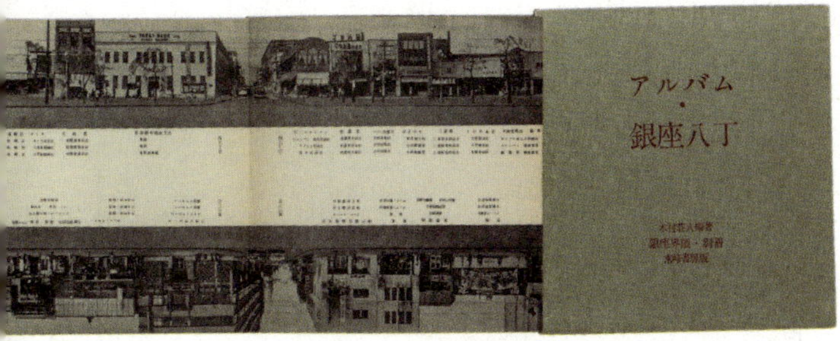

Ginza Haccho (Every Building on 8 Blocks in Ginza) by Yoshikazu Suzuki proved to be the missing link for opening up this collection to books before Ruscha. Just as Ruscha's *EVERY BUILDING ON THE SUNSET STRIP*, but published in 1954, that is, twelve years earlier, its Japanese predecessor contains photographs of opposing street views, and its execution as a twelve-foot-long leporello makes it very likely that Ruscha knew this work, although he never acknowledged it.

3. Books and ideas after Seth Siegelaub

Another example is *Books and ideas after Seth Siegelaub*, which was featured in the 2013 exhibition *My Gallery is the World Now* at Center for Book Arts in New York and shortly thereafter published in the anthology *Books and Ideas after Seth Siegelaub*. The publications collected there, after Seth Siegelaub, were almost exclusively created in the twenty-first century.

4. Books and ideas after Stéphane Mallarmé

Besides artists, it appears to have been primarily antiquarians such as Stefan Schülke and bibliophiles such as Reiner Speck, Robert Bolick and myself, who have assembled collections of Mallarmé appropriations and organized related exhibitions. Bolick also runs the excellent blog *books-on-books*, where appropriations after Mallarmé prominently figure and which were recently assembled in an online exhibition.[18]

18 See *Stefan Schülke zeigt Künstlerbücher"* at BQ Berlin, November 26, 2009, Michalis Pichler *Exposition littéraire autour de Mallarmé* at Kunstverein Milano, December 15, 2016–January 28, 2017 and Center for Book Arts NY, January 18–May 1, 2024, *Bookmarking Book Art – 'Un Coup de Dés Jamais N'Abolira l'Appropriation' — An Online Exhibition*, https://books-on-books.com/2022/05/01/bookmarking-book-art-un-coup-de-des-jamais-nabolira-lappropriation-an-online-exhibition/; *Footprints of a Collector: Reiner Speck – Mallarmé, Broodthaers et les Autres* at Michael Werner Gallery, Cologne, May 2–July 23, 2022, Berlin, December 2022, and New York, February 2 –March 25, 2023, and *Casting Letters: Art, Books, Chance* at West Court Gallery, Jesus College, Cambridge, May 26–June 26, curated by Jessica Berenbeim; and *Homage to Mallarmé's* UN COUP DE DÉS at Turn the Page Artists' Book Fair, The Forum, Norwich, May 27–28, 2022, curated by Jules Allen.

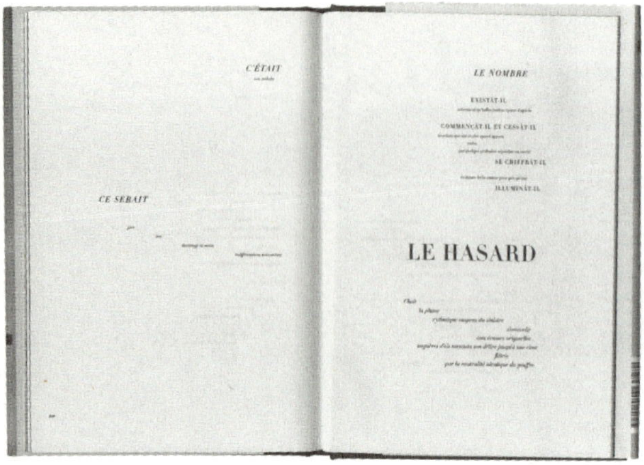

Fig. 10. (Seattle: Wave Books, 2015), 50.

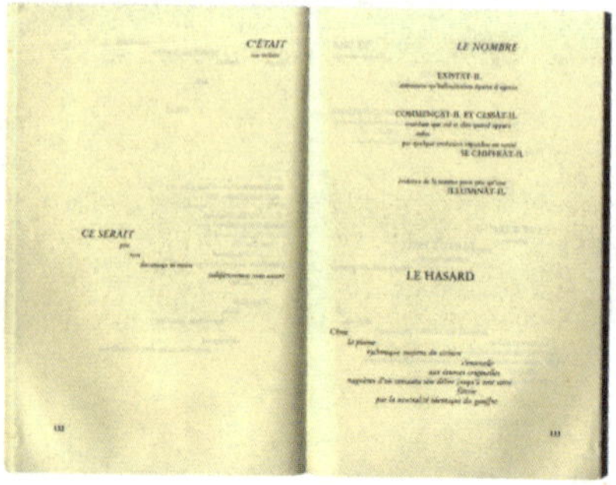

Fig. 11. (Munich: Hanser, 1992), 132–33.

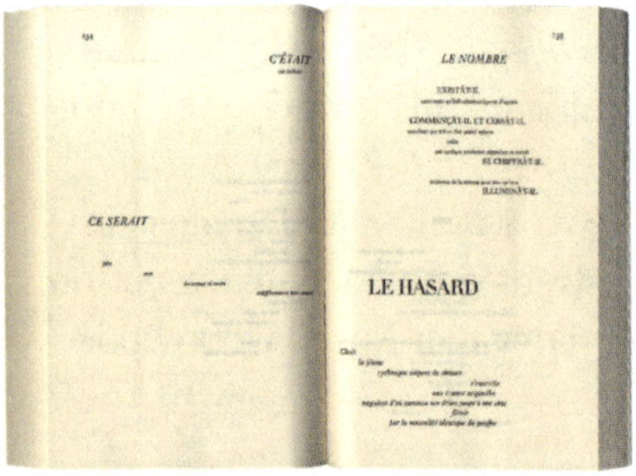

Fig. 12. (Oxford: Oxford University Press, 2008), 154–55.

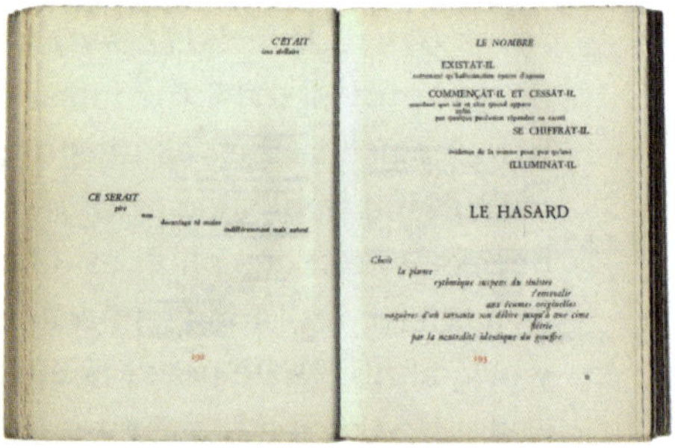

Fig. 13. (Lausanne: Éditions Du Gran-Chêne, 1943), 192–93.

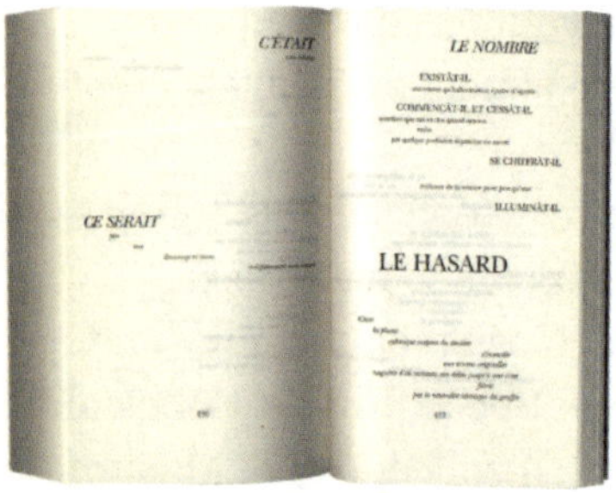

Fig. 14. (Paris: Éditions Gallimard, 2003), 436–37.

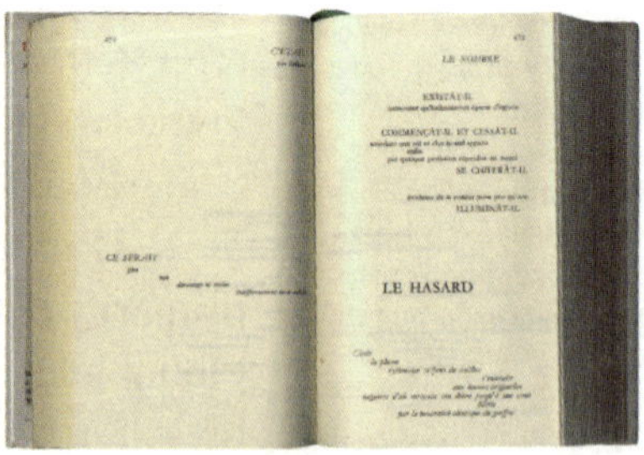

Fig. 15. (Paris: Éditions Gallimard, 1965), 472–73.

Fig. 10–15. LE HASARD spread of *UN COUP DE DÉS* with paginations.

Liberature and the New Art of Making Books

The way Mallarmé composed the poem on opposing pages treated these spreads as compositional entities, much like how a painter treats a canvas or even how an astrologist looks at the sky. Constellations of words on a page or spread and the interplay of the text fragments with the surrounding white, much like how a constellation of stars interplays with in the sky, is a metaphor that was explicitly used and introduced into literature by Mallarmé.

> The visual structure and semantic potential differs depending on order and density of the text fragments, from the position of singular words [...], on the contrasts in letter size and type style, on the resulting basic geometrical shapes (circle, diagonal, line, vortex, star etc.). Last but not least the interplay of a spread with the preceding or following spreads has an decisive influence to the rhythm of leafing through,[19]

as Annette Gilbert writes about approximating Mallarmé's notion of *constellation* to Ulises Carrión's vision of a "new" book. "In the old art, to read the last page takes as much time as to read the first one. / In the new art the reading rhythm changes, quickens, speeds up."[20]

The recto-verso sensitivity of the poem is challenged by some of the numerous print-on-demand editions, where recto pages end up being printed on the left and verso pages on the right, just because there was a page missing in the initial scan, say the "dispensable" blank page on the back of the half-title page. This minor omission can then cause a major tectonic shift of the whole book, enacting hasard at its best. A particularly beautiful case is the reprint of *Cosmopolis* 6 by NABU Press, where different print runs are different in regard to recto-verso-sensitivity, making up a beautiful diptychon of suspense and delay.

Many of the re-editions, either monographic or anthologized, only consider the twenty-one pages "from text to text," starting on the first recto page with text and ending on a page with text, which happens to also be a recto page. That appears to me as if the poem was only cited in an excerpt and as secondary information, as if the blank pages preceding and following could be disregarded.

Quentin Meillassoux has criticized Mitsou Ronat's thesis that the number twelve dominates *UN COUP DE DÉS* and guides the hidden logic of the poem as outdated. He criticizes it as outdated but acknowledges the book is comprised of eleven spreads plus two blank pages, one preceding and one following, and that, therefore, the Alexandrinian metrum finds asylum in the surroundings of the text, for instance, the materiality of the book.

19 Annette Gilbert, "Afterword" in Michalis Pichler, *Der Einzige und Sein Eigentum* (Berlin: "greatest hits," 2009), 455.
20 Ulises Carrión, "The New Art of Making Books," *Kontexts* 6–7 (1975) and *Plural* 41 (1975).

prince amer de l'écueil

s'en coiffe comme de l'héroïque
irrésistible mais contenu
par sa petite raison virile
en foudre
soucieux
expiatoire et pubère
muet

rire

que

SI

(La lucide seigneuriale aigrette de vertige
au front invisible
scintille
puis ombrage
une stature mignonne ténébreuse debout
en sa torsion de sirène
le temps
de souffleter
par d'impatientes squames ultimes bifurquées
un mystère

faux roc évaporé en brume

qui imposa

une borne à l'infini)

c'était

issu stellaire

le nombre

EXISTÂT-IL

autrement qu'hallucination éparse d'agonie

COMMENÇÂT-IL ET CESSÂT-IL

sourdant que nié et clos quand apparu

enfin

par quelque profusion répandue en rareté

SE CHIFFRÂT-IL

évidence de la somme pour peu qu'une

ILLUMINÂT-IL

ce serait

pire

non

davantage ni moins

mais autant indifféremment

LE HASARD

(Choit

la plume

c'était

issu stellaire

le nombre

EXISTÂT-IL

autrement qu'hallucination éparse d'agonie

COMMENÇAT-IL ET CESSÂT-IL

sourdant que nié et clos quand apparu

enfin

par quelque profusion répandue en rareté

SE CHIFFRÂT-IL

évidence de la somme pour peu qu'une

ILLUMINÂT-IL

ce serait

pire

non

davantage ni moins

mais autant indifféremment

LE HASARD

(Choit

la plume

rhythmique

suspens du sinistre

s'ensevelir

aux écumes originelles

naguères d'où sursauta leur délire jusqu'à une cime

flétrie

en la neutralité identique du gouffre)

RIEN

de la mémorable crise

ou se fut l'évènement accompli

en vue de tout résultat nul

humain

N'AURA EU LIEU

une élévation ordinaire verse l'absence

QUE LE LIEU

inférieur clapotis quelconque comme pour disperser l'acte vide

abruptement qui sinon

par son mensonge

eût fondé

la perdition

dans ces parages

du vague

où toute réalité se dissout

Such an acknowledgement is already informed by practitioners such as Carrión, bpNichol, and Steve McCaffery, all of whom question the notion of the book as a neutral container of language (or images). They have elaborated on the ways in which the material form of text—including, in most cases, the form of the book itself—can and should be consciously engaged and explicitly considered as an integral part of the overall work of art. In this tradition, Zenon Fajfer believes that the crisis of contemporary literature has its roots in its focus on the text[21] (in negligence of the physical shape and structure of the book) and invented the term "liberature," a portmanteau/ *Wolpertinger* combining "liber" and "literature" in order to signal a literary practice that makes conscious use of the book as a compositional entity.

Many of the editions that have appeared in the last one hundred years under Mallarmé's authorship treat the paratext that often goes with it as neutral and as if it were invisible: but column titles are not invisible, and neither are footnotes, nor is pagination, nor the blank pages, nor its famous foreword.

Why would one even pay attention to the format, font, or pagination of a poem if the text is the same? Because it is not the same. One of the arguments to be made here is that the materialization of a text matters; when we consciously consider language as material, and how text is embodied on a page (or screen) or in a book not just as an abstraction in a metaphysical void, we can begin to discuss poetics in terms of *Materialzärtlichkeit*. The *materialization of ideas* puts the supposed *dematerialization of art* (or literature) from head to feet. The materialization of ideas on pages, consciously treated, insists that text is not indifferent or immune to its typographic realization and questions the contingency of how a text is put or viewed on a page (or screen). The medium that embodies text is not neutral, invisible, or transparent, and neither is language.

Fig. 16–17. Previous two spreads: *Cosmopolis* 6, ed. Fernand Ortmans, in different print runs of the POD Publisher NABU Press (Charleston, SC: NABU Press, 2010), 424–25 and 425–26. 1:1.

21 Zenon Fajfer, "Liberature: Appendix to a Dictionary of Literary Terms," translated by Katarzyna Bazarnik, in *Publishing Manifestos*, ed. Michalis Pichler (Cambridge, MA: MIT Press / Berlin: Miss Read, 2019), 100–03, 101.

Annette Gilbert
Appropriation (&) Literature around Mallarmé

Literary (Post-)Production in "a Culture of Use"[1]

Like many other areas of life, contemporary literature is under the pressure of an affluent society, which gives rise to new strategies of artistic production and the creation of meaning. According to Nicolas Bourriaud back in 2006, the crucial question is no longer "'what can we make that is new?' but 'how can we make do with what we have?'"[2] Now, the realization that "in the realm of culture, recourse to a state of nature of any kind is logically impossible"[3] has already formed the cornerstone of postmodern and poststructuralist theory since the 1970s. However, it has become more radicalized in recent years, for which Felix Stalder sees three main reasons:

> First, it has changed the standard method of cultural production. If once the author in his parlor, sitting in front of the blank page (the nothing), struggling with himself (the will), and then filling the page with his thoughts (the creation), was considered the paradigmatic model of artistic work […] this image has noticeably receded into the background. […] Secondly, the circle of cultural producers has widened enormously. […] Third, today we are confronted with less and less "nature" and more and more "culture."[4]

Against this background, a form of "literary ecology"[5] has also emerged in literature, which goes hand in hand with a determined rejection of any kind of genuine, i.e., primary textual production in the

1 Nicolas Bourriaud, *Postproduction. Culture as Screenplay: How Art Reprograms the World* (New York: Lukas & Sternberg, 2005), 19.

2 Bourriaud, *Postproduction*, 17.

3 Felix Stalder, "Who's afraid of the (re) mix? Autorschaft ohne Urheberschaft," in *Der Autor am Ende der Gutenberg Galaxis* (Zurich: buch & netz, 2014), 97–107, 100f (translated by the editor).

4 Stalder, "Who's afraid of the (re)mix?," 102f (translated by the editor).

5 Craig Dworkin, "The Fate of Echo," in *Against Expression: An Anthology of Conceptual Writing*, eds. Craig Dworkin and Kenneth Goldsmith (Evanston, IL: Northwestern University Press, 2010), xxiii–liv, xlii.

sense of a *creatio ex nihilo* of an author glorified as genius, starting from a blank, white sheet of paper. The literary practice has long since ceased to consist merely in authors themselves writing "new" texts—and in the future, perhaps even less so. There are many other methods of producing text, from copying, editing, and rearranging, to translating, reframing, and compiling, to computer generating, rewriting, annotating—and reprinting or appropriating. Following Marjorie Perloff's suggestion, one could speak of "poetry by other means."[6] Considering this multitude of literary production methods, we must think beyond the absolutization of writing, as Austrian experimental poet H. C. Artmann has already called for in his "eight-point proclamation of the poetic act" by stating: "there is a premise which is unassailable, namely that one can be a poet even without ever having written or spoken a single word."[7]

Appropriation & Literature = Appropriation Literature

Media-historical Caesura and Discursive Environment

From this perspective, appropriation literature—a term I introduced a decade ago to describe the expansion and radicalization of strategic appropriation as a literary strategy within the literary system since the 1960s[8]—would be simply another variety of "literature in the second degree"[9] in the post-postmodern and postproduction era, and nothing more than another case of "dispersed" authorship. The term "appropriation literature" captures the appropriation of texts and books in books, in other words, a form of extensive appropriation of other people's works that originates in books and at the same time takes place in books themselves, and thus falls equally within the realm of literature and the artist's book.

This genre reached its first peak, avant la lettre, around 1970 with works by Carl Fredrik Reuterswärd, Åke Hodell, Marcel Broodthaers, Emilio Isgrò, Gerhard Rühm, Jarosław Kozłowski, Tom Phillips, and Ulises Carrión. The explosive development of appropriations in the field of literature right before the turn of the millennium is due to a particular historical moment. To begin with, the infinitely growing number of published and accessible texts positively calls for recycling and a literary ecology, whose motto might be a statement by Douglas Huebler from 1969, which has recently been repeated like a mantra and transferred onto literature by the replacing of the word "objects" with "texts": "the world is full of objects, more or less interesting; I do not wish to

6 Marjorie Perloff, *Unoriginal Genius: Poetry by Other Means in the New Century* (Chicago: University of Chicago Press, 2010), 12.

7 H. C. Artmann, "eight-point proclamation of the poetic act (April 1953)," in *Poems for the Millennium, Volume Two, The University of California Book of Modern and Postmodern Poetry, From Postwar to Millennium*, eds. Jerome Rothenberg and Pierre Joris (Berkeley, CA: University of California Press, 1998), 116–17, 116.

8 See Annette Gilbert, ed., *Reprint. Appropriation (&) Literature* (Wiesbaden: luxbooks, 2014).

9 Gérard Genette, *Palimpsests: Literature in the Second Degree*, trans. Channa Newman and Claude Doubinsky (Lincoln, NE: University of Nebraska Press, 1997).

add any more."[10] This in turn brought about a new approach to texts and textuality, as well as a new approach to canon and intellectual property. Thus, appropriation literature is fostered and characterized by the post-postmodern play with references, which has become even more important in the digital age. For, "in the digital condition, one of the methods (if not the most fundamental method) enabling humans to participate […] in the collective negotiation of meaning is the system of creating references."[11]

Of course, "the impulse is not new" (Nick Thurston, Craig Dworkin, and Simon Morris cite James Joyce as a grantor: "'I am quite content to go down to posterity as a scissors and paste man'"). "[B]ut the ease and scale of scissoring and pasting are unprecedented."[12] Digital availability of texts and new techniques for word processing made it possible to copy, edit, and publish larger amounts of text effortlessly and quickly.

From Thought Experiment to Reality

This form of appropriation, described here as appropriation literature, can point to a famous—albeit fictional—literary predecessor that is unlikely to be absent from any discussion of artistic appropriation of other people's works: Jorge Luis Borges's famous 1939 short story *Pierre Menard, Author of the Quixote*, at the center of which (fictitious) writer Pierre Menard decides, at the beginning of the twentieth century, to write *Don Quixote* anew and in whose estate are actually found three chapters that match Cervantes's *Don Quixote* word for word. It always fascinated both literary and philosophical discourses that have tried to explain how Menard's work differs from Cervantes's original.

The question as to the ontological status and the identity of the work has to some extent already been discussed in the debate between Nelson Goodman and Arthur C. Danto. Nelson Goodman argued on the basis of the allographic nature of literature, which enables multiple inscriptions of a single text, all of which must then be seen as individual cases of one and the same work ("the sameness of spelling"[13]). He concluded: "who wrote *Don Quixote* or when simply does not matter to the identity of the work."[14] According to this reading, Menard's *Don Quixote* is not a new work but only a further inscription of Cervantes's text, that is, a further manifestation of the same work, similar to every textually identical copy of *Don Quixote* by Cervantes.[15]

10 Douglas Huebler, [untitled], in *On Art. Artists' Writing on the Changed Notion of Art After 1965/Über Kunst. Künstlertexte zum veränderten Kunstverständnis nach 1965*, ed. Gerd de Vries (Cologne: DuMont, 1974), 117. Huebler's statement is quoted, for instance, in Dworkin, "The Fate of Echo," xliii; Kenneth Goldsmith, "A Week of Blogs for the Poetry Foundation," in *The Consequence of Innovation: 21st Century Poetics*, ed. Craig Dworkin (New York: Roof Books, 2008), 137–150, 144, Michalis Pichler, "Statements on Appropriation," 2009, *UbuWeb*, https://www.ubu.com/papers/pichler_appropriation.html.

11 Felix Stalder, *The Digital Condition* (Cambridge: Polity Press, 2018), 96 (emphasis in the original).

12 All citations Craig Dworkin, Simon Morris, Nick Thurston, *Do or DIY* (York: information as material, 2012), 14.

13 "Let us suppose that there are various handwritten copies and many editions of a given literary work. Differences between them in style and size of script or type, in color of ink, in kind of paper, in number and layout of pages, in condition, etc., do not matter. All that matters is what may be called *sameness of spelling*: exact correspondence as sequences of letters, spaces, and punctuation marks." Nelson Goodman, *Languages of Art: An Approach to a Theory of Symbols* (Indianapolis, IN: Bobbs-Merrill, 1968), 115f (emphasis in the original).

14 Nelson Goodman and Catherine Z. Elgin, *Reconceptions in Philosophy and Other Arts and Sciences* (Indianapolis, IN: Hackett, 1988), 65.

15 "To deny that I have read *Don Quixote* if my copy, though correctly spelled in all details, happens to have been accidentally produced by a mad printer in 1500, or by a mad computer in 1976, seems to me utterly untenable." Nelson Goodman, *Of Mind and Other Matters* (Cambridge, MA: Harvard University Press, 1984), 141.

In contrast, Arthur C. Danto, who examines the ontological status of works of art and their copies that can't be superficially distinguished from the original, concluded that a copy is never the same thing as the original, since it has a different history of production and is the result of a different historical situation. Menard's work already includes Cervantes's work as a historical reality, so that it can make reference to it. We are thus no longer negotiating Cervantes's story about the valiant Knight of the Sorrowful Countenance, but a work about a novel of Cervantes's about the valiant Knight. What defines Menard's work, and individuates it from Cervantes's story, is this doubled "aboutness."[16]

Borges himself would have surely subscribed to this second reading.[17] In the end, however, this philosophical dispute was not satisfactorily settled. Critics too often dismissed the philosophical or literary-theoretical concerns of Borges's story as mere "speculation" or "idle" discussion of an extreme case that "would never really occur," as exemplified by the following contribution to the debate:

> Speaking to Goodman: Menard's *Quixote* is not an *interpretation* in the sense of literary theory, nor, speaking to Danto: is it a *work* in the sense of literary theory. Menard's *Quixote* doesn't exist in the world of literary theory—at least not as a subject of interpretation—and thus, every literary theoretical (i.e., philosophical) speculation that treats it as a part of this world is pointless.[18]

So, one got rid of the problem by dismissing the case as pure fiction, the realization of which seemed to be inconceivable. Fittingly, the collection in which this story appeared is entitled *Ficciones*.

In the face of recent developments in literature and art, this philosophical debate needs to be taken up anew, as we are now dealing not only with a purely fictional case but also with concrete, real, existing entities. Today's appropriation literature draws much of its effect from the fact of its realization. It translates Borges's vision of recreating an existing literary work under new authorship into reality and action. Even the story of Borges, in fact even Menard's *Quixote*, has now become the object of real appropriation, as Sturtevant's *Author of the QUIXOTE* and Pierre Ménard's [Aurélie Noury] *Don Quijote* (both 2009) show.[19]

As a result, the philosophical debate between Arthur C. Danto and Nelson Goodman as to the status of Menard's *Don Quixote* and the possibility

16 Arthur C. Danto, *The Transfiguration of the Commonplace. A Philosophy of Art* (Cambridge, MA: Harvard University Press, 1981), 52 (original emphasis deleted).
17 At the very least, the narrator concludes a comparison between the two Quixotes: "The text of Cervantes and that of Menard are verbally identical, but the second is almost infinitely richer." Jorge Luis Borges, "Pierre Menard, Author of the Quixote" (1939), in Borges, *Collected Fictions*, trans. Andrew Hurley (London: Penguin Books, 1999), 88–95, 94.
18 All citations Axel Spree, "Borges, Danto, Goodman," *Sprache und Literatur* 33/1 (2002): 52 (emphasis in the original).
19 See Pierre Ménard [Aurélie Noury], *El ingenioso hidalgo Don Quijote de la Mancha* (Rennes: Éditions Lorem Ipsum, 2009), and STURTEVANT, *Author of the QUIXOTE*, ed. Museum für Moderne Kunst Frankfurt and Udo Kittelmann (London: Koenig Books, 2009).

of two autonomous works with the exact same text loses its speculative-hypothetical character. It can be observed that it does indeed make a difference whether one is negotiating the categories of originality and authorship with reference to a real book or with reference to a fictitious case: Only the former really attacks the usual order of things. It raises the stakes and the emotional involvement, and it demands, with a very different urgency, concrete, pragmatic decisions in dealing with this work. That is why it can reveal much more about our real, deeply internalized, often unacknowledged concepts of literature than any thought experiment could. No wonder, then, that the institutions of the literary world are proving unable to cope with these works: Not only philosophers, but also librarians disagree about how to deal with these works, even more so the literary world. The best evidence of this is the bibliographical indexing of such works, which becomes the arena for conflicting normative ideas about authorship when librarians take it upon themselves to override such provocations and to restore "order."[20]

Defining Appropriation Literature

Within the slow and traditionalist literary scene with its more or less candid dictate of originality, and its all-dominant focus on content and meaning, appropriation literature unfolds its full momentum only when it takes place within the same system, in other words, if the source material is taken from the belles lettres.[21] This is the crucial difference to so-called found poetry, where authors appropriate everyday, non-literary texts and incorporate them into literature.[22]

Aside from the criterion that concerns the origin of the source text, a quantitative criterion will help to distinguish appropriation literature from established literary procedures and genres such as quotation, pastiche, cut up, collage or cento. In contrast to most of these procedures or genres, works of appropriation literature as specified here don't merely consist of selectively transferring foreign texts into a larger textual context in a manner that is either contrasting (collage) or assimilating (cento). Instead, appropriation literature uses by preference whole texts or books, i.e., the appropriations are made from these only. Given the scale and the exclusive nature of the appropriation, this can hardly be called quotation anymore. Neither can we speak of collages or centos

20 The Bibliothéque nationale de France has no concerns about listing the fictional author "Pierre Ménard" as the author of the (real) books published by éditions lorem ipsum, while German libraries negate Sherrie Levine's claim to authorship for *gustave flaubert, un cœur simple*—Gustave Flaubert continues to be listed as author here, relegating Levine to the role of designer or editor. See chapter nine in Annette Gilbert, *Literature's Elsewheres: On the Necessity of Radical Literary Practices* (Cambridge, MA: MIT Press, 2022).

21 The opening up towards intellectual history, philosophy, theory, and science is based on the growing permeability of discourses and intellectual cultures, initiated in general by postmodernism, and by conceptualisms in the arts and by experimental literature specifically.

22 See Peter Handke's poem "Die Aufstellung des 1. FC Nürnberg" (in *Die Innenwelt der Außenwelt der Innenwelt* [Frankfurt: Suhrkamp, 1969]), the standard example of found poetry in German-language literature, which Handke took from a soccer team's starting lineup notice in the sports section of a newspaper. For English-language literature, the takeover of weather reports in literary works can be cited as an example, as conceived by Ulises Carríon as an idea and presented by Vito Acconci, for example, in "Act 3, Scene 4," *0 TO 9* 5 (1969): 65–70, and Kenneth Goldsmith in *Weather* (Los Angeles: Make Now Press, 2005). Goldsmith's transcription of an edition of the *New York Times* in *Day* (2003) can be considered another classic of this genre.

since this would require the conflation of at least two texts. A limit seems to have been reached, where literary studies lack the right terms for describing this phenomenon.

A further noticeable difference between the narrow concept of appropriation literature and other forms of using source material in literature lies in the qualitative focus of the appropriation. Genuine appropriation literature is less concerned with usurping and further developing the style, theme, plot, or content of a text without regard to its concrete form and the materiality of its printing or book form, such as one finds in parodies made "in the style of ...," or in pastiches, which treat "the text like a model—that is, a genre."[23] Appropriations, however, are much more strongly attached to the materiality, mediality, and paratextuality of the original texts and books from which they draw. This can encompass many aspects, including the pure linguistic material (grammatical and syntactic structures, statistics of the text, lexis, the repertoire of signs), the concrete form of a text (the text as image, typography, the positioning of linguistic signs), but also paratexts (running header, page numbers, front matters, indexes, footnotes) or the design and characteristics of a specific edition, or of a specific book (paper, cover, format, color, blurb, publisher).

This basic focus on the materiality, mediality, and paratextuality of a book or text is even more prevalent in every appropriation that is published as an autonomous entity, because in this case the author, editor, or publisher has to include not only the actual text but also further parameters, like typesetting, paratexts, cover design, and imprint into the artistic means of expression—all of which can induce a deeper confrontation with the medium of the book and open up the scope for further interventions in the literary system.

Thus, the making or the design of the book quite often plays a crucial role besides the text itself—much as the book artist Ulises Carrión postulated in 1975 that in "the new art of making books [...] the writer assumes the responsibility of the whole process" and amongst the "sequential laws of language" now also has to follow "the sequential laws of books," which is why books are no longer "accidental container[s] of a text" but rather "an autonomous and self-sufficient form." For Carrión, this entailed a totally new (self-)understanding of the author: "in the old art the writer writes texts, in the new art the writer makes books." It should be understood that the text—in its contentual, semantic dimension—in such books is only one element amongst many: it is the "book, as a totality, that transmits the author's intention."[24]

Works that in this sense result from intense reflection on the medium, and factor it into the artistic conception, could be called "bookworks" as

23 Genette, *Palimpsests*, 84. One could think of Kathy Acker's update of *Don Quixote* in *Don Quixote, Which was a Dream* (1986) or of Ulrich Plenzdorf's *The New Sufferings of Young W.* (1972/73).

24 All quotes from Ulises Carrión, "The New Art of Making Books" (1975), in *Second Thoughts* (Amsterdam: VOID Distributors, 1980), 5–22.

Carrión and Clive Phillpot suggest.[25] Zenon Fajfer's neologism "liberature" (where the emphasis is intentionally shifted from "litera" (letter) to "liber" (book)) has the advantage that it relocates the phenomenon more clearly from the realm of artists' books to that of literature: "the material book, which can be of any shape and structure, ceases to be a neutral container for a text, but becomes an integral component of the literary work. It becomes its spatial-temporal foundation shaped by authors just as they shape the fictional world represented through language."[26]

Appropriation Literature and Appropriation Art

Within the category of books sketched here—that is, of books that appropriate other texts and books in their entirety and in their materiality, mediality, and paratextuality—a further distinction is to be made, on the one hand, between book objects that are one of a kind (or occasionally also exist in multiple copies), and, on the other hand, reissued books where the books, after having been appropriated, are reprinted and, potentially with an ISBN, published in a (at least small) print run. This makes a difference since the change of status and authorship as described above does not affect only a single copy of a work. Rather, the reprint addresses the work as such.

Unlike in singular art (in which usually only a single entity comes into being, with which we identify the work of art), multiple arts such as literature (in which the work exists in several copies) raise intricate questions of what is actually to be addressed here as the work of art, for "there is no physical object that can with any plausibility be identified as the work of art: there is no object existing in space and time (as physical objects must) that can be picked out and thought of as [...] a novel."[27] Here literary studies, in conjunction with the philosophy of art, is called upon to develop aesthetic and ontological criteria for the specific oscillation between identity and difference of original and appropriation, and at the same time to consider the diverse ethical, political, and legal implications of reproducing procedures, which have by no means been fully spelled out for the literary system.

Thus, one must be cautioned against prematurely assigning appropriation literature to the realm of artists' books or deducing appropriation literature as a derivative of appropriation art. After all, the difference between art and literature manifests itself not only in different media and discourses but also in the various levels and speeds of their respective developments. Even if one is familiar

25 While Phillpot uses the term to describe "'books in which the book form is intrinsic to the work,'" Carrión maintains that "the work cannot but exist as a book." All citations Ulises Carrión, "Bookworks Revisited," in *Second Thoughts* (Amsterdam: VOID Distributors, 1980), 56–70, 67. See also Clive Phillpot, *Booktrek: Selected Essays on Artists' Books since 1972* (Zurich: JRP|Ringier, 2013).

26 Katarzyna Bazarnik, "Time for Liberature," in Zenon Fajfer, *Liberature or Total Literature: Collected Essays 1999–2009*, ed. Katarzyna Bazarnik (Kraków: Ha!art, 2010), 7–8, 7. Alexander Starre suggests another "authorial construction of the literary bibliographer," that is to say, "book writers" in a literal sense who tell their story not just in the book but through the book. Both citations Alexander Starre, *Metamedia: American Book Fictions and Literary Print Culture after Digitization* (Iowa City: University of Iowa Press, 2015), 169, 263.

27 Richard Wollheim, *Art and Its Objects: An Introduction to Aesthetics* (New York: Harper & Row, 1968), 4.

with the differences and the chronological autonomy of these two systems, it is remarkable to notice the extent to which, for example, "practices long unremarkable in the art world are still striking, controversial, or unacceptable in the literary arena."[28] "The same techniques applied to literary texts, in contrast, are likely to elicit the response that such works [...] do not qualify as poetry tout court."[29] It is therefore indicated to inspect the phenomenon of appropriation in literature against the specific background of literary traditions, values, discourses, and institutions from which appropriation literature has emerged, as well as to pursue the fundamental and controversial questions that haven't been raised in such a radical nature within the literary system for a long time.

Michalis Pichler's COUP DE DÉS (COLLECTION) *in the Context of Appropriation Literature*

This literary perspective also seems advisable in dealing with Michalis Pichler's *COUP DE DÉS (COLLECTION)*, which was presented for the first time in 2016 as part of an exhibition entitled *Exposition littéraire autour de Mallarmé* at the Kunstverein Milano and will now travel to Center for Book Arts in New York and other places. These venues show that this artistic project has so far been located and received more in the art world than in a literary context. *Exposition littéraire autour de Mallarmé* was titled after Marcel Broodthaers's eponymous exhibition held at Wide White Space in Antwerp, Belgium, in 1969. Pichler used the title and the design of the original invitation card, but replaced Broodthaers's name, the exhibition location and date with his own dates, while replacing the passport portrait of Mallarmé on the recto of the card with a portrait of Broodthaers. A faithful appropriation of a historical exhibition, Pichler's *Exposition littéraire autour de Mallarmé* is, in his own terminology, a "greatest hit" in its own right, which he defines as follows: "If a work paraphrases one explicit historical or contemporary predecessor in title, style and/or content, this technique is what I would call a 'greatest hit.'"[30] This and other statements were distributed as a giveaway at the entrance of the show, which featured Pichler's book *UN COUP DE DÉS JAMAIS N'ABOLIRA LE HASARD (SCULPTURE)* in juxtaposition with Broodthaers's *UN COUP DE DÉS JAMAIS N'ABOLIRA LE HASARD (IMAGE)* and Mallarmé's *UN COUP DE DÉS JAMAIS N'ABOLIRA LE HASARD (POÈME)*.[31] Much as Broodthaers's *IMAGE*, where the verses have been replaced by black stripes, Pichler's *SCULPTURE* is a copy of the 1914 edition of Mallarmé's poem, but with all the words cut out by laser, in a way that

28 Dworkin, "The Fate of Echo," xl.
29 Ibid., xli.
30 Michalis Pichler, "Appropriation," 2009, https://www.printedmatter.org/programs/critical-essays/5-appropriation.
31 This lineage is taken up in Jean-Nicolas Illouz, "Noli me legere: Stéphane Mallarmé, Marcel Broodthaers, Michalis Pichler, Un coup de dés jamais n'abolira le hasard," *Poésie* 172–73 (2020): 211–22. A broader discussion of greatest hits and strategies of positioning can be found in Annette Gilbert, "The Signature of the Author," in Michalis Pichler, *Thirteen Years: The Materialization of Ideas from 2002 to 2015*, ed. Annette Gilbert, Clemens Krümmel (Leipzig: Spector Books / New York: Printed Matter, 2015), 10–15.

Marcel Broodthaers
à la Deblioudebliou/S

Exposition littéraire
autour de Mallarmé

Vernissage dinsdag 2 december 1969
Tentoonstelling van 3 tot 20/12/69
Wide White Space
Schildersstraat 2, Antwerpen
Open 14-18 u. - Tel. 03 / 3813 55

Fig. 1. Invitation card (front) from *Exposition littéraire autour de Mallarmé*, Wide White Space, 1969. 1:1.

Michalis Pichler

Exposition littéraire
autour de Mallarmé

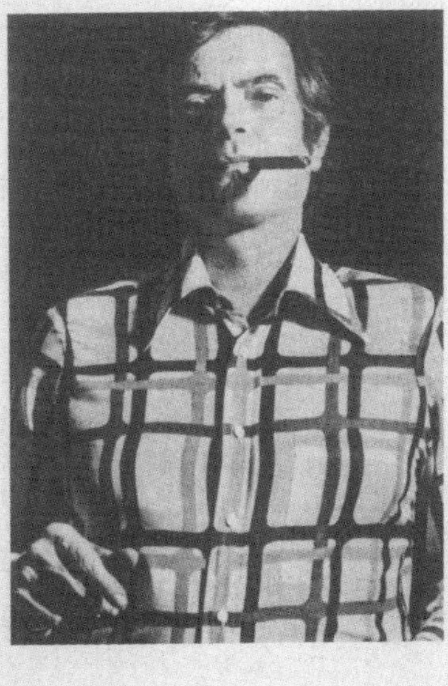

Inaugurazione 14 dicembre 2016
Mostra dal 15/12/16 al 28/01/17
Kunstverein Milano
Il Lazzaretto, Via Lazzaretto 15, Milano
Aperto lu-ve 10-16 e su appuntamento
www.kunstverein.it

Fig. 2. Invitation card (front) from *Exposition littéraire autour de Mallarmé*, Kunstverein Milano, 2016. 1:1.

Fig. 3. Invitation card (back) from *Exposition littéraire autour de Mallarmé*, Wide White Space, 1969.

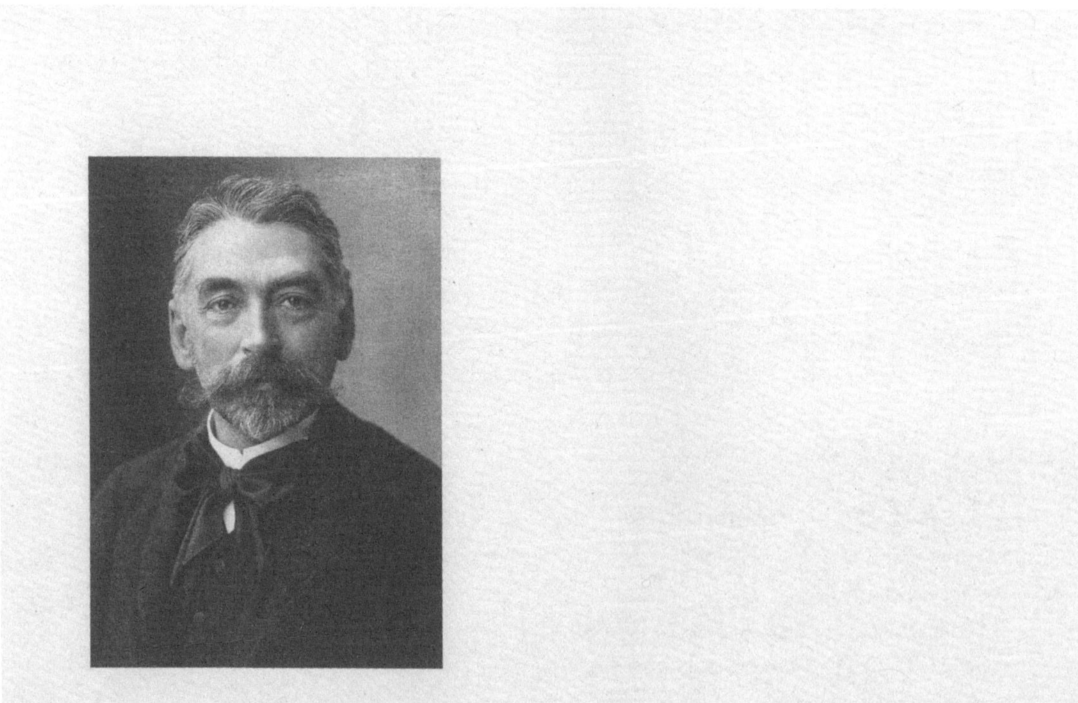

Fig. 4. Invitation card (back) from *Exposition littéraire autour de Mallarmé*, Kunstverein Milano, 2016.

corresponds directly to the typographic layout used by Mallarmé. Broodthaers, in his *Exposition littéraire autour de Mallarmé*, had presented three different versions of *UN COUP DE DÉS JAMAIS N'ABOLIRA LE HASARD (IMAGE)*: as a book on plain paper mimicking the 1914 edition of Mallarmé's poem (three hundred copies), as a book on translucent paper (ninety copies), and engraved on (each twelve) aluminum plates (ten copies) to be installed in the exhibition space. Broodthaers's edition numbers (300/90/10) were echoed in Pichler's *SCULPTURE*, with five hundred copies printed (lasered) on plain paper, ninety copies on translucent paper, and ten copies engraved on (each twelve) Plexiglas plates.

Pichler's show also featured these Plexiglas plates as a spatial installation of *SCULPTURE* installed in the airspace of the gallery and a musical installation *UN COUP DE DÉS JAMAIS N'ABOLIRA LE HASARD (MUSIQUE)* running a paper roll of the cut-out verses through the barrel of a player piano. In addition, the show included an 8mm film modeled after Broodthaers's *Une Seconde d'eternité*, two collages—and a large display of *COUP DE DÉS (COLLECTION)*, a work in progress that even then, in 2016, comprised a variety of authors and artists and that now finds a temporary conclusion here in the exhibition and catalog of 2024.

The context of this first public presentation, which has been described in detail here, seems to prove the clear positioning and reception of this project in the art world. But there was another, rather inconspicuous part of the exhibition that gives a decisive indication of the artist's own attempt to cross the border into literature, namely a reading room, which juxtaposed the mode of beholding with reading as a further possible mode of reception. This offer will be taken up in the following, and Pichler's collection will be viewed from a more literary-historical perspective.

This is not a matter of drawing a new artificial boundary between literature and art, which would be a futile endeavor in the age of the dissolution of boundaries between the arts anyway. On the contrary, the boundary between art and literature is highly permeable, just as the boundary between literature and science can hardly be maintained. In Pichler's collection, this is probably most clearly manifested in the remarkable analyses that the scholars Camille Soula (1931) and Ernest Fraenkel (1960) gave to Mallarmé's poem. For the purpose of gaining knowledge, they resorted to methods of graphic visualization, which show strong similarities to later artistic works. Pichler's collection can thus also be read as an implicit appeal to the scientific community to expand the usual range of methods and, for example, to give room to speculative, explorative approaches, for which Pichler's project itself can stand alongside Soula and Fraenkel: It positions itself decidedly both as an independent *artistic* work and as artistic *research*, which demonstratively opens itself up to chance and serendipity through its collection policy—in resonance with a dice roll as the object of the collection—when, for example, it assembles books in Section 3 that are united only by the phrase "COUP DE DÉS" in the title.

Experience teaches that such literary-inspired or literary-based projects can receive a gratifying amount of attention in the art world—often even more than in the literary world, especially if they are experimental or avant-garde in nature. There, however, they do not always find the specific forms of reception, presentation, and mediation they require—as the example of Marcel Broodthaers shows, who realized this as soon as he switched from poetry to art and held his first exhibition in 1964, when no one was interested in the literary texts that were plastered into his sculpture *Pense-Bête*. He reports:

> Everyone [...] has perceived the object either as an artistic expression or as a curiosity. "Look! Books in plaster!" No one had any curiosity about the text; nobody had any idea whether this was the final burial of prose or poetry, of sadness or pleasure. No one was affected by the prohibition.[32]

In this sense, I would like to consider Pichler's curatorial project from a literary studies perspective, since otherwise certain aspects and potentials would remain under the radar, which contributes decisively to its specific relevance for art and literary history. For it is only when one takes Pichler's *COUP DE DÉS (COLLECTION)* seriously as an undertaking that emerged from engagement with literature and its discourses, traditions, conventions, and institutions, can it play out its differential quality to similar projects.

First and foremost, Ed Ruscha, who in recent years has virtually assumed the role of *Übervater* (dominant father figure) in the discourse on the artist's book, is to be mentioned here. An expression of this is the explosion of Ruscha appropriations documented in collections such as *VARIOUS SMALL BOOKS: Referencing Various Small Books by Ed Ruscha*, edited by Jeff Brouws, Wendy Burton, and Hermann Zschiegner. It is appropriately advertised as: "With his books, Ruscha expanded the artist's field of permissible subjects, approaches, and methods. With *VARIOUS SMALL BOOKS*, various artists pay tribute to Ed Ruscha and extend the legacy of his books."[33]

Stéphane Mallarmé as the reference point of Pichler's *COUP DE DÉS (COLLECTION)* undoubtedly forms an equal counterpart to this. Mallarmé's *UN COUP DE DÉS* can be considered at least as pioneering and epoch-making in its radicalism and innovativeness. As Pichler's collection clearly shows, it has not only had a decisive influence on literature but continues to have an impact on the other arts and inspires

32 Marcel Broodthaers, "Ten Thousand Francs Reward, 1974," in Marcel Broodthaers, *Collected Writings*, ed. Gloria Moure (Barcelona: Ediciones Polígrafa, 2012), 413–19, 417.

33 Publisher's blurb for *VARIOUS SMALL BOOKS: Referencing Various Small Books by Ed Ruscha*, ed. Jeff Brouws, Wendy Burton, Hermann Zschiegner (Cambridge, MA: MIT Press, 2013), https://mitpress.mit.edu/9780262018777/various-small-books.

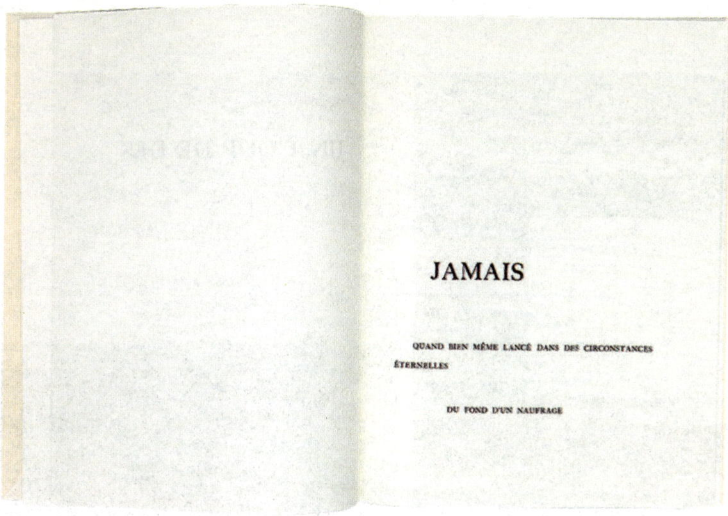

Fig. 5. Stéphane Mallarmé, *UN COUP DE DÉS JAMAIS N'ABOLIRA LE HASARD (POÈME)*, 1914.

Fig. 6. Marcel Broodthaers, *UN COUP DE DÉS JAMAIS N'ABOLIRA LE HASARD (IMAGE)*, 1969.

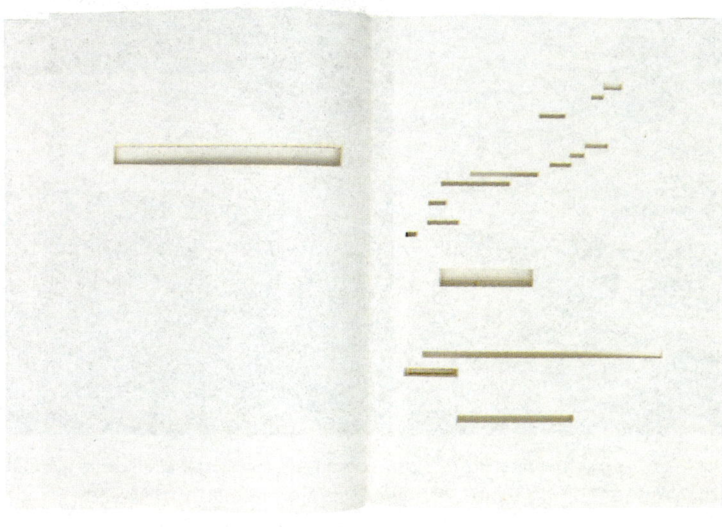

Fig. 7. Michalis Pichler, *UN COUP DE DÉS JAMAIS N'ABOLIRA LE HASARD (SCULPTURE)*, 2008.

Figs. 8–11. Top: UN COUP DE DÉS JAMAIS N'ABOLIRA LE HASARD (MUSIQUE); bottom left: open letter at the entrance; bottom right: reading room, installation views at *Exposition littéraire autour de Mallarmé*, Kunstverein Milano 2016.

Fig. 12. UN COUP DE DÉS JAMAIS N'ABOLIRA LE HASARD (SCULPTURE), glass edition, installation view at *Exposition littéraire autour de Mallarmé*, Kunstverein Milano 2016. Photo: Massimo Monnecchi. Courtesy of Kunstverein Milano.

Fig. 13. COUP DE DÉS (COLLECTION), installation view at *Exposition littéraire autour de Mallarmé*, Kunstverein Milano 2016. Photo: Massimo Monnecchi. Courtesy of Kunstverein Milano.

artists of all kinds. This radiance, which extends far beyond the literary field, is impressively demonstrated in Pichler's collection, both in the quantity of publications that echo Mallarmé's work and œuvre in one way or another—consciously or unconsciously, explicitly or mediated, strongly or weakly, in title, design, concept, or content—and in the impressive number of revivals Mallarmé's work has experienced in appropriation literature. They clearly exceed the number of appropriations using works by William Shakespeare, Marcel Proust, Immanuel Kant, Jorge Luis Borges, and other classics of literary and intellectual history.

Pichler's *COUP DE DÉS (COLLECTION)* thus fills a gap in the critical and historical treatment of artistic strategies of appropriation; at the same time, it expands the discourse around the artist's book, which is still narrowed to a few pillar saints and into which manifestations from other arts, epochs, and cultures are only gradually flowing. Pichler's collection, especially in its part two, can also be considered a meritorious contribution to the reflection and historiography of both the artist's book and appropriation literature, as the abundance of material presented gives rise to differentiations and accentuations, even corrections. Thus, the tradition-forming effect of Marcel Broodthaers's appropriation *UN COUP DE DÉS (IMAGE)* from 1969 is traced and impressively documented by means of countless successors. At the same time, however, Broodthaers's work is re-situated and re-constellated by means of the carefully assembled collection, thus significantly opening up and diversifying the field. Broodthaers's well-known Mallarmé appropriation was by no means the first, nor the only one of those years—after Pichler's *COUP DE DÉS (COLLECTION)*, one will no longer be able to go back behind this realization. Here, too, it is necessary to rewrite history and thus also the canon—not least the canon that has emerged within appropriation literature itself. For Pichler's *COUP DE DÉS (COLLECTION)* also helps to realize that a canon of its own seems to be developing within appropriation literature, with second-tier appropriations, i.e., appropriations of appropriations, being of particular importance—a genre that points towards a form of self-reflective historicity amongst the appropriationists. At the same time, however, in its exclusionary focus on a few key works, it is in need of a reappraisal, for which Pichler's field research may provide important impulses.

Pichler has already moved in this direction once before when, in 2011, he published his collection *Printed Matter and Other Visible Things on Paper Not Necessarily Meant to Be Viewed as after Ruscha aka: One Hundred Views of One Hundred Views of Mount Fuji, if Someone Says So* made public under the title *Six Hands and a Cheese Sandwich*. This project not only preceded the aforementioned Ruscha collection *VARIOUS SMALL BOOKS*. It looked beyond the canonical, European and US centric horizon and included examples of eighteenth and nineteenth century Japanese book art from Hokusai to Kiyonaga to Hiroshige as equal-ranking expressions and predecessors of that photo book tradition often associated primarily with the name of Ed Ruscha. Even then, Pichler accompanied his collection with the plea: "Eventually this perception, to relate them all 'back to Ruscha,' has to do also with the historical attention span of the viewer. It is certainly possible to span a larger arc of tension."[34]

Mapping the Field

Accordingly, Michalis Pichler's *COUP DE DÉS (COLLECTION)* was also taken as an opportunity to reconsider, re-weigh, and, where necessary, expand the principal methods and procedures of appropriation literature, which were first tentatively developed in 2014 on the basis of the works collected in the anthology *Reprint: Appropriation & Literature*.[35] In addition, recent trends and manifestations of literary appropriation strategies were taken into account and included in the "taxonomy."[36]

Reframing

"Reframing" probably describes the simplest and at the same time most complex case of appropriation literature, namely that a work is reproduced without further intervention, albeit under a different authorship, and thus declared a new, autonomous work. The only, but crucial, change then lies in the altered paratextual framing, which places the work in a new historical context, as when Sherrie Levine moves Flaubert's name into the title of the work (*gustave flaubert, un cœur simple*), or when Sturtevant puts her name in the place of Menard's (STURTEVANT, *Author of the QUIXOTE*). In doing so, they assign a different history of production as well as another level of "aboutness" (Danto) to the text, which is otherwise no different from its predecessors. Accordingly, this paratextually grounded identity of the work becomes itself the material, sometimes even the sole material, which is critically examined, artistically formed, and staged in this subgenre of appropriation literature.

Selection

Selection is the most widespread procedure, where certain elements are selected from a given body of text, mostly according to predetermined rules. This often shifts the reader's focus to certain aspects or elements of a text or book. The use of lexical, grammatical, or content-based criteria for selection is just as possible as there are works based on aleatory constraints or on selections made by a computer. Jérémie Bennequin, for example, lets the number of pips of a dice—and thus, appropriately, chance—

34 Pichler, *Appropriation*, 2009.
35 Not all the categories listed hereafter can be illustrated with examples from Pichler's collection. This has to do with the source text, in this case Mallarmé's *UN COUP DE DÉS*, that particularly suggests certain procedures, questions, approaches.
36 It must be noted that a certain degree of abstraction was unavoidable while creating concepts for the groups of procedures. This means that the categories are not sharply separable, but merge into each other, and that works can naturally fall into more than one category as they often unite multiple procedures.

decide which words of Mallarmé's poem remain. In the best-case scenario, concept and result, rule and effect, intention and chance, should all complement one another, so that, as the Oulipian writer Oskar Pastior formulated, the "rules of the game and the stroke of luck fit so optimally that they make each other necessary *and* possible."[37]

Erasure

A further, relatively large subset of the selection procedure is erasure, which may well be regarded as one of the oldest and most established forms of appropriation literature, and which has even been granted its own name: erasure poetry.[38] The difference between selection and erasure lies mostly in the strictness of the selected criteria. In creating new poetic texts that make further use of some part of the linguistic material and allow the rest of the material to more or less disappear, erasure poetry tends towards arbitrary criteria (i.e., not pre-determined constraints). In doing so, the sequence and position of the given words on the page of the original text are mostly roughly retained. It would therefore not suffice to say that these works deal with the pure linguistic material. Non-linguistic aspects like the position of the text on paper, the white space of the page, and the materiality of the color application and the deletions are deemed equally important. Particular attention is paid not only to the poetic quality of the new texts, but also to the shifting of the meaning of the extracted words in their new context.

The procedure and handling of the source material differ enormously depending on the work: the focus can be on the deleted, i.e., no longer necessary, linguistic material or on the preservation of the "useful" words. While the original text is still visible or legible in some of the works, resulting in a sort of dialog between it and the extracted text, others emphasize the independence of the newly generated text.

For our readings, it makes a great difference whether the retained words were highlighted (positive selection) or if the unnecessary words were erased (negative selection); whether the preserved words were determined according to rather liberal or "objective" strict constraints; whether the discarded linguistic material is still legible or whether it has been liquidated, that is, materially removed from the book, as, for example, in the case of Michalis Pichler's UN COUP DE DÉS (SCULPTURE); or whether it has been blacked out or whited out, as, for example, in the case of Michael Maranda's UN COUP DE DÉS JAMAIS N'ABOLIRA LE HASARD (LIVRE).

Reduction

Every selection implies a reduction of the given material, which is why a clear demarcation between

37 Oskar Pastior, "Spielregel, Wildwuchs, Translation. Regle du jeu, Ulcérations, Translations," in *La Bibliothèque Oulipienne*, ed. Oulipo, vol. 5 (Bégles: Castor Astral, 2000), 281 (emphasis in the original).

38 Of course, not every work of erasure poetry represents a case of appropriation. See Craig Dworkin, *Reading the Illegible* (Evanston: Northwestern University Press, 2003). See also Álvaro Seiça, "The Art of Deleting: A Study of Erasure Poetry, Practices of Control, Surveillance, and Censorship," *ARTDEL*, 2021, https://artdel.net.

reduction and selection is difficult. One difference between the procedures can be postulated as follows: whereas in *selection* something from the given material is chosen and preserved, in *reduction* the actual text is indiscriminately and radically omitted, as is the case in Mario Diacono's *JCT 1 a MeTrica n'ABOOlira*, so that the book is merely a container of a text comprised of parameters, such as format, number of pages, typesetting, pagination, front matter, etcetera. In extreme cases, nothing from the original text remains, and in other cases the "emptied" book is furnished with additional elements such as annotations, proofreader's marks or punctuation marks.

Interpolation

Usually, interpolation refers to a subsequent (unauthorized) insertion of words or sentences in the text of a work. This can be done conventionally by adding extra passages of text, or by adding punctuation, annotations, underlining, and corrections. One can also subsume under this procedure works where the book rather than the text has experienced a subsequent insertion and addition.

Rearrangement

A different form is reflected in books where the raw material of a work is fully maintained but newly organized. Besides the division of a text into vowels and consonants and the arrangement by means of chance procedures, alphabetization is the most common case. Its basic unit can be a single verse, a word, or a single letter. Consequently, also non-linguistic material (like numbers, punctuation, diagrams, and tables) is often affected by this dissection and realignment. The different ways that authors deal with punctuation and emphasis, like case sensitivity and italicization, are telling. Interesting observations as to the statistical frequency of certain words as well as to the vocabulary of authors and genres can be made in these new arrangements. In spite of the annihilation of the original order, meaningful relationships, even the beginnings of new narrations, surprisingly flash up again and again.

The idea of a consciously triggered but nevertheless uncontrollable self-producing character of language was something Mallarmé searched for in his vision of a "pure work": "the pure work implies the disappearance of the poet as speaker, yielding his initiative to words [...]; they light up with reciprocal reflections like a virtual stream of fireworks over jewels."[39] It is in this sense that the play with elements in some of the appropriations comes of its own accord, such as when surprisingly sensible statements or diverse visual compositions emerge from alphabetically organized texts. Such visual compositions lead away from a standard linear, successive, and

39 Stéphane Mallarmé, "Crisis in Poetry," trans. Mary Ann Caws, in *Manifesto: A Century of Isms*, ed. Mary Ann Caws (Lincoln: University of Nebraska Press, 2001), 25.

meaning-orientated reading, and open up new facets of aesthetic perception, where even the turning of the page becomes its own experience.

Variation
This procedure seems to be particularly suitable for short and lyrical texts and is often used by the authors associated with concrete poetry and Oulipo. Usually, a single poem is the starting point for a series of transformations and procedures. One could rightly question the novelty of this procedure in literary history, since there have always been variations such as parodies of famous poems (one example of such textual variations, bordering parody, would be Jim Clinefelter's *A THROW OF THE SNORE WILL SURGE THE POTATOES*). What distinguishes radical appropriation poetry from these historical examples, other than the magnitude, is the greater interest in the exploration of the material of the poem than in the exploration of its content. This material is exhausted in as many variations as possible, making use of syntax, sound, lexis, grammar, typography, etcetera, such that an entire series can make up a whole book, as Derek Beaulieu, for example, explores to some extent in *tattered sails (after un coup de des)* (2018).

Rewriting
Rewriting refers to the replacement of individual elements of the text while also retaining its skeleton. This skeleton can be of a syntactical and grammatical nature. The conservation of the sound structure or typographical design, as in Klara Vith's layout of speeches by Donald Trump, is also conceivable. Often, key concepts or words are exchanged. In contrast to other works in the history of literature that seem to be similar, these works of appropriation literature remain much closer to the text, its structure, and its materiality.

Transcript
On the one hand, transcript applies to the production of a copy of an available text. This is done primarily by hand, which might seem anachronistic today; but it may also be carried out with a typewriter, or a computer. In all these cases, the act of writing stands in the center. On the other hand, transcript also subsumes works which stray from the process of writing in a narrow sense and rather emphasize the "one more time" aspect: here, an already existing text is set and entirely published one-to-one. The focus, then, is more on the result, and it is irrelevant whether the text was laboriously copied by hand or retyped.

Texture
The works subsumed here foreground questions of visual-iconic dimensions. This can mean the staging of the contrasts between handwriting and

print. But it can also mean a palimpsest with a plurality of (handwritten or printed) layers of script or color, one on top of the other, which often entails a limitation of legibility, as in the case of Maranda's *UN COUP DE DÉS (LIVRE)*. Likewise, there are also examples of works in which the writing was printed deliberately blurred or pixilated, so that the text resists the act of reading and rather stages the image-like qualities of a text or writing.

Materiality

This class has some overlap with that of texture. Here, it is the materiality of the printing or book that stands at the center, for example, when the amount of ink used per page is indicated or the browned paper color of the original is mimicked, as in Maranda's *UN COUP DE DÉS (LIVRE)*. In other works, the ink or paper were removed with a rubber eraser or by laser cutting, as in *UN COUP DE DÉS (SCULPTURE)* by Pichler. At the same time, works that reproduce a book in photos or by scanning (and thereby show the book as a three-dimensional object) also fall into this rubric.

Transposition

In general, transposition means the transferal into another context: here, it means the transfer from one medium to another. In some cases, one could also speak of remediation. This can apply to the transfer of normal print into 3D (see Eric Zboya's and Brian Larosche's appropriations), of an audio book back into written words, of a text in another type and font, of typographic patterns into corresponding visualizations, of color words into colors, of the statistical distribution of letters into corresponding graphs, of punctuation marks into words, or of written text in sound waves (see Sammy Engramer's book).

Translation

Frequently encountered are also appropriations that ostentatiously identify themselves as translations, for instance into a playful Internet slang or a fictitious backwoods dialect. The provocation here lies in the fact that translations are traditionally regarded as derivative works for which the translator, subject to the still valid ideal of invisibility, cannot claim sole authorship. Given the rapid advancement of automated translation, there are also more and more works that present (machine) mistranslations. They follow an aesthetics of error, of alienation and disruption, which clearly has its roots in the classic avant-garde and is meant to inspire creativity and innovation. Or they may see themselves as a critique of technology, which documents the loss and violence to which translated texts are subjected when they are fed automatically "through the eyes and ears of the machine, whose misunderstanding serves as a source of sudden meaning."[40]

40 Hannes Bajohr, *Blanks* (Denver: Counterpath, 2021), 120.

Editing

Another category is formed by those works that actually seem to owe their existence to traditional editorship—another variety of derivative work—but for which their makers claim full authorship, because they no longer see editing and publishing itself as part of post-production, but as genuine literary *production*. They thus oppose the traditional model of "production-then-reproduction" with a concept of "reproduction-as-production."[41] This counters the traditional, but still prevalent, paradigm of the division of labor in the book trade, which Roger Chartier expressed in the well-known dictum: "Authors do not write books: they write texts that become written objects, which may be hand-written, engraved, or printed (and, today, electronically reproduced and transmitted)."[42]

Compilation

Works in this category are based on the processing and montaging of multiple sources. This is not a fundamentally new principle in the history of literature—there have always been collages or montages. Nevertheless, what seems to be new here is the amount of foreign material. The works are not made up of quotations that are tightly woven together, but they consist entirely of full texts by others. Moreover, the linguistic material is no longer simply quoted and strung together, rather, a given text is assembled as a series of "images" in its concrete materiality and scriptorial visuality. While in some works the points of rupture of the different materials are immediately visible, in others the compiled character cannot be seen at first glance.

Curating

There is a curatorial moment in every compilation. However, in view of the growing number of authors who understand their literary, editorial, or collecting practice as curatorial and/or label them as such, a separate category of curating seems appropriate. This reflects "the curatorial paradigm" that shapes our postindustrial and post-material consumer society. The curatorial projects within appropriation literature avowedly place centrally "the skill—or, if you will, the 'art'—of choosing," which "has become a cultural practice in its own right."[43] If the curatorial practice was previously at home in the exhibition business of museums and galleries, it can now also be found in the world of literature, books, and libraries. Following Hanna Kuusela, curators in the literary field can be described as ators "who mainly mediate, distribute, (re)present, publish, or exhibit in new contexts texts that have been

41 Nick Thurston, "Publishing as a Praxis of Conceptualist Reading Performances," *Journal of Writing in Creative Practice* 6, no. 3 (Winter 2013–14): 421–29, 425.

42 Roger Chartier, *The Order of Books: Readers, Authors, and Libraries in Europe Between the Fourteenth and Eighteenth Centuries* (Stanford: Stanford University Press, 1994), 10.

43 Dorothea von Hantelmann, "The Curatorial Paradigm," *The Exhibitionist* 4 (2011): 6–12, 8. For the parallels between publishing and curating, see Michael Bhaskar, *The Content Machine: Towards a Theory of Publishing from the Printing Press to the Digital Network* (London: Anthem, 2013).

produced by people other than themselves and who thereby create literary phenomena in the public."[44] Along the lines of the art world, where curating has now ascended to a full-fledged artistic practice in its own right, literary curators are also increasingly succeeding in creating "a new artist-like identity"[45] for themselves and inscribing their "collections" as autonomous works of their own right in their own œuvre, of which Michalis Pichler's *COUP DE DÉS (COLLECTION)* presented here is a striking example. At the same time, his artistic collections—from Ruscha to Siegelaub to Mallarmé—stand for the claim of respecting the integrity of the assembled material as artworks in *their* own right.

Dealing with Appropriations

Besides the questions of categorization and definition, appropriation literature also raises the question of how these books are to be received. How does one *read* a book that copies another book word for word? How does one read a book in which all the words are listed alphabetically or organized according to chance? How to read books in which almost all the linguistic material is cut out, blacked out, or white, i.e., invisible, or which are comprised entirely out of punctuation marks? In this way, appropriation literature "push[es] us to reformulate new tactics for reading,"[46] which require a certain openness as well as the willingness to adapt the reading to the respective work. Each of these books seems to demand a very unique, specifically tailored form of reading, much as Carrión suggested:

> In the old art all books are read in the same way.
> In the new art every book requires a different reading.
> In the old art to read the last page takes as much time as to read the first one.
> In the new art the reading rhythm changes, quickens, speeds up.[47]

This raises the fundamental question whether one can even speak of "reading" these books. In the end, according to Carrión, "knowing the alphabet is" not "enough." Yet, he allays, one does not need a PhD for the reading of these "new types" of books: "in order to be able to read the new art, and to understand it, you don't need to spend five years in a faculty of English."[48] Nevertheless, a willingness for reflection and a sense of gratification from intellectual challenges are certainly helpful to approach appropriations, just as a basic understanding of literature (its history, materiality, mediality, and its defining discourses) is not detrimental to

44 Hanna Kuusela, "Publisher, Promoter, and Genius: The Rise of Curatorial Ethos in Contemporary Literature," in *Publishing as Artistic Practice*, ed. Annette Gilbert (Berlin: Sternberg Press, 2016), 118–33, 119 (emphasis deleted).
45 Kuusela, "Publisher, Promoter, and Genius," 123.
46 Sianne Ngai, *Ugly Feelings* (Cambridge, MA: Harvard University Press, 2005), 272.
47 Carrión, "The New Art of Making Books," 20.
48 Both citations, ibid., 20 and 21.

the engagement with these books. In this respect, this new way of making books seems to confirm that the growing need for commentary in contemporary art also has validity for parts of contemporary literature where it has become increasingly more common to speak of "thinkership" rather than "readership."[49] The parallels to conceptual art and conceptual writing are obvious. Yet, such concept-driven text production can also be traced back to a long literary tradition of "formalized" texts that experienced a rebirth in the second half of the twentieth century in movements like Oulipo or digital literature.

Double Reading

Ideally, such a new kind of reading is not limited to the appropriation itself but also stretches out towards the original. Frequently, the authors themselves hold the opinion that the complexity and manifest nature of their books as well as their details are only opened up once a comparative analysis with the originals is completed. Janet Holmes—author of *The ms of m y kin*, an erasure of Emily Dickinson's poems—for example, admits: "in my ideal imaginary, a reader would feel compelled to go back to the original poems, and would experience some resonance between the originals and the erasures."[50] Here, Holmes suggests a sort of double reading, which simultaneously takes both (source and derivative, original and appropriation) into consideration, and thus reads the appropriated material with regards to its original context, as well as to its new context.

This double way of reading often opens a new view of the originals since the appropriations highlight specific aspects of the source text. Depending on the aim and the applied procedure, sudden insights about the underlying text can be generated, for example, in relation to the visual elements of Mallarmé's UN COUP DE DÉS, or monumental texts can be thawed from their historical frozen state, or original characteristics can be brought back into consciousness, or, finally, the works can also be interpreted against the grain, giving them unexpected and often completely opposite meanings than what the original statements elicited. Indeed, this subversive "double meaning" that the reused elements received "by the coexistence within them of their old and new senses" was something that the Situationists had already noted as "a peculiar power"[51] of *détournements*.[52]

49 See, for instance, Robert Fitterman, "Foreword," in *Notes on Conceptualisms*, ed. Robert Fitterman, Vanessa Place (New York: UDP, 2009), 10; as well as Kenneth Goldsmith, "We move from assuming a readership to embracing a *thinkership*," in *Uncreative Writing: Managing Language in the Digital Age* (New York: Columbia University Press, 2011), 100 (emphasis in the original).

50 Janet Holmes, about her book *The ms of m y kin* (Exeter: Shearsman Books, 2009) on the publisher's website https://www.shearsman.com/store/Janet-Holmes-The-ms-of-m-y-kin-p102838791.

51 All citations "Détournement as Negation and Prelude," trans. Ken Knabb, in *Situationist International Anthology*, ed. and trans. Ken Knabb, revised and expanded edition (Berkeley, CA: Bureau of Public Secrets, 2006), 67–68, 67.

52 By this, the Situationists mean "the reuse of preexisting artistic elements in a new ensemble," ibid.—the ideas and writings of the Situationists have had a recent revival and are often quoted in connection to appropriation. Thus, also Antoine Lefebvre's *La Bibliothèque Fantastique* has a series entitled La Bibliothèque Situationiste, and Michalis Pichler calls upon Guy Debord in his "Statements on Appropriation" (2009), *UbuWeb*, https://www.ubu.com/papers/pichler_appropriation.html.

New Understanding of Originality and Creativity

It follows from this that one must always focus on the specific handling of the appropriated material and the interplay between the appropriated and the appropriation method. This also means one must concede to the authors that even appropriations that seem disrespectful and destructive are the result of a deep engagement with the original. In this context, Bernhard Metz suggests "a specific form of truth to the materials and faithfulness to the original work"[53] that the appropriations keep to the originals in spite of everything. With Pichler, one could also speak here of a special form of *Materialzärtlichkeit* (material tenderness) that is often found in appropriations.[54] His *UN COUP DE DÉS (SCULPTURE)* (2008), with its cut out lines of verse, seems to embody this concept at its best. Besides the beauty and grace that emanates from this fragile object, even this book without any text invites reading, albeit a creative and exploratory one: through the holes it is now easy to see how the various strands of Mallarmé's poem are connected and continued throughout the entire book—an effect which inevitably remains under the threshold of perception in Mallarmé's original.

Tomasz Waszak also argues for recognizing the intensive preoccupation with the original, which can take on features of immersion, and for bringing "values such as [...] empathy, fidelity, preservation, care, reproduction"[55] into the discussion of appropriations. This seems surprisingly conservative, but it could invalidate the often-raised accusation against appropriations of treating literary masterpieces with little respect, and could be used as a criterion for the aesthetic evaluation of appropriations. Appropriation, then, would be first and foremost a critical transfer, indeed translation, of an artifact into the present, reintroducing linguistic works into artistic-literary discourse and renegotiating them.

These criteria would at the same time provide a point of reference for the evaluation of originality in the case of appropriations. Certainly, writing one's own new texts, which had served as the foundation for the creative act, is dismissed by appropriation literature as a relic of the old art. But of course, originality—despite the advertising rhetoric of unoriginality and uncreativity[56]—has not disappeared, it has merely shifted to other areas. The act of creativity takes place elsewhere. Often the innovative character of these "translations" is based "on the discovery of gaps, of still unoccupied places in the cultural archive,"[57] as Magnus Wieland has shown discussing exemplarily six different appropriations of one and the same source text:

53 Bernhard Metz, "The kite is nothing without the string: Appropriation und Contrainte/Appropriation als Contrainte," in *Wiederaufgelegt. Zur Appropriation von Texten und Büchern in Büchern*, ed. Annette Gilbert (Bielefeld: transcript, 2012), 315–30, 330 (translated by the editor).

54 Michalis Pichler, "Bibliophagia," *CounterSignals* 4: *Identity is the Crisis* (2021): 184–85.

55 Tomasz Waszak, "Der Fall Menard als Provokation oder wie die Textappropriation von der Literaturwissenschaft appropriiert werden kann," in *Wiederaufgelegt. Zur Appropriation von Texten und Büchern in Büchern*, ed. Annette Gilbert (Bielefeld: transcript, 2012), 87–102, 89 (translated by the editor).

56 See Perloff, *Unoriginal Genius*, and Goldsmith, *Uncreative Writing*.

57 Wieland, Magnus, "about:blank. Appropriationen des Leerraums seit Mallarmé," in *Wiederaufgelegt. Zur Appropriation von Texten und Büchern in Büchern*, ed. Annette Gilbert (Bielefeld: transcript, 2012), 193–216, 215 (translated by the editor).

Mallarmé's *UN COUP DE DÉS*. For the "reading" of these works, this of course means an immense change. What is called for is a discerning attitude to reception that includes the margins of the books, presupposes a certain knowledge of the original (in text and book) and its (production and reception) history, and is aware of recent discourses and developments in art and literature.

Enriching and Rewriting Literary History

In this context, the reading instruction that Borges's narrator provides might also prove helpful for dealing with appropriation literature. He attests to the fictional Pierre Menard that with his *Don Quixote* he has invented "a new technique" which—purely through the power of appropriation and repetition—"fills the calmest books with adventure" and "enrich[es] the slow and rudimentary art of reading."[58] This kind of reading would be tantamount to a rewriting of literary history and a new kind of history of influence that reverses the usual direction of the writing of history—a perspective that Sherrie Levine claims for herself when she says: "'I have the same relationship to van Gogh as Pierre Menard had to Miguel de Cervantes, that is to say, I have influenced him.'"[59]

This history of influence is less concerned with the dependence of the later work on its antecedents than with the fact that from now on this antecedence can be mediated only through what comes after it. Instead of a linear, future-oriented history of art and literature, in which the past predetermines the future—that is to say, shapes and forecasts it—here a form of historiography is conceptualized in which what comes later recasts what has passed. Because of its anachronism, this idea of a "preposterous history"[60] has so far been problematized mostly in literary hermeneutics. Jerrold Levinson, for example, is resolute: "[T]he future, I suggest, is rightly left aside in understanding the artistic past."[61] A prominent proponent of the inverted concept of the history of influence can, however, be found in T. S. Eliot, who argues in "Tradition and the Individual Talent" that

> what happens when a new work of art is created is something that happens simultaneously to all the works of art which preceded it. […] and so the relations, proportions, values of each work of art toward the whole are readjusted; and this is conformity between the old and the new. Whoever has approved this idea of order […] will not find it preposterous that the past should be altered by the present as much as the present is directed by the past.[62]

58 Jorge Luis Borges, "Pierre Menard, Author of the Quixote," 95.
59 Levine, cited in Howard Singerman, "Sherrie Levine's Art History," *October* 101 (Summer 2002): 96–121, 115.
60 Mieke Bal, *Quoting Caravaggio: Contemporary Art, Preposterous History* (Chicago: University of Chicago Press, 1999), 7 (emphasis deleted).
61 Jerrold Levinson, *Music, Art, and Metaphysics: Essays in Philosophical Aesthetics* (Oxford: Oxford University Press, 2011), 195.
62 T. S. Eliot, "Tradition and the Individual Talent," in *Selected Prose of T. S. Eliot*, ed. Frank Kermode (New York: Faber and Faber, 1975), 37–44, 38f.

In recent years, this has also been reinforced theoretically, above all in art history; for example, through Mieke Bal, who argues that "the work performed by later images obliterates the older images as they were before that intervention and creates new versions of old images instead." In the revision of the past through what follows it, Bal does not, however, see "a problem, a liability of history," but "an enrichment of our cultural habitat as a whole"; she thus emphasizes, as do Borges and Levine in the quotes above, the "enriching" potential of these kinds of processes.[63] Michael Baxandall also represents this position in his thoughts against influence: "'Influence' is a curse of art criticism primarily because of its wrong-headed grammatical prejudice about who is the agent and who the patient."[64] As in a game of billiards in which, with each hit, not just one ball is bumped and moved but all the balls are forced into a new relationship with one another, every artistic reference to a predecessor also ensures new constellations not only between the predecessor and the successor, but also in their relationship to all other actors: "What happens in the field, each time Y refers to an X, is a rearrangement. [...] Arts are positional games and each time an artist is influenced he rewrites his art's history a little."[65]

Concept of Authorship

This should make it clear: Although it may seem natural to speak of plagiarism, fakes, deception, or counterfeit when first encountering appropriation literature, this is misguided in most cases. Not excluded from this are the cases where the authors provoke our old conception of authorship by, for instance, never mentioning the original and its author, which is probably unnecessary in most cases due to the canonical works that are being used. Appropriation literature functions only on the basis of a strong concept of authorship, which, despite all of the swan songs of authorship, is still able to unfold a highly organized discursive force. Thus, authorship is in no way repealed but put into the spotlight.

It should also be mentioned here that, despite the prevalent prejudices against the motives for appropriations, a great majority of these works should be understood more as contribution to analyzing, interpreting, commenting on, updating, translating and, as a result, also canonizing the works rather than an act of destruction or desecration. At the same time, according to Pichler, it would be too simple "to dismiss appropriation of books within books as homage, fandom, and subaltern prostration to masters of art history," as is often done in defense of appropriation literature. His counterproposal, born out of his engagement with Oswald de Andrade's *Manifesto Antropófago*, reads: "It is time to counter homage with bibliophagia."[66]

63 She defines: "This reversal, which puts what came chronologically first ('pre-') as an aftereffect behind ('post') its later recycling, is what I would like to call a *preposterous history*." All citations Bal, *Quoting Caravaggio*, 1, 7, and 6f (emphasis in the original).

64 Michael Baxandall, *Patterns of Intention: On the Historical Explanation of Pictures* (New Haven: Yale University Press, 1986), 58f.

65 Baxandall, *Patterns of Intention*, 60.

66 Michalis Pichler, "Books and Ideas after Stéphane Mallarmé," in this volume.

Copyright: Jurisprudence, Adaptations, Translations

Of course, legal questions of copyright and ethical questions of copying and appropriating inevitably arise. Legal aspects continue to play a role, for instance, whenever: an old translation from the public domain is preferred to another translation that is not available due to copyright issues; the legal information as to the unresolved status of the present work is attached; the book is purposefully not for sale; or whenever authors suggest, for their own security, that the publication could be withdrawn should someone own the copyrights to any of the used works.

All this shows that the authors are aware that they are moving in a gray area, which is marked by countless inadequacies and inconsistencies as well as imponderables and cases of doubt. Even proven copyright experts come to confusingly different judgments about the permissibility of artistic appropriation practices, as shown by the example of a fictitious court hearing at which, at the invitation of The Piracy Project (Eva Weinmayr and Andrea Francke), lawyers from three legal systems (US, Great Britain, Europe) were to discuss case studies and create clarity.[67]

The jurisprudence thus offers little help and knows no answer to the latest developments in society, technology, media, and art. Thus, for example, the relationship between work and adaptation is becoming increasingly distorted when authors declare their translations, typographical creations, editorial work, spin-offs, etcetera, full-fledged, autonomous works of their own although, according to common standards, they are considered derivatives of a work and thus second-rate manifestations in the service of the original. This presumption of sole authorship may seem particularly provocative in the case of curated collections or translations, where the ideal of the "invisible" translator[68] is still widespread as an unspoken norm. According to common expectations, the only goal of the translator is "to preserve, capture and convey the original work, and not to create a new work having no precedent in the source. Therefore the goal of translation is reproduction."[69] According to copyright law, the translation is certainly treated in the same way as the original work: that is to say, as a personal, intellectual creation it meets the necessary threshold of originality to count as an original work and enjoy protection under copyright. In Article 2, Para. 3 of the Berne Convention for the Protection of Literary and Artistic Works (1971), it states unambiguously that "[t]ranslations, adaptations, arrangements of music and other alterations of a literary or artistic work shall be protected as original works without prejudice to the copyright in the original work." But,

67 The discussion is documented in Andrea Francke, Eva Weinmayr, eds., *Borrowing, Poaching, Plagiarising, Pirating, Stealing, Gleaning, Referencing, Leaking, Copying, Imitating, Adapting, Faking, Paraphrasing, Quoting, Reproducing, Using, Counterfeiting, Repeating, Cloning, Translating* (London: AND Publishing, 2014).

68 Ideally, the impression should be created "that the translation is not in fact a translation, but the 'original'": "the translator works to make his or her work 'invisible,' producing the illusory effect of transparency that simultaneously masks its status as an illusion: the translated text seems 'natural,' i.e., not translated." Lawrence Venuti, *The Translator's Invisibility: A History of Translation* (London: Routledge, 1995), 1 and 5.

69 Jiří Levý, *The Art of Translation*, ed. Zuzana Jettmarová, trans. Patrick Corness (Amsterdam: John Benjamins, 2011), 57f.

as a derivative or "secondhand" work, the translation remains by definition strictly related to the source text, the "original work" whose protection under copyright has priority. Declaring that a translation is an autonomous work under its own authorship is thus a clear declaration of war against the established hierarchy between translator and original author, which is also deeply anchored in a legal practice "that systematically identifies translators as non-authors."[70]

In the context of appropriation literature, similar tendencies can be observed among typographers, book designers, editors, and literary curators, who increasingly claim full authorship for themselves. Thus Kuusela states that, in their drive for recognition and authorship, literary curators "not only make public others' texts but also seek publicity for their *own* practices, and thus accumulate and create cultural capital for themselves."[71] This profiling threatens to be at the expense of authors whose texts—whether they consent or not—are used in the curator's project: "the praxis of curating is also, or above all, an act of reterritorialization, i.e., an act of designing a new power"[72] that can take on ethically dubious and exploitative traits "when taken to the extreme."[73]

Ethics of Appropriation

This already indicates that over the years ethical questions have gained weight in dealing with literary-artistic appropriations. In the discussion led by theorists such as Benjamin H. D. Buchloh and Hal Foster in the context of appropriation art, the conviction of the critical potential of appropriation is strongly anchored. However, the question increasingly arises as to "whether appropriation is a critical instrument or part of the system that needs to be criticized."[74] At least, it can be said—also on the basis of the material presented in Pichler's *COLLECTION*—that there can be no question of unlawful expropriation and presumption of authorship in the sense of plagiarism or forgery. After all, in most works of appropriation literature the act of appropriating another's source is clearly marked and staged, and the original authorship by the first authors is usually not denied. Still, any appropriation remains an encroachment on other people's property, often perceived as an illegitimate expropriation, which is why intertextual as well as appropriative modes of writing and production, which until a few decades ago were an accepted and widespread aesthetic strategy, especially in postmodern narrative, are increasingly met with resistance and protest.

The extreme polarization of society, which is also a result of the ever more accelerated, monopolistic attention economy and platform capitalism that

70 Anthony Pym, "The Translator as Non-Author, And I'm Sorry About That," in *The Translator as Author: Perspectives on Literary Translation*, ed. Claudia Buffagni, Beatrice Garzell, Serenella Zanotti (Berlin: LIT, 2011), 31–44, 42.
71 Kuusela, "Publisher, Promoter, and Genius," 119 (emphasis in the original).
72 Ibid., 132.
73 Ibid., 130.
74 Stefan Römer, "Wem gehört die Appropriation art?," *Texte zur Kunst* 26 (June 1997): 129–37.

characterize the last decade, has also given rise to a new politicization and recalibration of artistic strategies. Appropriation is now by definition under suspicion. It is no longer suitable means for addressing power structures: instead of being accepted as a tool for criticism or self-empowerment, it is now perceived as simply part of the power apparatus itself. It has also become evident that artists must constantly reflect on and reassess their own artistic practice, however tried and tested, critical, or well-intentioned it may be, as shown by the example of Vanessa Place, whose œuvre underwent a complete reevaluation in a short period of time. For four years, her project *Gone with the Wind* (2011)—which consisted of posting Margaret Mitchell's 1937 novel sentence by sentence under her own name on Twitter—ran almost unnoticed, or in any case unchallenged. As Place later explained, she wanted the project to bring attention to the novel's inherent racism and question its hitherto little-disputed place in America's cultural heritage.[75] In 2015, however, during a rampant public debate, she was accused of reproducing racist language and imagery, ultimately leading Place to discontinue the project. An even bigger dismissive debate—albeit related to the appropriation of a *non-literary* text—ensued, when Kenneth Goldsmith performed "The Body of Michael Brown," an appropriation of Brown's autopsy report in 2015.[76] These two artistic projects based on appropriation clearly show how the sociopolitical discourse has shifted fundamentally in just a few years, so that the implications and stakes inherent in appropriation as an artistic strategy are now being evaluated on completely different terms.

Sometimes this also leads to the authors and artists themselves rethinking and (self-) critically examining their own artistic strategies. As an example, Paul Soulellis can be mentioned, whose view of his long-preferred strategy of appropriation, which he once further differentiated with the verbs "hunting, grabbing, and performing," has fundamentally changed:

> This past summer, as I was preparing to give a talk in Italy, I wrote out the word "grabbing," and thought, How, in this era of Trump, can we talk about grabbing other peoples' work? Suddenly, grabbing didn't feel right at all, and I realized that my feelings about how and when appropriation should be used had changed.[77]

At another place, he elaborates on this consideration and problematizes the use of appropriative strategies by means of some questions that should necessarily accompany any appropriation and that I, too, would like to place at the end of my reflections on appropriation:

75 See Vanessa Place, "Artist's Statement: Gone With the Wind @VanessaPlace," *Genius*, May 19, 2015, https://genius.com/Vanessa-place-artists-statement-gone-with-the-wind-vanessaplace-annotated.

76 See, for example, David Kaufmann, *Reading Uncreative Writing: Conceptualism, Expression, and the Lyric* (Cham: Palgrave Macmillan, 2017), and Priscilla Frank, "What Happened When A White Male Poet Read Michael Brown's Autopsy As Poetry," *Huffpost*, March 17, 2015, https://www.huffpost.com/entry/kenneth-goldsmith-michael-brown_n_6880996.

77 All citations Paul Soulellis, "Library of the Printed Web," interview by Meg Miller, November 21, 2017, https://www.are.na/blog/paul-soulellis.

Post-Trump, it's difficult to see the word "grabbing" and not recognize an imperialist move. Taking material in a way that disturbs authorship remains an intriguing strategy for artistic practice, but not without these urgent questions: Who controls the narrative? To what end will the found material be used? Does the act of appropriation work to reveal an imbalance of power, or amplify an underrepresented voice, or expose a site of oppression? Might the work even repair or stitch together broken relations?[78]

78 Paul Soulellis, "Urgent Archive," in *Library of the Printed Web. Collected Works 2013–2017*, ed. Paul Soulellis (Self-published: POD Lulu, 2017), 501–16, 511.

Craig Dworkin
Materiality as Interpretation

"Le monde" (the world), Stéphane Mallarmé famously reiterated, was "fait pour aboutir à un beau livre" (made to end up in a beautiful book). But the specifics of that *bookness*, the form a book might take, was left unspecified even as Mallarmé was thinking through its most radical transformations. I have argued elsewhere for the particular ways in which Mallarmé was attuned to the material properties of paper as a physical, three-dimensional substrate and the how he extrapolated from the basic logic of the rhythm of the fold—for him, the fundamental origin of poetic verse—to imagine folded sheets of paper in mobile permutation as a poetic form in and of itself.[1] Ultimately, indeed, he imagined the structure of that book projected beyond even the folio to stacks of paper dispersed into the six compartments of a bespoke cabinet. As the measure of the poetic line transmigrates to the arrangement of pages on which it is printed, the book imagined by *UN COUP DE DÉS* and *Le Livre* was to be three-dimensional and unbound. The former was meant to be printed in nested folios but unbound along the spine, so that the sheets could be shuffled. The latter was to be a theatricalization of the reading that follows from drawing unbound sheets in permutational and aleatory combinations from the cubby-holes of a filing cabinet. Beyond understanding these two particular poems, recognizing the specifics of Mallarmé's radical experiments with the forms of the book has implications for how we think not only about the situation of poetry in his own moment, but how we might evaluate the many works that position themselves explicitly within the lineage of Mallarmé's legacy.

However unusual Mallarmé's conception of the book might have been in terms of poetry publishing, the procedure he envisioned shares surprising affinities with another cultural practice of his moment. While Mallarmé was at work on his late poems and essays, Alphonse Bertillon was establishing the

1 Craig Dworkin, "Pli Selon Pli: Mallarmé and the Significance of the Fold," *Inscription: The Journal of Material Text – Theory, Practice, History* 3 (November 2022).

identification bureau of the Parisian Préfecture de Police, bringing together biometrics, photography, and archival interfaces to promote what came to be known as the Bertillon system, or bertillonage. The method met with spectacular success in the arrest of the anarchist Ravachol (sc. François Claudius Koenigstein) for attacks on the judiciary. He was publicly executed by guillotine a few months later, and the sensational publicity surrounding the affair helped to spur the adoption of Bertillon's system worldwide. It also garnered Bertillon the decoration of *la Légion d'honneur*.

Organizing more uniform poses for the sorts of mugshots the police had been using haphazardly for some years, Bertillon combined the newly stylized portrait photography with a series of standardized bodily measurements, demographic information, and physical descriptions; the various data were recorded on cards which were then filed and cross-referenced in bespoke cabinets. Like the séance leader in the performances described in *Le Livre*, an investigator would retrieve certain sheets from the cabinet and arrange them to arrive not at a poem, but at an identification. Indeed, one of the popularizing demonstrations of the systems suggests the theatricality cultivated in Mallarmé's notes: After "printing a partial list of the descriptions that are in this cabinet […] cards were distributed to the audience, containing the descriptions of several noted characters in figures."[2] The séance leader then worked bureaucratic magic, like guessing the playing card in a parlor trick, to dramatically produce the name of the person whose attributes had been called out by the audience. Nor was the furniture used in the performance incidental; as in Mallarmé's schema, with its *meuble du laque*, Bertillon's system places a cabinet center stage. As Allan Sekula recognizes, in his consideration of the integration of photography and its optical model into the larger ensemble of the Bertillon system, "the central artifact of this system is not the camera but the filing cabinet."[3] Max Houck comes to the same conclusions: "the central instrument of the system was not the camera but the filing cabinet."[4] Paul Knepper and Clive Norris concur, arguing that for all the innovations in standardized photography, "Bertillon's chief accomplishment, however, was a card file catalog of criminal records or 'search cabinet'."[5] The police themselves came to the same conclusion. An officer in Columbus, Ohio, reported in 1905 that the department had "laboured under a serious disadvantage, owing to a lack of necessary equipment, for the purpose of filing the Bertillon record cards, but then made the valuable addition […] of a nine-drawer Bertillon filing and classification cabinet."[6] Indeed,

2 Robert W. McClaughry: "The Bertillon System for Identification of Criminals," *The Prevention and Repression of Crime: Being a Report of the Fifth Section of the International Congress of Charities, Correction and Philanthropy, Chicago, June, 1893*, ed. Frederick H. Wines (Baltimore: The Johns Hopkins Press, 1894): 79.

3 Allan Sekula, "The Body and the Archive," *October* 39 (Winter 1986): 16.

4 Max M. Houck, *Forensic Science: Modern Methods of Solving Crime* (Westport, CT: Praeger Publishers, 2007), 27. A forensic reader might wonder whether Houck has lifted the line, leaving Sekula's fingerprints.

5 Paul Knepper and Clive Norris, "Fingerprint and Photograph: Surveillance Technologies in the Manufacture of Suspect Social Identities," *Urban Crime Prevention, Surveillance, and Restorative Justice: Effects of Social Technologies*, ed. Paul Knepper, Jonathan Doak, and Joanna Shapland (Boca Raton, FL: Taylor and Francis, 2009), 79.

6 Columbus Police Benevolent Association, *History of the Police Department of Columbus, Ohio: From the Earliest Times to the Present with a Record of the Principal Crimes Committed* (Columbus, 1908), 111.

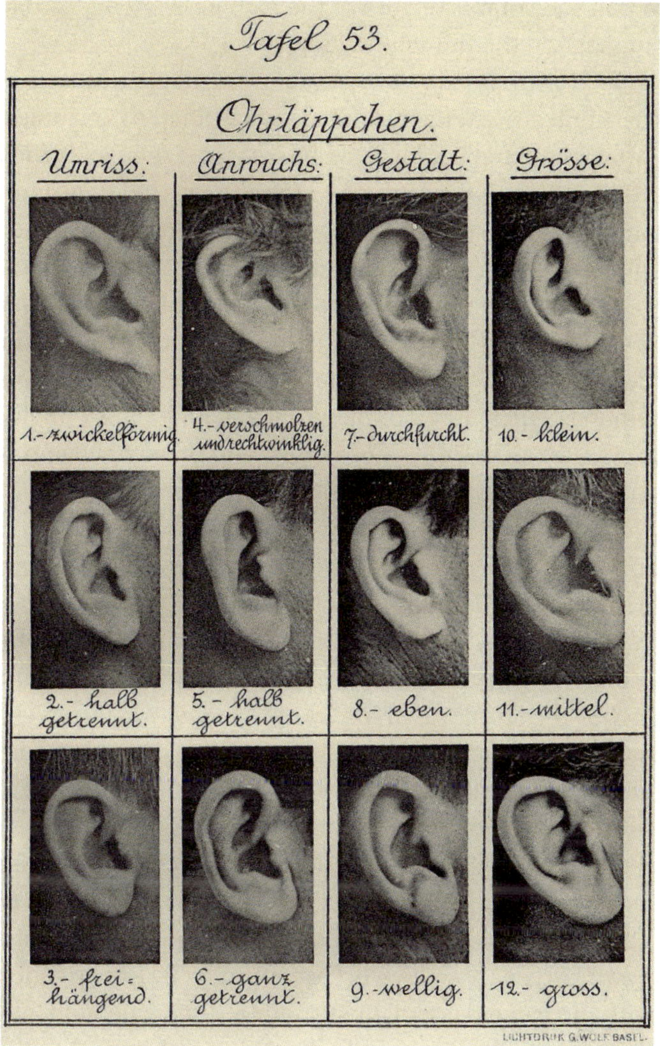

Fig. 1. Alphonse Bertillon, *Das anthropometrische Signalement*, 2nd edition with an album (Bern/Leipzig: Dr. v. Sury, 1895), plate 53: "Classification of an earlobe."

"the Bertillon cabinet became the distinguishing mark of the modern police organization," and the furniture was such an essential tool that Bertillonage was at times referred to as the "filing cabinet method," with companies specializing in the bespoke furniture known as "Bertillon cabinets."[7]

The combinatory possibilities of withdrawing sheets from the cabinet—what for Mallarmé was the rhythmic essence of the new poetry of the exploded book, allegorized by the aleatory thematics of *UN COUP DE DÉS*—was both the power and problem of Bertillonage. One reformer, who proposed refining

7 Raymond Fosdick, "The Passing of the Bertillon System of Identification," *Journal of the American Institute of Criminal Law and Criminology* 6, no. 3 (1915): 364; Dana Seitler, *Atavistic Tendencies: The Culture of Science in American Modernity* (Minneapolis: University of Minnesota Press, 2008): 72; Michelle Caswell, *Archiving the Unspeakable: Silence, Memory, and the Photographic Record in Cambodia* (Madison, WI: University of Wisconsin Press, 2014), 35.

the system so that the compartments of the cabinet were adjustable rather than fixed, summarized the branching factorials:

> In the Bertillon system the records are classified by dividing them four times into three groups with fixed limits. For example, we may have a few thousand cards on each of which is recorded four dimensions of one individual. Let us say, to fix our ideas, that these dimensions are length of head, breadth of head, height of head, and stature. The bundle of cards is first divided into three groups by arranging them in a series according to lengths, and choosing two lengths as the limits of the middle group, which will make the number of cards in each group approximately equal. Each of these groups is again sub-divided into three groups by means of the breadths, and the subdivision is further carried out by means of the other two dimensions.[8]

The description gives a good sense of the method, which is why I quote it at length, although the cards were in fact indexed by six measures, out of eleven taken.[9] The number, which would be *l'unique nombre* for Bertillon, is significant because the specific furniture that results from its permutations uncannily matches the structure of Mallarmé's *meuble de lac* (even if the Bertillon cabinet were more likely to be "made of golden quartered oak, in handsome dull finish," as one manufacturer touted their product).[10]

More substantively, the manufacturer explained that "a Bertillon cabinet cannot be made with less than nine drawers [...] and these drawers must be arranged three wide by three high," so that every one of the six principal measurements can be further subdivided into small, medium, and large groupings.[11] Larger cabinets were required by larger precincts, but they scaled with the same triplets illustrated by Mallarmé in his notes; "the sizes of cabinets have to be increased by multiples of three," as the Y & E Company explained their series of nine-, twenty-seven-, eighty-one-, and 243-drawer cabinets. "When we take such a large cabinet we multiply the subdivisions," conceded the Chicago police chief, but however massive the database, "gathering the vast cabinet" always required the fundamentally nonologic tripartite division that was Bertillon's great advance in efficiency. As one forensic physician explained, the cross-referencing method "enables the search to be made with great rapidity, and the exact position in the cabinet of any previous record of the same individual to be determined with a minimum amount of labour in examining other records not relating to him."[12] Or, as a parliamentary committee summed it up, suspects "could be found

8 J. Gray: "Anthropometric Identification: A New System of Classifying the Records," *Man: A Monthly Records of Anthropological Science* 52 (1905): 85.

9 *Criminal Identification by "Y and E" Bertillon and Finger Print Systems: Including Record of Arrests, Anatomical Index, Lost and Stolen Property, Rogues' Gallery* (Rochester, NY: Yawman and Erbe Manufacturing Company, 1913), 15.

10 Ibid., 15.

11 Ibid., 16.

12 J.G. Garson, "The Metric System of Identification of Criminals, as Used in Great Britain and Ireland," *The Journal of the Anthropological Institute of Great Britain and Ireland* 30, no. 3 (London, 1900): 165.

in M. Bertillon's cabinet as certainly and almost as quickly as an accurately spelt word could be found in the dictionary."[13]

Mallarmé, famously, was looking for words that were *not* in the dictionary, and for all their similarities, *Le Livre* and *Bertillonage* were fundamentally inverse practices.[14] The former developed its system of *feuilles* and *casiers* in order to multiply indeterminacy and ambiguity, while the latter developed its similar system of *fiches* and *tiroirs* in order to narrow possibilities to an unambiguous certainty. Nonetheless, the two spheres of avant-garde literature and police surveillance overlapped in the Belle Époque. Perhaps the best-known point of intersection was Félix Fénéon, the anarchist art critic who worked days as an obscure clerk in the Ministère de la guerre. Arrested for the bombing of the fashionable Restaurant Foyot in 1894, Fénéon—who had been under surveillance for some weeks because of his political views—was photographed by Bertillon as part of his processing by the authorities. Against the protocols for mugshot uniformity, a hallmark of Bertillon's bureau, Fénéon poses in one of the photographs with his head at a quarter turn, signaling a haughty indifference. He would be acquitted by a divided jury, after a trial in which Mallarmé testified as a character witness. In his defense of Fénéon, Mallarmé conflated writing and bombing, declaring "certes il n'y aurait pas pour Fénéon, de meilleurs détonateurs que ses articles" (for Fénéon there would certainly be no better detonators than his articles).[15] The remark, ultimately as undecidable as Fénéon's guilt, echoed Mallarmé's earlier comment on Auguste Vaillant's bombing of the Chambre des députés the previous year: "Je ne sais pas d'autre bombe qu'un livre" (The only bomb I know about is a book).[16] Mallarmé's next book of poetry was to be *UN COUP DE DÉS*; he may have thought of it as a *coup de détonateur*. The repercussions of that explosion are still being felt. Indeed, the influence of Mallarmé's late poetics, we should remember, extends beyond typographic experiments; the revolutionary social implications of his poetics were not lost of a writer like Norman H. Pritchard, who would explain: "I'm going to go out with a revolution that's going to change the form of the book [...] I am concerned with a revolution that involves the transformation of the book itself."[17]

For Allan Sekula, collections like those housed in Bertillon's cabinets were a shadow archive cast by the twin discourses of physiognomy and phrenology converging in archival taxonomies:

> We can speak then of a generalized, inclusive archive, a shadow archive that encompasses

13 C. E. Troup, "Report of a Committee Appointed by the Secretary of State to Inquire into the Best Means Available for Identifying Habitual Criminals," *Parliamentary Papers* 72 (1893–94): 29.

14 On Mallarmé's use of the reference book, see my *Dictionary Poetics: Toward a Radical Lexicography* (New York: Fordham, 2020), 27–31.

15 Interview in *Le Soir* (Bruxelles), April 27, 1894.

16 Stéphane Mallarmé, *Œuvres Complètes* 2 (Paris: Gallimard, 1951): 1722–23. For more thorough considerations of Mallarmé's relation to contemporary politics, see Howard G. Lay, "'Beau geste!' (On the Readability of Terrorism)," *Yale French Studies* 101 (2001): 79–100, and Patrick McGuinness: "Mallarmé and the Poetics of Explosion," *MLN* 124, no. 4 (September 2009): 797–824.

17 Interview with Judd Tully, Comprehensive Employment Training Act/ Cultural Council Foundation Artists Project, September 11, 1978.

> an entire social terrain while positioning individuals within that terrain. This archive contains subordinate, territorialized archives: archives whose semantic interdependence is normally obscured by the "coherence" and "mutual exclusivity" of the social groups registered within each. The general, all-inclusive archive necessarily contains both the traces of the visible bodies of heroes, leaders, moral exemplars, celebrities, and those of the poor, the diseased, the insane, the criminal, the nonwhite, the female, and all other embodiments of the unworthy.[18]

Accordingly, snapshots such as quotidian bourgeois holiday pictures of the family, for instance, are always implicitly measured against the extremities of the shadow archive. If we pose, with more or less self-awareness, in imitation of celebrities, or conform our appearance to models of class aspiration and solidarity, we also pose in avoidance of the policed and pathologized bodies recorded in the libraries of disciplinary institutions.

Within the dynamic play of deviation and imitation we can discern another parallel between Bertillonage and Mallarméan poetics. Written in response to contemporaneous trends in free verse and prose poetry, and probing their inherent poetics with a spatialized layout measured in pages rather than syllables, *UN COUP DE DÉS* bolstered and sharpened the definition of the new forms—not to mention more conventional verse—by the extremity of its deviation. The signification of a form such as the alexandrine sonnet, for instance, arises not only from its similarity to other lyrics but also through its divergence from other forms and the distance it maintains between itself and the horizon of the most radical anomalies. Functioning for verse in the way *Finnegans Wake* has functioned for prose, *UN COUP DE DÉS* has stood for over a century as a limit case of visual prosody, with the air of being simultaneously both foundational and unsurpassable (although less well-known, *Le Livre* sets a similar boundary for the idea of "The Book"). At the same time, as Bertillon knew from the posturing of certain detainees, there are always those who intentionally shun the guise of bourgeois respectability and cultivate the attitude of the dangerous classes. Certain writers, similarly, would take Mallarmé's late works as models to engage rather than grotesqueries to avoid. The periphery of the conventional, established canon serves as the displaced center of other traditions, and Mallarmé's late books have been taken up in part because of their reputations as the limit cases that established them as foundational works for the counter-canon of the avant-garde.

In addition to that counter-canonical status, Mallarmé's late works have been fruitful interlocutors for artistic dialogue in part because they are works, as Mallarmé himself left them, to be realized: from the page-proof annotations for the projected but unpublished Didot/Vollard edition of *UN*

COUP DE DÉS to the hermetic notebook jottings toward *Le Livre*, these texts are, by definition, notes and instructions for future instantiations. Furthermore, they each have an abstraction and obscurity that invites a formal (rather than semantic) intervention and leaves suitable play for multiple reinterpretations without an attendant loss in meaning. Finally, *UN COUP DE DÉS* and *Le Livre* each in their own ways constitute discrete works commensurate with the self-contained unit of "the book," while still being brief enough to tackle. The task of the translator, in these instances, is impressive, but not daunting. In other words, to transpose or translate or restage Mallarmé's late works leaves an artist with a complete, stand-alone publication, a work easily compared with its celebrated original, and a sense of substantial but not overwhelming labor. Like Ed Ruscha's series of photo books, which includes *Twentysix Gasoline Stations* and *EVERY BUILDING ON THE SUNSET STRIP*, the interchange between new works and Mallarmé's late books now comprise their own genre.[19] The editions and appropriations of *UN COUP DE DÉS* alone are substantial enough to have led to an exhibition, and a sense of the assembled collection, *UN COUP DE DÉS (COLLECTION)*, as an artistic work in its own right.[20] Such works of appropriation obviously invite comparison to their sources, so the formal specifics of Mallarmé's texts that I have argued for here bear on the significance of the formal restagings they have inspired. Changing understandings of Mallarmé's books, in short, change our sense of their derivatives, bringing certain elements into sharper focus or more pronounced salience while others recede and become less relevant by comparison.

For one instance of this dynamic, consider Klaus Scherübel's edition of *Le Livre*, which wraps a Styrofoam block with a simulated dustjacket, replete with title and author, publisher's mark, pull quote ("Everything in the world exists in order to end up in a book"), cover copy, and ISBN. Begun in the late 1990s, translated versions have appeared in French, English, German, Dutch, and Portuguese. The brilliance of the project—to actually realize Mallarmé's tantalizingly unfinished *Livre*—is a stroke of gratifying and deliberate wit. Like the original notes on which it is based, Scherübel's version emphasizes the formal, financial, commercial, material, and cultural aspects of a book detached from the particulars of its literary language or narrative: a material object sold, catalogued, and discussed within the institutions of literature. In this way, Scherübel

18 Sekula, 10.

19 Beyond the established artists represented in the exhibition, a number of print-on-demand projects were curated by Danny Snelson as part of a seminar on poetic infrastructures: LaPod Press, 2018, https://lapodpress.tumblr.com (accessed May 28, 2022). Most of these works are a subset of the appropriations discussed by Annette Gilbert in her edited collection of republication as an artistic practice: *Reprint: Appropriation (&) Literature* (Berlin: Luxbooks, 2014); as cited below, Gilbert reads *UN COUP DE DÉS* and its bibliographic offspring as "site specific" texts in *Literature's Elsewheres* (op. cit.). For more thorough considerations of the genre, in addition to Gilbert's *Literature's Elsewheres*, see Karen Donnachie and Andi Simionato: "Mallarmé's Self-replicating Machine," *Materialidades de literatura* 81 (2018): 38–49, and Barbara Bourchenin, "Du Texte à la Texture chez Marcel Broodthaers, Michalis Pichler et Jérémie Bennequin: Une relecture de Stéphane Mallarmé à l'ère du glitch," *Études Stéphane Mallarmé* 6 (2018): 23–46. For Ruscha's books as the source of a genre of derivative books, see *Various Small Books: Referencing Various Small Books by Ed Ruscha*, ed. Jeff Brouws, Wendy Burton, and Hermann Zschiegner (Cambridge, MA: MIT Press, 2013).

20 See Michalis Pichler, *Exposition littéraire autour de Mallarmé* (Milan: Kunstverein Milano, 2016; New York: Center for Book Arts, 2024).

offers a fixed version of the variable schema developed by Dan Graham, who constructed a template for recording various characteristics of the text itself, depending on the specifics of its publishing venue: number of pages, typeface, paper stock, parts of speech, etcetera. Graham's "Poem Schema" (alternately *Schema (March 1966)*) in fact, might be considered an updated version of *Le Livre*, given its publication in *Aspen* 5 + 6, which was dedicated to Mallarmé, who had been of particular importance and inspiration to Graham at the time.[21] By following Mallarmé in neglecting any written contents, Graham and Scherübel engineer a reversal of the status usually accorded to the "main text" in relation to its material substrate. Where Graham describes, Scherübel manufactures, replacing the body of the book with its paratext, and this dialectic is what allows Annette Gilbert to see the theoretical and philosophical challenge the project poses to pervasive notions of literariness and the presumption that the literary *work* precedes the *book*.[22] Furthermore, Scherübel's figuration of the codex as a solid, stolid, unopenable block, emphasizes the sculptural physicality of "the book," a term too often abstracted and dematerialized, and he emphasizes the dimensions of his edition (sixteen by twenty-four centimeters) as a trim "specified by Mallarmé."[23] As with the texts collected and transcribed by Scherer as *Le Livre*, in which "not a word of the notes can be said to belong to the *Livre* itself," Scherübel's *Livre* materializes the notes without attempting to reconstruct the *Livre* itself.[24] At the same time, however, as we have seen, such a work is the very epitome of the structure Mallarmé was rejecting with *Le Livre*, which sought to amplify the mobility of pages bound in the tomb of the old-fashioned tome and to take a form that was not even a codex at all.

John McDowall's *Biblioteca Universalis* (2018), in contrast, offers a symbolic depiction of the loose sheets distributed in Mallarmé's imagination of *Le Livre*, and it gives a palpable sense of his interest in the fold; the book is structured with triple-pamphlet binding that enhances the hinges of its switchbacks and a disorienting sense of scale and sequence in its full-bleed photographs of the stacked stock in a high-end stationer's shop. Like the Styrofoam mannequin of Scherübel's book, those sheets are blank: prepared paper seen as literature in the future perfect tense, they are the form of *writing to come*. Conveying a symbolic sense of vertiginous permutation and sublime infinity, McDowall leverages the affect of the potential in Mallarmé's schema at the expense of the technical limits that he was at pains to note. For Mallarmé, the multiplication of aleatory permutations was key, but so was their limit: as a set number of

21 See Dan Graham: "The Artists As Bookmaker: The Book As Object," *Arts Magazine* 41, no. 8 (Summer 1967): 23. For a discussion of Mallarmé's similar influence on Sol LeWitt, see Anna Lovatt: "The Mechanics of Writing: Sol LeWitt, Stéphane Mallarmé and Roland Barthes," *Word & Image* 28, no. 4 (2012): 374–83.

22 Gilbert, *Elsewheres*, 279–86. Note the particularly smart, thorough reading of the Styrofoam dummy in relation to Mallarmé's poetic, which qualifies my hasty characterization of neglected content.

23 Klaus Scherübel, http://klausscheruebel.com/index.php?/projets/8/ (accessed May 26, 2022).

24 Trevor Stark, *Total Expansion of the Letter: Avant-Garde Art and Language after Mallarmé* (Cambridge, MA: MIT Press, 2020), 232.

sheets distributed across nine pigeonholes, "The Book" was to be expanded, but not infinitely.

Our understanding of *UN COUP DE DÉS* has similar implications for its many artistic interlocutors, beginning in the 1960s with a series of graphic abstractions of Mallarmé's poem. To begin with, Ernst Fraenkel issued a suite of strangely psychologized patterns in *Les Dessins trans-conscients de Stéphane Mallarmé* (1960), each of which cancels the words of the poem in various ways, from geometrically printed blocks to hand-spread inking, in order to form a series of what appear to be geometric shadow projections, primitive modernist abstractions, concatenated ladders, or the trace of the eye's saccadic path across the page. That page, however, was not the opening of the folded sheet with its shadowed gutter, but the single page of the deprecated *Cosmopolis* edition of the poem, which Mallarmé disavowed. Fraenkel's experiments thus privilege a sense of the text separable from the folio form of the book which Paul Valéry, for one, understood to be integral to the very conception of the poem. In his analysis, the form of the print is coeval with the composition of the poem:

> I do not think we should consider *UN COUP DE DÉS* as having been executed in two successive operations: one consisting of writing the poem in the usual way, that is, without regard to its visual pattern or spatial arrangement, and the other then giving that definitive text a fixed and attractive disposition on the page. Mallarmé's endeavor must necessarily have been much deeper, extending back to the very moment of conception.[25]

Indeed, Mallarmé himself wrote, in a letter to André Gide, that "le poème (sc. *UN COUP DE DÉS*) s'imprime, en ce moment, tel que je l'ai conçu; quant à la pagination, où est tout l'effect" (the poem is to be printed, now, just as I conceived it; as to the pagination, that is where all the effect lies).[26] At the same time, the set of folded, loose sheets in the unusual publication of *Les Dessins*, with its assembled essays and broadsides housed in thick stock wraps that are more of a box than a codex, nonetheless capture two of the fundamental poetic principles essential to Mallarmé's very rejection of the *Cosmopolis* edition: folds and mobility.

Recognizing the *Cosmopolis* edition as an aborted, false start, both Mario Diacono and Marcel Broodthaers produced versions of *UN COUP DE DÉS* based on the Gallimard edition of the poem, replacing the lines of Mallarmé's text with geometric bars in sizes scaled to the relative point size of the original type. The results—constructivist geometric forms floating in space— align Mallarmé's graphic design with the Russian avant-garde that would follow hard on the edition published in

25 Quoted in *Poésure et peintrie: "d'un art, l'autre"* (Marseille: Musées de Marseille, 1993), 507, and translated for this essay by the author.

26 Henri Mondor, *Autres precisions sur Mallarme et inedits* (Paris: Éditions Gallimard, 1961), 236.

1914. The results look like a mashup of Mallarmé and Malevich. Broodthaers published three formats of his "image" version of the poem, which has become the locus classicus of *UN COUP DE DÉS* restagings: a facsimile of the Gallimard pamphlet on standard art paper; another using translucent paper, producing a composite view of the poem in a single simultaneous view of layered depths of gradated greys; and series of machine-etched aluminum plates that abandon the codex form to gesture toward sculpture. In contrast to the booklets, those plates further emphasize the three-dimensional materiality of the work and the mobility of the unbound sheets that Mallarmé envisioned, but in the process they lose the gutter fold and the play of recto and verso highlighted by the transparent paper edition (since the metal is etched on only one side). Conversely, Derek Beaulieu's *tattered sails (after un coup de des)* (2018), incorporates the logic of the fold—as well as aleatoric procedure—into the production of its two-dimensional images, which are derived from copies of Broodthaers's (*IMAGE*). Beaulieu folds photocopies of the Broodthaers page spreads, paper-airplane style, as if they were folded flags or trimmed sails angled from the mast. The chance cropping of lines that results—juxtaposed in canted sets across the space of the page—again suggests the legacy of Constructivism in the geometric abstractions of an Earle Brown graphic score or mid-century works such as Almir Mavignier's *Interpenetração* (1954).

Beaulieu's xerography, evident in the granular inking of nth-generation images preserved in the small-press pamphlet publication of his book, works to flatten any sense of the original pages with an insistent two-dimensionality, even as they are folded and creased; the reproduction of pages manipulated in space, paradoxically, cancels the necessarily spatial aspect of Beaulieu's procedure. In contrast, as Gilbert has argued, the essential three-dimensionality of the book is also key to understanding the contributions of those who have taken up *UN COUP DE DÉS*, such as Rainier Lericolais and Michalis Pichler, each of whom excised the rectangular forms of Broodthaers's edition with die-cut perforations.[27] In a related work, with a stroke of pataphysical genius, Pichler then rotated the perforated pages, printed on a continuous sheet, so that they could be played as pianola roll. Corroborating Pichler's instinct, R. Howard Bloch has seen a similarity between *UN COUP DE DÉS* and

> the original punch cards that Joseph-Marie Jacquard invented at the end of the eighteenth century for the programming of textile looms, that the English polymath Charles Babbage adapted for the calculating "Analytic Engine" (1864), that Herman Hollerith used for the tabulation of census data in the 1880s, or that Mallarmé encountered in the barrel organ, organette, and player piano rolls, that were popular in fin-de-siècle France.[28]

27 Given that it is not presented as a book, Gilbert does not discuss Liricolais, pairing Pichler instead with the visionary vector tracing of Eric Zboya's computational versions of the text; for a similar reading of Zboya, see Donnachie and Simionato, 41.

28 R. Howard Bloch: *One Toss of the Dice: The Incredible Story of How a Poem Made Us Modern* (New York: Liveright, 2017), 22.

Fig. 2. *UN COUP DE DÉS JAMAIS N'ABOLIRA LE HASARD (MUSIQUE)* at Musikinstrumenten-Museum, Berlin 2009.

Furthermore, following Mallarmé's own proposition that "la nature des caractères employés et la position des blancs suppléent aux notes et aux intervalles musicaux" (the nature of the typographic characters used and the spacing of the blanks substitute for musical notes and rests)—a partition that emerges once one equates the white of the unprinted page with poetic silence—Bloch imagines that "Mallarmé's manuscript looks in places like sheet music, and the poet saw the layout of his poem as a musical score whose ups and downs indicate the rising and falling intonation of the voice."[29] Pichler's pianola version concretizes such speculations, returning Mallarmé's musically-inspired poetics, with its ultimate grounding in Richard Wagner's operas, to the realm of the audible. That we are able to hear the discontinuous, atonal notes and clusters of a performance of the pianola *coup* as music is only thanks to the experiments of twentieth-century composers who expanded the range of what constitutes the musical. The piece thus invites comparison with the post-war musical developments directly inspired by *un coup de dés* and *Le Livre*, which served as the point of departure for compositions by Pierre Boulez and John Cage. Famously feuding over the nature of chance in music, both Boulez and Cage transferred what they understood as the compositional principles of Mallarmé's poetics to musical composition, which Pichler more directly and literally transposes while abandoning his poetics. In order to be playable, the piano-roll scroll loses any sense of the fold that was the essence of musical rhythm for Mallarmé; the single continuous roll achieves its musicality at the expense of the aleatory mobility of the multiple sheets of Mallarmé's proposed *cahier*. And yet, with the punches, the scroll opens little windows onto the fact that the recto and verso of the sheet, trimmed to whatever length, are two inseparable faces of the same strata (the very model of Ferdinand de Saussure's contemporaneous theory of the linguistic sign).

Further examples could be adduced—there are scores of directly bibliophagic works—but my point is less that any particular aspects of their designs are more or less accurate or valid than that once we understand the materiality of the substrate to be an integral part of the literary work, engagements with that work can be expected to take the substrate into consideration. Moreover, every subsequent engagement then renders its own materiality a matter not of exigency, but of interpretation.

29 Mallarmé, *OC*, 392; Bloch, *One Toss*, 22. Bloch's reading of Mallarmé, one should note, is already inflected by Broodthaers's editions; the interpretive networks are looping and recursive. Similarly, if Mallarmé found compositional inspiration for his poetics in musical models, his poetry was in turn the inspiration for developments in post-war music. Kate van Orden documents the ways in which both *un coup de dés* and *Le Livre* were the direct point of departure for compositions by Pierre Boulez and John Cage; see "Modern Poetics of Chance: Boulez, Mallarmé, Cage," *Yearbook of Comparative and General Literature* 42 (1994): 70–82, and "On the Side of Poetry and Chaos: Mallarmean *Hasard* and Twentieth-Century Music," *Meetings with Mallarmé in Contemporary French Culture*, ed. Michael Temple (Exeter, UK: University of Exeter Press, 1998), 166 *et seq*. For Mallarmé's texts as a "mode of notation" and their "musicalization of poetry," see Stark, 203, 206 *et passim*.

Luc Boltanski, Arnaud Esquerre
Collectors' Items[1]

Things that have been overlooked or forgotten, even trash—that is, things whose principal characteristic is precisely that they have low prices or are deemed worthless[2]—can become collectors' items alongside "valuable objects," "beautiful things," or "noteworthy works" acquired at high prices. The former may have been acquired at low prices, or "found"—that is, extracted from the environment for free, or even stolen. Nevertheless, if we acknowledge that things to which value has already been attributed, things that have been the object of a monetary exchange, often owe this status to the very fact that they had been included in earlier collections (this is made evident when their itinerary has left material or memorial traces), then we can postulate that there are very few collected or collectable objects that, at some stage of their existence, have not existed as trash before being noticed, gathered up, classified, and taken in hand. This is eminently clear in the case of archaeological, prehistorical, or paleontological collections, all of which comprise things that have been extracted from the soil in which they lay. Still, this property can doubtless be extended to most if not all objects in collections, so that it would not be an exaggeration to say that collections are the result of *digs*.

Things that are collectors' items *already exist*. Thus they come from the past, although the past in question may be remote or (as in the case of contemporary art) recent. By and large, these things were not produced for the purpose of collecting; thus the economy in which they are inserted is one in which production does not play a determining role in valuation, unlike the economy associated with the standard form. It is rare for a collector to acquire such objects by placing an order with a supplier,

1 Excerpt from Luc Boltanski, Arnaud Esquerre, *Enrichment: A Critique of Commodities* (Cambridge: Polity, 2020), translated by Catherine Porter.
2 Like the stoneware once produced industrially whose trajectory has been reconstituted in minute detail by Thierry Bonnot in *La vie des objets* (Paris: Éditions de la MSH, 2002).

although certain things (for example, high-end luxury cars) can be produced in limited series intended specifically for collectors.

Collected items are not subject to use. This is equally true for things taken from so-called natural environments (for example, pebbles) and for articles that result from human activity (for example, pots or buttons). None of these things is acquired in order to perform practical functions corresponding to needs (unlike stones acquired in order to build a house or shoes purchased for walking). They are not acquired even for the purpose of display, in a logic of social distinction (for example, boots of a certain brand and at a certain price). In other words, interest in the items collected is not dictated by considerations that rely on externalities, whether these considerations are material (sturdy shoes for walking in the rain) or social (eye-catching shoes that make a statement). To be sure, if we wanted to remain within a neoclassical framework, we could say that these things do have a certain utility. But this utility is related exclusively to the place they can occupy in a given collection.

While objects brought together in a collection do not give rise to use, they arouse two types of interest that are generally closely connected. The first sort of interest is stimulated by what the item, considered in terms of what is singular about it, is capable of evoking. The second sort of interest is focused on the tension, made evident when the items collected are juxtaposed, between *repetition* and *difference*—that is, between what a certain number of things have in common and what distinguishes them from one another. The "beauty" of things, often evoked by collectors to justify what they call their "passion" (a property that does not belong to things as such but, rather, refers to the sentiments they arouse), takes shape at the intersection between these two types of interest.

Let us start by examining the first type, which may apply, moreover, to objects brought together in "curio cabinets" as well as to objects situated in what we are calling *systematic collections*. Stemming from the past, the objects gathered up and collected bring up memories of persons, events, or states of affairs with which they are thought to have been formerly associated. In this way they are comparable to what are called "souvenirs," a term designating things capable of arousing mental states on the order of evocation or recollection.

This is the case, for example, of a dip pen that once belonged to Marcel Proust, a paving stone ripped out of the rue Soufflot during the "night of the barricades" in May 1968, or "the watch my grandfather wore" that was taken from him on his deathbed. Such things are charged with a *memorial force* whose gradient is a function of the importance granted by collectivities of any size to the person, thing, event, or state of affairs whose memory the things evoke.[3]

3 This valorization through reference to the past differs from the "memorial value" (Erinnerungswert) proposed by Aloïs Riegl in that it is a justification of prices, not a value incorporated in things. See Aloïs Riegl, *The Modern Cult of Monuments: Its Character and its Origin*, trans. Kurt Walter Forster (Cambridge, MA: MIT Press, [1903] 1982).

The second type of interest, which is particularly evident in systematic collections, is what distinguishes a collection from a *heap*. A collection is generally presented in the form of an accumulation of things whose juxtaposition is justified through reference to a property that is said to belong to each of the things brought together. What these things have in common is most often a visible property. This property may be self-evident to a nonexpert viewer, who will perceive something like a *family resemblance* (for example, among pots, watches, or keys), taking into account the functions these things fulfilled when they were still in use; alternatively, the property may be perceptible only to the viewer who knows something about the history of the objects assembled (as in the case of things originating in the same place, from the same period, and so on). A systematic collection is thus based on a premeditated *repetition*. The property that is presumed to be shared by the things brought together makes it possible to say what the collection is collecting: *its state of things*. In the absence of that something that the objects are presumed to have in common, the accumulation would break down into a *heap*—that is, a group of objects in a proximity that nothing justifies, that results from contingency, chance, or the deleterious action of time. *Being in a heap* is the mode of being of trash. It is only when things are removed, by human hands, from the contingent proximity of other things with which they had appeared together in a heap, and then placed in contiguity to things with which the object in question has something in common, that an object gains access to the field of the collectable.

But the figure of repetition does not suffice to characterize the collection arrangement. Things made in factories, according to certain standards, intended to be as similar as possible to a prototype (for example, bolts made from the same mold) and brought together in a single place, do not constitute a collection. Here again we are in the presence of a heap, but a heap of bolts of the same kind. There are, then, two types of heap. In one case, heaps bring together heterogeneous things among which differences are perceptible and innumerable; in the other, heaps bring together things presumed to be similar (even if close examination—through a microscope, for example—might reveal differences). Collections fall between these two opposing types of heap: the one in which everything is different (a jumble) and the one in which everything is the same (a stockpile of specimens from a single prototype).

The distinction between accumulation and collection can be spelled out in yet another way. Accumulations are in principle open or unlimited. To things already accumulated, one can endlessly add other things that bear some degree of resemblance. But adding on the basis of similarity may lead to an accumulation of more and more divergent things, because resemblance can be spread from one thing to another—for instance, in relation to the order in which interest is paid to one feature and then another (as for example in children's word games based on associations of sounds: "fire truck" "truck stop" "stoplight" "lighthouse," and so on). In this type of accumulation, the connection between each new thing chosen and the previous ones may be made on the basis of properties that can vary. But the more slippage there is from one property to another, the more the accumulation as a whole will resemble a heap (as in displays of second-hand goods where there is a jumble of everything, including a kitchen sink).

The objects that figure in a given collection have to present not only resemblances but also systematic *differences* in relation to one another. Thus each of the things brought together on the basis of a certain similarity must also present features that differentiate them from the others, although these differences must not be so vast as to outweigh the family resemblances. The proper form toward which a collection tends is thus that of an accumulation of small differences among things that, considered from a greater distance, as it were, can be envisaged in their similarities. This form is unstable. If the differences among things are too significant, the collection regresses toward the heap form of the first type (a jumble). But if the differences are too hard to discern, the collection tends to approach the heap form of the second type (a stockpile). An analogy from cartography may help to clarify this: depending on the scale adopted, a map may represent the contours of an island in the form of a continuous line or a broken line.

The differences among the things that figure in a single collection have to be susceptible to organization in the form of a system of pertinent differences. The collection form thus sketches out a certain ontological framework within which a plurality of entities, *a priori* indefinite in number, is ordered by the relation of these entities to a *governing principle* that, as it is realized in their juxtaposition, blurs their relation to other things in the world, things that are generally kept at a distance from the environment in which the things collected are placed. The collected objects are thus detached from a *remainder* and placed in the perspective of their relations to one another. By the same token, the differences that nevertheless separate them must be explicitly described. Still, the descriptions can never account for all the differences among the things assembled, for these differences are always heterogeneous and excessive. The work of interpretation thus consists in distinguishing among several types of difference. Some of these are not noted. Others are attributed to contingency and treated as accidental defects that have an individual character. Still others, finally, are deemed *pertinent* and evaluated according to a certain gradient of solidity and stability. They can be indicated by a term in such a way that the presence of the specified difference can be reidentified on an *a priori* indefinite number of things likely to bear such a difference.

The relation between what we have called the *governing principle* (which specifies what type of thing is accumulated in the collection) and the *differences* deemed pertinent under a given governing principle can prove variable. What we call the governing principle is never more than one difference among others, placed for a time in a position that makes it possible to close the list of collectables. Thus, to take a very simple example, air mail can be the governing principle of a certain stamp collection in which the differences between countries will be treated as the pertinent differences. But if the governing principle selected is a particular country, then the difference between regular mail and air mail will become pertinent. Finally, the various types of difference we have just indicated are not necessarily stable. A previously unnoticed feature may become a pertinent difference, while differences once deemed pertinent may stop being taken into account or may come to be viewed as defects, and so on. In other words, the *conventions* according to which a certain field of collectables is organized, and the length of time these conventions last, depend first and foremost on the actions of operators, the length of time the field has been in existence, the power relations manifested in the field, the presence or absence of specific institutions, and especially, no doubt, the number of exchanges and their level in terms of price. Conventions and exchanges are in a circular relationship. The principal role of conventions is to facilitate agreements concerning the appreciation of the things in question under the circumstances of an exchange. But, at the same time, the conventions are shaped and solidified in the course of officially completed exchanges.

When *patterns* organizing a certain field of collectables are put into place (which is not always the case, especially if the field in question is relatively new), the accumulation of objects undertaken by operators is governed by a more or less shared representation of the totality to be constituted by the collection once it is complete. We need to distinguish, then, between *objective totalizations*, those on which the various accumulators embark, and *ideal totalizations*, which, even if they are never completely achieved by anyone, constitute the vanishing points toward which the various accumulations are oriented. The interactions within a community, whether it is a well-established and durable community or one that is still being formed, make it possible to establish a system of principles of juxtaposition and of pertinent differences that, through reference to shared conventions, can regulate geographically "scattered enterprises, each of which is rightly experienced as personal and even as singular. In fact, the constitution of a field of collectable things within which a plurality of systematic collections is developed presupposes that individual accumulations—which owe a great deal, of course, to chance encounters, the diversity of tastes, and even fantasies on the part of an individual collector—are nevertheless governed by reference to an *ideal collection*. Such a collection includes the complete series of objects subject to a single governing principle and distinguished from one another by the fact that each bears differences judged pertinent according to modalities that are themselves conventional.

In a format of this type, an accumulation that gives rise to a collection governed by reference to an ideal totality does not simply contain things as such (if it did, it would be hard to distinguish from a heap). A collection properly so called includes three sorts of entity. First of all, necessarily, there are *things*. But, secondly, there must be *differences*, and we can even go so far as to say that a collection is above all a *collection of differences*, even if those differences become pertinent only insofar as they are deposited in things. Considered in this light, the things in question matter less for themselves than in relation to the *differences* of which they are the material *supports*. In the logic of collecting, then, two things characterized by the fact that they are supports for the same pertinent differences constitute *duplicates*, so that one of the two is deemed excessive; it can be removed from the collection and be exchanged—a common outcome—for a thing that is lacking, a thing that supports differences not yet present in the collection understood as an objective totalization. Let us add that, while different things bearing pertinent differences may turn out to be valued differently and exchanged for very unequal prices, the differences that constitute a certain field of collectables all have equal weight.

A collection, as an objective totalization, includes a third sort of entity that can be designated by the term *lack*. It is a question of pertinent differences in the system of the ideal collection, differences that are supported by things that do not figure, or do not yet figure, in a given collection seen as an objective totalization.[4] Each collector operating within a certain field of collectables, oriented toward a single ideal totality, will seek to fill in what is lacking—that is, will try to acquire new things which bear certain pertinent differences that are not present in the things he or she already possesses. To say that every collection is composed at once of things that bear differences and of lacks means that things that are missing are always present, at the heart of the collections, but precisely in the form of lacks. It follows that the activity of collectors is above all guided by a concern for supplying what is lacking. It is because they are imbued with this concern that collectors engage in exchange.

For the collector, these lacks may be quite precise, in the sense that the things on which they figure are already identified, even if it is difficult to gain access to them and to incorporate them into the ongoing collection. But they may also have a relatively uncertain representational presence. Their existence may, sometimes, be only postulated (as when one speaks, in paleontology, of a "missing link"). In such cases they are sufficiently hypothetical for the things on which they might figure to be the

4 What we are calling "lack" here is close to what Serge Reubi calls "lacunae." See Serge Reubi, "La lacune, miroir des pratiques de collections," *Traverse*, no. 3 (2012): 81–90.

object of research, often lengthy and uncertain, but at the same time they may be anticipated with enough assurance to orient the research in certain directions rather than others. In either case, it is the dynamics of the collection itself, guided by the contours of the ideal totality taking shape (which each objective totalization helps to specify), that orients the research.

Thus all collectors, in order to pursue their accumulations, must meld two very different states of mind. On the one hand, they must set out in search of new things with an unbiased outlook: they must be "openminded" enough to welcome and acquire (when they encounter by happenstance) an object whose pertinence might have escaped them, as it had escaped others, because it had not up to that point been registered with reference to the ideal totality. On the other hand, they must orient their choices in a way that gives primacy to things that are capable of filling gaps, supplying what is lacking, with reference to the contours of an ideal totality that they, as collectors, are helping to draw. When they speak of what motivates them, collectors generally conflate these two orientations by grasping them in a single idiom, that of "desire," understood as a sort of impulse that grips and guides them in an almost involuntary way toward objects that they have to acquire "at any price." Yet this sort of subjectivization of the impulse that inspires them leaves aside the fact that they are especially attracted by lacks—that is, by entities that, even though they are absent, nevertheless have an *objective* mode of being, since the objects to which they correspond figure in the *pattern* of the ideal collection. Thus their "desires" are not internal, not rooted in their subjectivity; they arise, rather, from the arrangement of the *state of things* with which collectors are confronted.

The fields of the collectable may be mutable, especially if they are recent and bear upon objects that are readily accessible and not very expensive, or, on the contrary, they may be stabilized and equipped with instruments, supported by catalogs, experts, associations, and so on. But they are rarely institutionalized in the narrow sense in which their contours and their functioning would be the object of legal stipulations or would be placed under governmental control. Institutions may have to rule on the authenticity of things—that is, on their attribution—so as to distinguish originals from copies or counterfeits. But it is not their place to rule on what is, or what ought to be, the way a given collection is organized. Or, in other words, a given field of collectables and the system of governing principles and differences on which this field is based are not *codified*: that is, neither the field nor the system is backed up by written instructions and definitions claiming legal authority. Their acceptability—as in the case of dialects, by contrast with national languages that have been stabilized under the authority of grammarians—thus depends above all on the tacit recognition granted them by those who participate in exchanges and on the capacity of those participants to maintain grounds of understanding, despite the slight displacements (especially spatial, in the case of dialects, and temporal, in the case of collections) that continue to modify the participants' interactions.

The fields of collectables

The passage from the state of trash to that of a sought-after object owes a great deal to the action of primary collectors who also hold artistic authority, whether they are recognized artists, patrons of the arts, or organizers of exhibits or other artistic displays. This authority, acquired during earlier tests in the various art worlds, confers enough power on the actors to elevate rapidly the status of the things that they have singled out; part of the worth attached to their names is transferred to the things in question. Collecting and preserving what they like (or, in the case of artists, what they say are sources of inspiration), these actors gradually generate—starting from random encounters with certain objects and their exchanges (exchanges of things or exchanges of statements about things)—the conventions that will allow tastes and desires, considered initially as the expression of individual originality, to be shared by others. This is the case even if, in the absence of previously established conventions, these primary collectors are at the outset more like accumulators who pick up things that suit them and put them side by side without any sort of systematic organization. The reference to their very person is what tends to transform such accumulations into collections. Indeed, when artists whose creative activity has gradually made them famous are involved, their identity and the features that turn out to be attached to that identity become the constitutive principle (the governing principle) of a collection that is designated by their names (as when we speak of the "Breton collection") and whose deployment of objects is thought to reveal the depths of the artist's personality. [....]

The initial accessibility of things that bear pertinent differences allows experienced collectors to fill a great number of lacks and, as a result, to move quickly to develop collections (which are, let us recall, collections of differences and not only of things). During the process of accumulation, these collectors presumably acquire a number of duplicates, which they can exchange for things bearing the differences that are so necessary in the logic of collection that they have undertaken but not yet objectivized in the things already present (or they can exchange duplicates for a monetary equivalent that will allow them to acquire items they lack). Still, the existence of lacks that are hard to fill does not stop nagging at them; it is an obstacle to their hope of one day seeing the objective totalization of their collection and the ideal totality in relation to which they are orienting their efforts—a totality whose representation, moreover, they often continued to shape.

Ryoko Sekiguchi
Nagori: Everything Flowing, Everything Flourishing, Leaves the Imprint of Its Waves[1]

Nagori (名残) stands, above all, for the trace, the presence of a past thing, a thing that is no longer there. In this sense, one would speak of a city that has retained a medieval flair, or of a house in which the taste and atmosphere of its former inhabitants can still be felt.[2] Also, the effects, damages, and consequences of an event are called nagori, such as the nagori of an earthquake, or of a disease.

More broadly, nagori can also refer to that which "remains"—whether a person or a thing—in the world in the place of a deceased person, such as a child who reminds one of its parents, for all those who knew them when they were alive.[3] Nagori can also refer to the moment of a separation, or to dying. Or to the state of that which endures, like those scattered blossoms that remain on the branches of trees at the end of the season.

Nagori is not only used in a specific situation, it can also be used in combination with the verb *oshimu* (惜しむ), as in, *nagori wo oshimu* (名残を惜しむ), "to regret a nagori" in the sense of "to become sad over the separation, the passing away," or "to part with a heavy heart." The object of the nagori can be either a place, a person, or a season, or things or actions reminiscent of these.

In Japanese, there exist countless idiomatic expressions with nagori. On the one hand, nagori describe a concrete phenomenon that, contrary to expectations, persists beyond its time, such as *nagori no yuki* (名残の雪), "the nagori snow," that remains after the beginning of spring, or that falls in spring; or *nagori no tsuki* (名残の月), "nagori moon," the moon that can still be seen at dawn.

1 Excerpt from Ryoko Sekiguchi, *Nagori. La nostalgie de la saison qui s'en va* (Paris: P.O.L. Éditeur, 2019). English translation by the editor and Misaki Kawabe.

2 The title of Kazuo Ishiguro's book, *The Remains of the Day* (1989), is *Hi no nagori* (日の名残り), meaning "nagori of the day" in Japanese.

3 To express this meaning, there is another term, *katami* (形見), which means "that which reminds us of a person (the shape: *kata*) when you look at (*mi*) them."

On the other hand, these phrases can express a longing or regret that is reflected in an object or landscape. As in the phrase *nagori no sora* (名残の空), "nagori sky," which refers not to the summer sky that stays bright for a long time but to the sky as it appears when one leaves someone with regret, or to the sky on New Year's Eve, which one views with the feeling of the year coming to an end. *Nagori no sakazuki* (名残の盃) means "the nagori drinking bowl," and in turn refers to the farewell drink: it evokes the situation of drinking one last glass with someone on the evening of separation, in a melancholic mood.

In the Japanese tea ceremony, there is a specific ritual called *nagori no cha* (名残の茶), "nagori tea": it is the tea ceremony organized in autumn, with the remains of tea leaves from the previous year. The new tea is drunk only from November onward. *Nagori no cha* thus marks, in the tea cycle, the end of the tea from the current year, before a new year is opened with the fresh tea. The month of October is therefore called the "month of nagori," and one chooses tableware, equipment, and clothing for this ceremony in a simple style and decoration flowers that are also in the style of nagori, that is, flowers left over from the previous season.

In nagori, attachment, longing, and temporality are interwoven.

Nagori hints at a longing within us, namely the nostalgic longing for a thing that is leaving us, or has left us, as well as the idea of something that is slightly delayed by a season, as if the thing itself (for instance, flowers or snow) was leaving this world and its accompanying season with only regret. Therefore, the thing as well as the person contemplating the thing are experiencing a pain of parting.[4]

The etymology of the word nagori is related to *nami-nokori* (波–残り), the "remains of waves," referring to the imprint left on the sand by waves as they retreat from the beach, as well as the traces of waves, the ephemeral furrows drawn into the sand by them, and also the algae, shells, small pieces of driftwood, and pebbles, which have been washed ashore and remain there. There is neither sense nor reason in these sediments but once they are there, they settle down for a short, transient time.

Nowadays the word is spelled *na-gori* (名–残), the "name that remains." Even if they don't reflect the origin of the word, these letters still appear to create a vivid image of nagori.

Our emotions are not moving ahead as easily. As expressive and reactive as they may be, when it is about bidding farewell to a being or a place, our emotions are still much slower than our body. They follow us, are always a few steps behind.

This complex and delicate concept is widely established in art and also in poetry and essays,

4 On the other hand, *Kokoro-nokori* (心–残り), "losing one's heart," an expression describing regret, is not applicable to things or natural phenomena; its sense is categorically homocentric and apprehended much more narrowly.

5 *Saudade* stands in for a particular, Portuguese form of *Weltschmerz* that only approximately translates to "sadness," "wistfulness," "longing," or "melancholy." It expresses the feeling of losing something beloved and the insatiable longing for something that does not return. Saudade is not a negative mood per se but is longed for in *fado* music, a type of Portuguese singing.

painting and theater, as if it was our Japanese *saudade*, that the emotion connected to it is another one.[5] Nagori carries some sort of resignation within itself, the idea of a fate that cannot be changed. One is giving a part of oneself to the thing, the world, the beauty, and the heart of the beloved being. The heart which experiences nagori is a generous heart, a brave heart. It is not afraid to give itself to marginal, not necessarily dramatic but fragile and tender things, which comprise our lives.

Catalog

Chapter One
Editions of *UN COUP DE DÉS* attributed to Mallarmé

New York, London: Cosmopolis. An International Review, 1897
165 x 258 mm
Offset, thread binding

Cosmopolis Vol. VI. May, 1897. Nr 17 featured the first printed edition of UN COUP DE DÉS JAMAIS N'ABOLIRA LE HASARD on pages 417–427, including a two-page preface by Mallarmé entitled *OBSERVATION RELATIVE AU POÈME*. The texts were preceded by the writing of Anatole France and followed by letters by Ivan Tourgeneff, including no blank pages in any instance.

Wishing to be as eclectic in literature as in politics and to justify itself against the criticism that has been made of it, of misunderstanding the new French poetic school, the editorial staff of *Cosmopolis* offers its readers a previously unpublished poem by Stéphane Mallarmé, the undisputed master of symbolist poetry in France. In this work of an entirely new character, the poet has endeavored to make music with words as elements.

Cosmopolis editor's note

Mallarmé, who in the chrystalline structure of his certainly traditionalist writing saw the true image of what was to come, was in the COUP DE DÉS the first to incorporate the graphic tensions of the advertisements in the printed page.

Walter Benjamin *One Way Street*

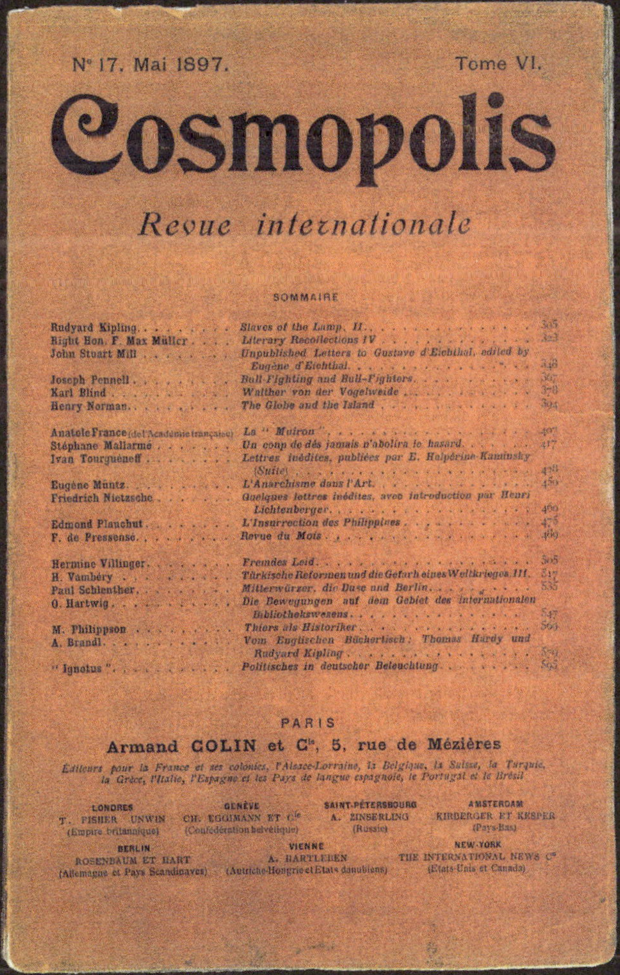

Nº 17. Mai 1897. Tome VI.

Cosmopolis

Revue internationale

SOMMAIRE

Rudyard Kipling	*Slaves of the Lamp. II.*	305
Right Hon. F. Max Müller	*Literary Recollections IV*	323
John Stuart Mill	*Unpublished Letters to Gustave d'Eichthal, edited by Eugène d'Eichthal*	348
Joseph Pennell	*Bull-Fighting and Bull-Fighters*	367
Karl Blind	*Walther von der Vogelweide*	378
Henry Norman	*The Globe and the Island*	394
Anatole France (de l'Académie française)	*La "Muiron"*	407
Stéphane Mallarmé	*Un coup de dés jamais n'abolira le hasard*	417
Ivan Tourguéneff	*Lettres inédites, publiées par E. Halpérine-Kaminsky (Suite)*	428
Eugène Müntz	*L'Anarchisme dans l'Art*	450
Friedrich Nietzsche	*Quelques lettres inédites, avec introduction par Henri Lichtenberger*	460
Edmond Planchut	*L'Insurrection des Philippines*	475
F. de Pressensé	*Revue du Mois*	489
Hermine Villinger	*Fremdes Leid*	505
H. Vambéry	*Türkische Reformen und die Gefahr eines Weltkrieges III.*	517
Paul Schlenther	*Mitterwürzer, die Duse und Berlin*	535
O. Hartwig	*Die Bewegungen auf dem Gebiet des internationalen Bibliothekswesens*	547
M. Philippson	*Thiers als Historiker*	560
A. Brandl	*Vom Englischen Büchertisch: Thomas Hardy und Rudyard Kipling*	579
"Ignotus"	*Politisches in deutscher Beleuchtung*	593

PARIS

Armand COLIN et Cie, 5, rue de Mézières

Éditeurs pour la France et ses colonies, l'Alsace-Lorraine, la Belgique, la Suisse, la Turquie, la Grèce, l'Italie, l'Espagne et les Pays de langue espagnole, le Portugal et le Brésil

LONDRES
T. FISHER UNWIN
(Empire britannique)

GENÈVE
CH. EGGIMANN ET Cie
(Confédération helvétique)

SAINT-PÉTERSBOURG
A. ZINSERLING
(Russie)

AMSTERDAM
KIRBERGER ET KESPER
(Pays-Bas)

BERLIN
ROSENBAUM ET HART
(Allemagne et Pays Scandinaves)

VIENNE
A. HARTLEBEN
(Autriche-Hongrie et États danubiens)

NEW-YORK
THE INTERNATIONAL NEWS Co
(États-Unis et Canada)

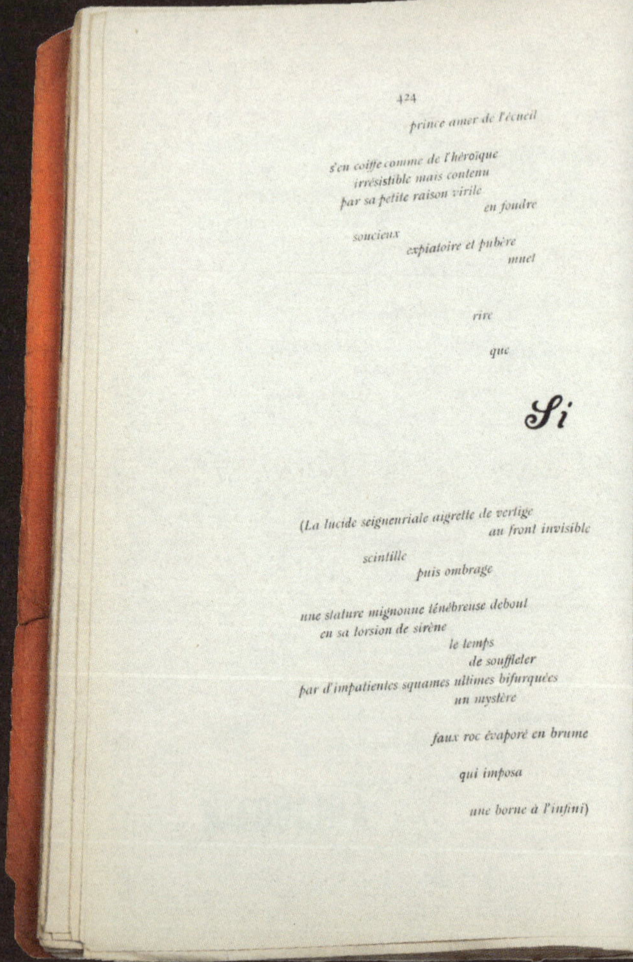

424

prince amer de l'écueil

s'en coiffe comme de l'héroïque
irrésistible mais contenu
par sa petite raison virile
en foudre

soucieux
expiatoire et pubère
muet

rire

que

Si

(La lucide seigneuriale aigrette de vertige
au front invisible

scintille
puis ombrage

une stature mignonne ténébreuse debout
en sa torsion de sirène
le temps
de souffleter
par d'impatientes squames ultimes bifurquées
un mystère

faux roc évaporé en brume

qui imposa

une borne à l'infini)

Stéphane Mallarmé

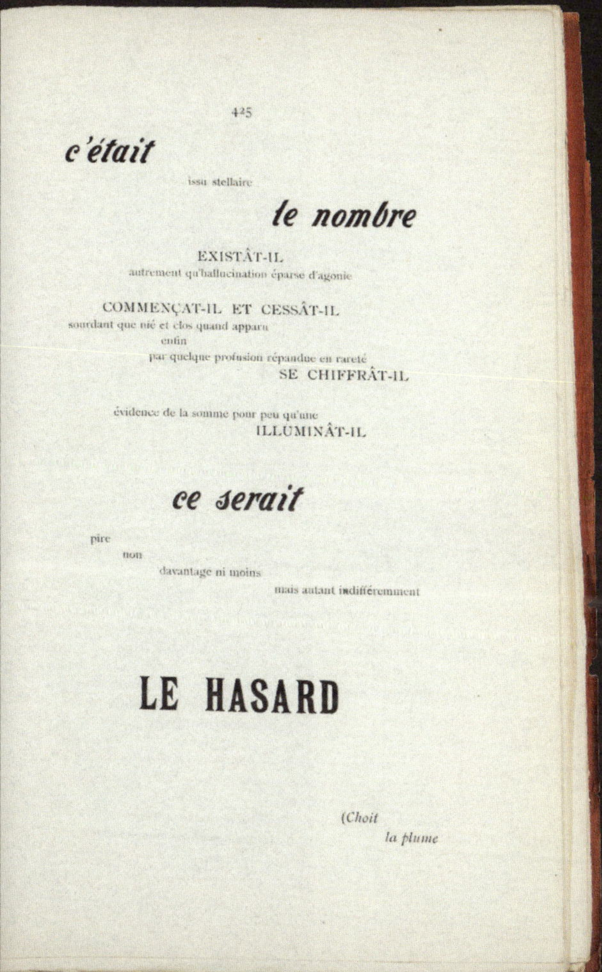

425

c'était

issu stellaire

le nombre

EXISTÂT-IL
autrement qu'hallucination éparse d'agonie

COMMENÇÂT-IL ET CESSÂT-IL
sourdant que nié et clos quand apparu
enfin
par quelque profusion répandue en rareté
SE CHIFFRÂT-IL

évidence de la somme pour peu qu'une
ILLUMINÂT-IL

ce serait

pire
non
davantage ni moins
mais autant indifféremment

LE HASARD

(Choit
la plume

1:2

Stéphane Mallarmé
UN COUP DE DÉS JAMAIS N'ABOLIRA LE HASARD. POÉME
Paris: Éditions de la Nouvelle Revue Française, 1914
330 x 255 mm
ed. 10 (numbered): letterpress on pure hemp paper, Papeteries de Monval
ed. 90: letterpress on Vellum D'Arches, thread binding
ed. 300: letterpress, thread binding

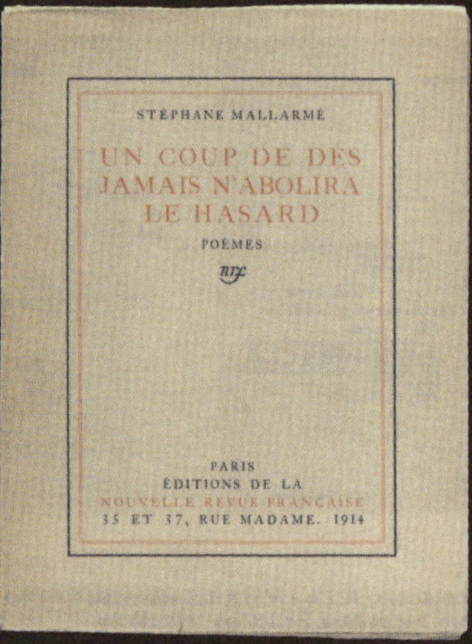

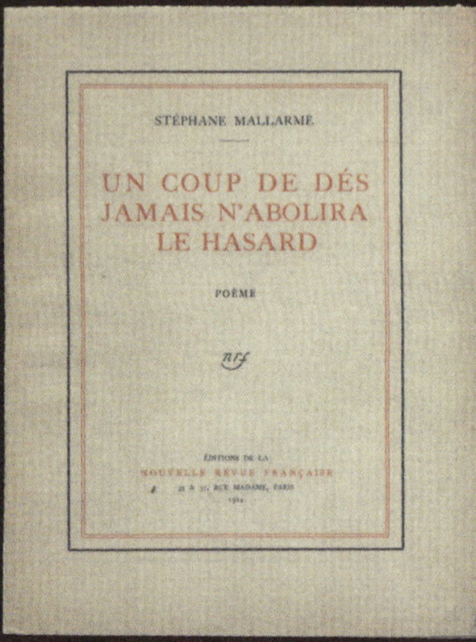

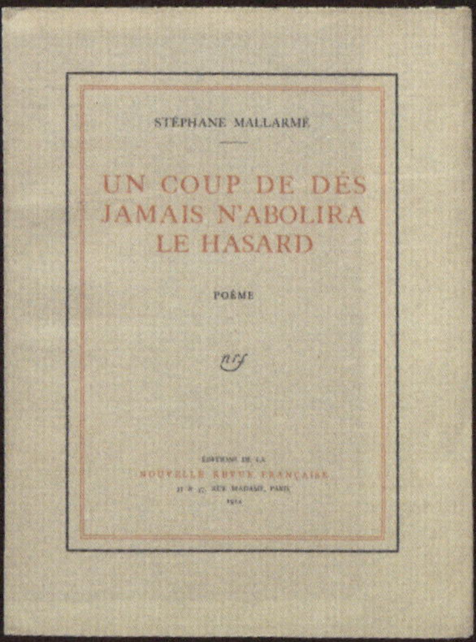

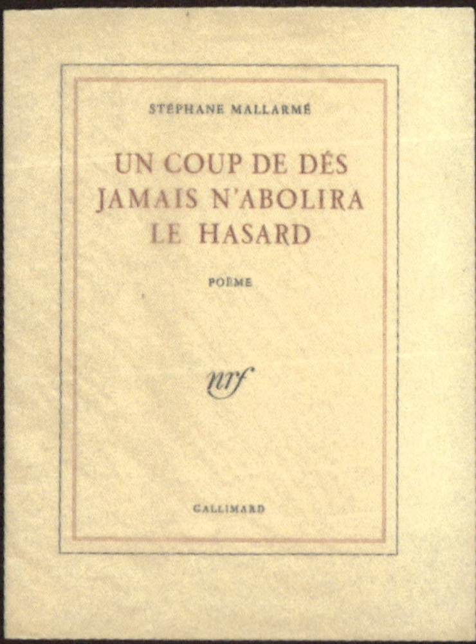

Stéphane Mallarmé
UN COUP DE DÉS JAMAIS N'ABOLIRA LE HASARD. POÉM
Paris: Éditions Gallimard, 1993, 2006, 2008
325 x 250 mm
Offset, thread binding

Stéphane Mallarmé
UN COUP DE DÉS JAMAIS N'ABOLIRA LE HASARD. POÈME
Paris: Éditions Gallimard, 1952
325 x 250 mm
Offset

Mallarmé's "PREFACE" from the *Cosmopolis* edition is reproduced in full in the monographic 1914 NRF edition: "This seemed to us to be of such comprehensive interest and significant enough for the author's thinking that it should be reproduced here, in front of the final edition, which he prepared with care, as it should have appeared at the moment when Death surprised him. The main innovation introduced by him in this last part of his work, to take up the expression he uses, seems to us to be that there are no longer two sides of a page, but that the reading is about both sides together done, just following the usual fall of the lines."

Editor's note, 1914 NRF edition

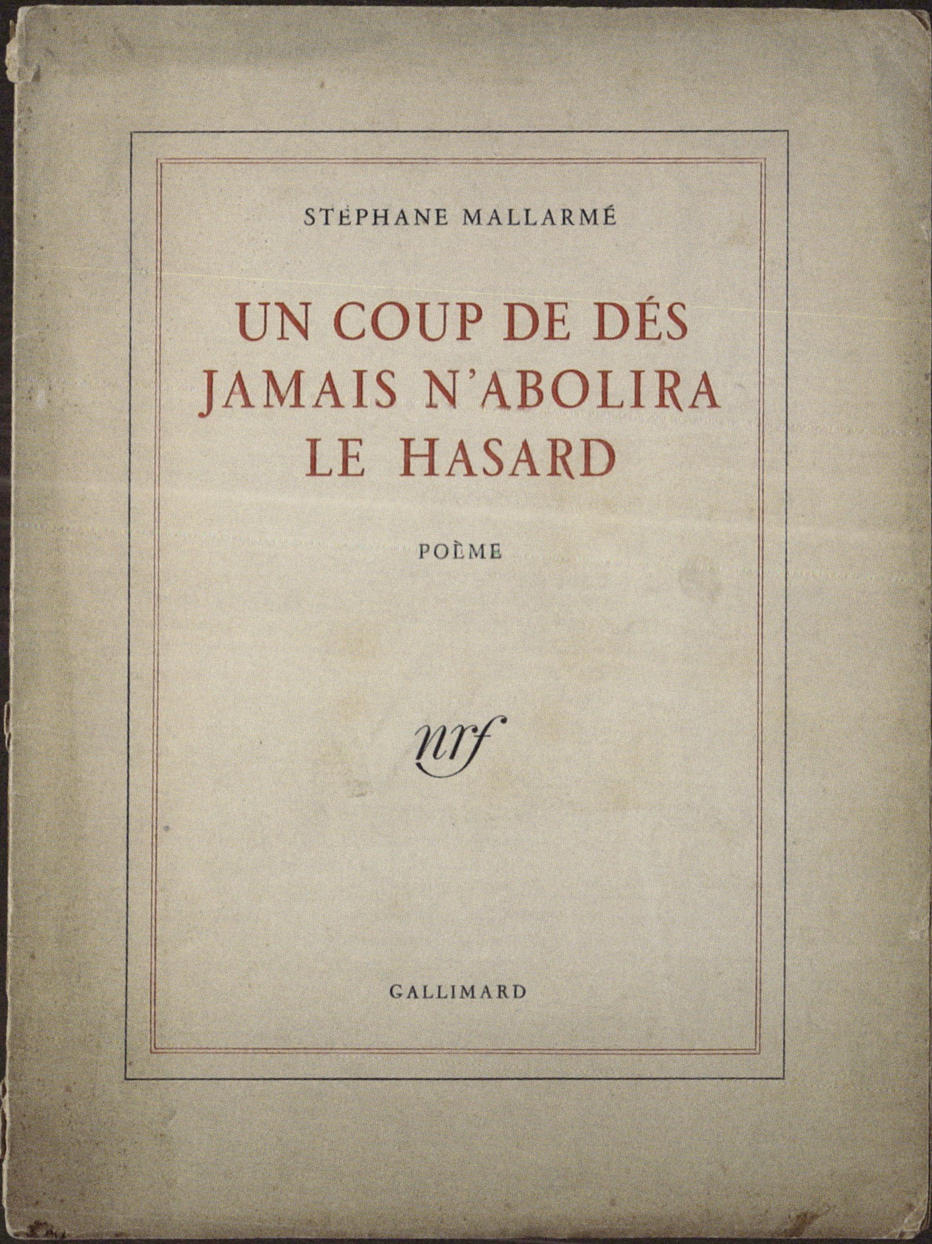

1:2

ne lût pas (NOT READING)
I would prefer that this Note was not read, or skimmed, was forgotten; it tells the knowledgeable reader little beyond their own penetration

espacement de la lecture (READING SPACE)
The ensuing words, laid out as they are, lead on to the last, with no novelty except the spacing of the reading.

"blancs" (WHITES)
The "blanks" indeed take on importance, at first glance; the versification demands them, as a surrounding silence, to the extent that a fragment, lyrical or of a few beats, occupies, in its midst, a third of the space of paper: I do not transgress the measure, only disperse it.

Le papier (PAPER)
The paper intervenes each time as an image, of itself, ends or begins once more, accepting a succession of others, and, since, as ever, it does nothing, of regular sonorous lines or verse

simultanée de la Page (PAGE as a spacial entity)
The literary value, if I may say it, of this span of empty space on the page, which mentally separates groups of words or words themselves, is to periodically accelerate or slow the movement, the scansion, the sequence even, given one's simultaneous view of the entirety of the page: the latter taken as unity, as elsewhere the Verse is or perfect line.

une partition (A SCORE)
In addition, this use of the bare thought with its retreats, prolongations, and flights, by reason of its very design, for anyone wishing to read it aloud, results in a score. The variation in printed characters between the dominant motif, a secondary one and those adjacent, marks its importance for oral utterance, and the scale, mid-way, at top or bottom of the page, will show how the intonation rises or falls.

PRÉFACE

J'aimerais qu'on ne lût pas cette Note ou que parcourue, même on l'oubliât ; elle apprend, au Lecteur habile, peu de chose situé outre sa pénétration : mais, peut troubler l'ingénu devant appliquer un regard aux premiers mots du Poème pour que de suivants, disposés comme ils sont, l'amènent aux derniers, le tout sans nouveauté qu'un espacement de la lecture. Les "blancs" en effet, assument l'importance, frappent d'abord ; la versification en exigea, comme silence alentour, ordinairement, au point qu'un morceau, lyrique ou de peu de pieds, occupe, au milieu, le tiers environ du feuillet : je ne transgresse cette mesure, seulement la disperse. Le papier intervient chaque fois qu'une image, d'elle-même, cesse ou rentre, acceptant la succession d'autres et, comme il ne s'agit pas, ainsi que toujours, de traits sonores réguliers ou vers — plutôt, de subdivisions prismatiques de l'Idée, l'instant de paraître et que dure leur concours, dans quelque mise en scène spirituelle exacte, c'est à des places variables, près ou loin du fil conducteur latent, en raison de la vraisemblance, que s'impose le texte. L'avantage, si j'ai droit à le dire, littéraire, de cette distance copiée qui mentalement sépare des groupes de mots ou les mots entre eux, semble d'accélérer tantôt et de ralentir le mouvement, le scandant, l'intimant même selon une vision simultanée de la Page : celle-ci prise pour unité comme l'est autre part le Vers ou ligne parfaite. La fiction affleurera et se dissipera, vite, d'après la mobilité de l'écrit, autour des arrêts fragmentaires d'une phrase capitale dès le titre introduite et continuée. Tout se passe, par raccourci, en hypothèse ; on évite le récit. Ajouter que de cet emploi à nu de la pensée avec retraits, prolongements, fuites, ou son dessin même, résulte, pour qui veut lire à haute voix, une partition. La différence des caractères d'imprimerie entre le motif prépondérant, un secondaire et d'adjacents, dicte son importance à l'émission

1:2

orale et la portée, moyenne, en haut, en bas de page, notera que monte ou descend l'intonation. Seules certaines directions très hardies *, des empiètements, etc., formant le contre-point de cette prosodie, demeurent dans une œuvre, qui manque de précédents, à l'état élémentaire : non que j'estime l'opportunité d'essais timides ; mais il ne m'appartient pas, hormis une pagination spéciale ou de volume à moi, dans un Périodique, même valeureux, gracieux et invitant qu'il se montre aux belles libertés, d'agir par trop contrairement à l'usage. J'aurai, toutefois, indiqué du Poème ci-joint, mieux que l'esquisse, un "état" qui ne rompe pas de tous points avec la tradition ; poussé sa présentation en maint sens aussi avant qu'elle n'offusque personne : suffisamment, pour ouvrir des yeux. Aujourd'hui ou sans présumer de l'avenir qui sortira d'ici, rien ou presque un art, reconnaissons aisément que la tentative participe, avec imprévu, de poursuites particulières et chères à notre temps, le vers libre et le poème en prose. Leur réunion s'accomplit sous une influence, je sais, étrangère, celle de la Musique entendue au concert ; on en retrouve plusieurs moyens m'ayant semblé appartenir aux Lettres, je les reprends. Le genre, que c'en devienne un comme la symphonie, peu à peu, à côté du chant personnel, laisse intact l'antique vers, auquel je garde un culte et attribue l'empire de la passion et des rêveries ; tandis que ce serait le cas de traiter, de préférence (ainsi qu'il suit) tels sujets d'imagination pure et complexe ou intellect : que ne reste aucune raison d'exclure de la Poésie — unique source.

* La partie comprise entre les mots "Seules certaines directions..." et "...suffisamment pour ouvrir des yeux" concernait plus spécialement l'édition de ce Poème donnée dans la revue *Cosmopolis* (mai 1897) pour laquelle cette Préface avait été faite. Celle-ci, du reste, nous a paru d'un intérêt assez général, et assez significative de la pensée de l'auteur pour être reproduite ici, en tête de l'édition définitive, préparée par ses soins, telle qu'elle allait paraître au moment où la mort le surprit. L'innovation principale établie par lui dans ce dernier "état" de son œuvre, pour reprendre le terme dont il se servit, nous semble consister en ceci qu'il n'existe pas de page recto ou verso, mais que la lecture se fait sur les deux pages à la fois, en tenant compte simplement de la descente ordinaire des lignes.

(Note de l'Editeur).

dans un Périodique (CONTEXT)
It is not for me, save by a special pagination or volume of my own, in a Periodical so courageous, gracious and accommodating as it shows itself to be to real freedom, to act too contrary to custom.

mieux que l'esquisse (A SKETCH)
I will have shown, in the Poem below, more than a sketch, a "state" which yet does not entirely break with tradition, will have furthered its presentation in many ways too, without offending anyone, sufficing to open a few eyes.

la Musique (MUSIC)
Their meeting takes place under an influence, alien I know, that of Music heard in concert; one finds there several techniques that seem to me to belong to Literature; I reclaim them.

sujets d'imagination (IMAGINATION)
This may be the preferred means (as follows) of dealing with subjects of pure and complex imagination or intellect: which there is no remaining justification for excluding from Poetry—the unique source.

les deux pages à la fois (SPREAD as an entity)
The main innovation established by him in this last "state" of his work, to use the term he used, seems to us to consist in the fact that there is no recto or verso page, but that reading is done on both pages at once, simply taking into account the ordinary descent of the lines.

1:2

SOIT

que

l'Abîme

blanchi

étale

furieux

sous une inclinaison

plane désespérément

d'aile

la sienne

par

Mallarmé

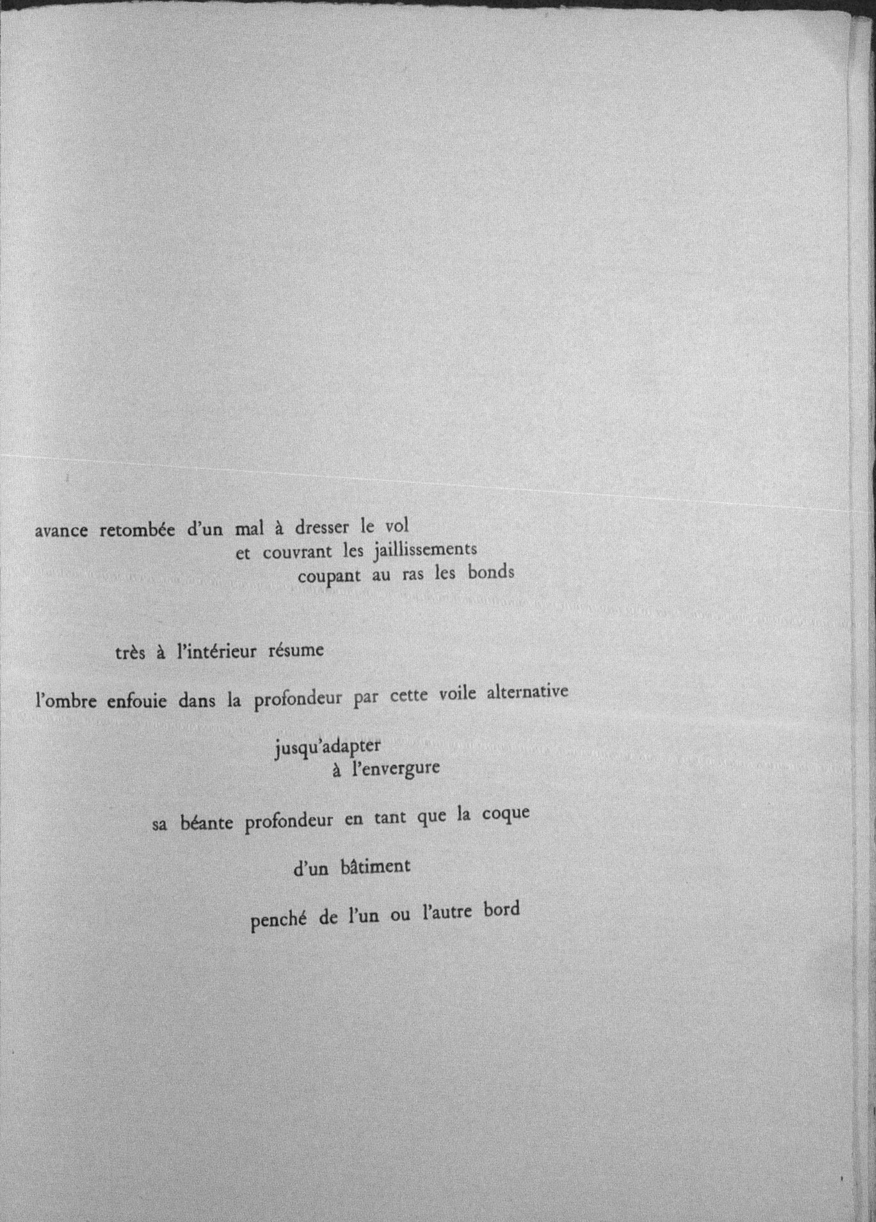

avance retombée d'un mal à dresser le vol
et couvrant les jaillissements
coupant au ras les bonds

très à l'intérieur résume

l'ombre enfouie dans la profondeur par cette voile alternative

jusqu'adapter
à l'envergure

sa béante profondeur en tant que la coque

d'un bâtiment

penché de l'un ou l'autre bord

1:2

C'ÉTAIT
issu stellaire

CE SERAIT
pire
non
davantage ni moins
indifféremment mais autant

Stéphane Mallarmé

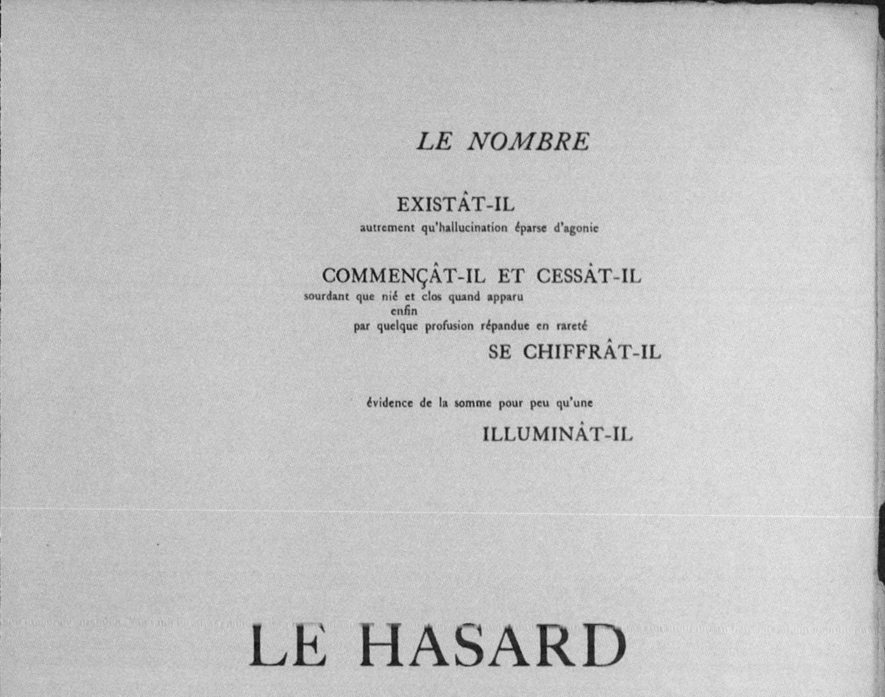

LE NOMBRE

EXISTÂT-IL
autrement qu'hallucination éparse d'agonie

COMMENÇÂT-IL ET CESSÂT-IL
sourdant que nié et clos quand apparu
enfin
par quelque profusion répandue en rareté
SE CHIFFRÂT-IL

évidence de la somme pour peu qu'une
ILLUMINÂT-IL

LE HASARD

Choit
la plume
rythmique suspens du sinistre
s'ensevelir
aux écumes originelles
naguères d'où sursauta son délire jusqu'à une cime
flétrie
par la neutralité identique du gouffre

1:2

C'ÉTAIT
issu stellaire

CE SERAIT
pire
non
davantage ni moins
indifféremment mais autant

LE NOMBRE

EXISTÂT-IL
autrement qu'hallucination éparse d'agonie

COMMENÇÂT-IL ET CESSÂT-IL
sourdant que nié et clos quand apparu
enfin
par quelque profusion répandue en rareté
SE CHIFFRÂT-IL

évidence de la somme pour peu qu'une
ILLUMINÂT-IL

LE HASARD

Choit
la plume
rythmique suspens du sinistre
s'ensevelir
aux écumes originelles
naguères d'où sursauta son délire jusqu'à une cime
flétrie
par la neutralité identique du gouffre

Claude Roulet
ÉLUCIDATION DU POÈME DE STÉPHANE MALLARMÉ,
UN COUP DE DÉS JAMAIS N'ABOLIRA LE HASARD
Neuchâtel: AUX IDES ET CALENDES, 1943
240 x 160 mm, 178 pp.
Offset, thread binding

Two volumes: secondary literature (scholarly essay) and facsimile of Mallarmé's *UN COUP DE DÉS*.

Image on previous spread: scale 1:1

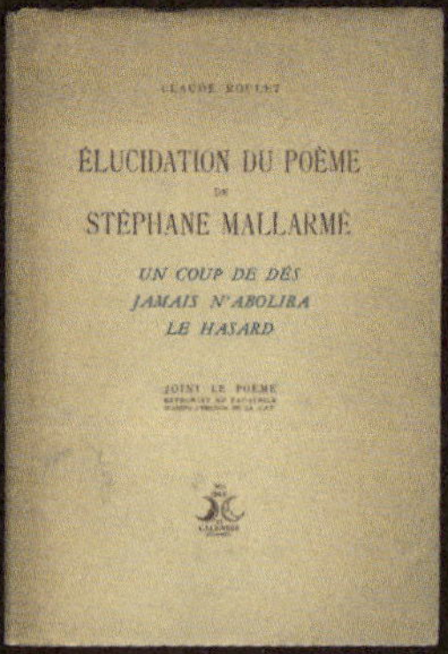

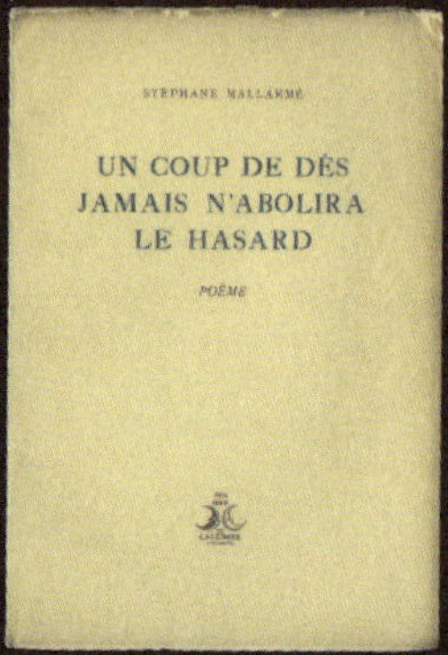

Stéphane Mallarmé
UN COUP DE DÉS JAMAIS N'ABOLIRA LE HASARD
Mailand: Il Balcone Rosa e Ballo, 1945
323 x 245 mm
Offset, thread binding

Stéphane Mallarmé, ed. Henri Kaeser
POÉSIES. UN COUP DE DÉS VERS DE CIRCONSTANCE
Lausanne: Aux Éditions Du Grand-Chêne, 1943
192 x 145 mm, 352 pp.
Offset, thread binding
ed. 2,000

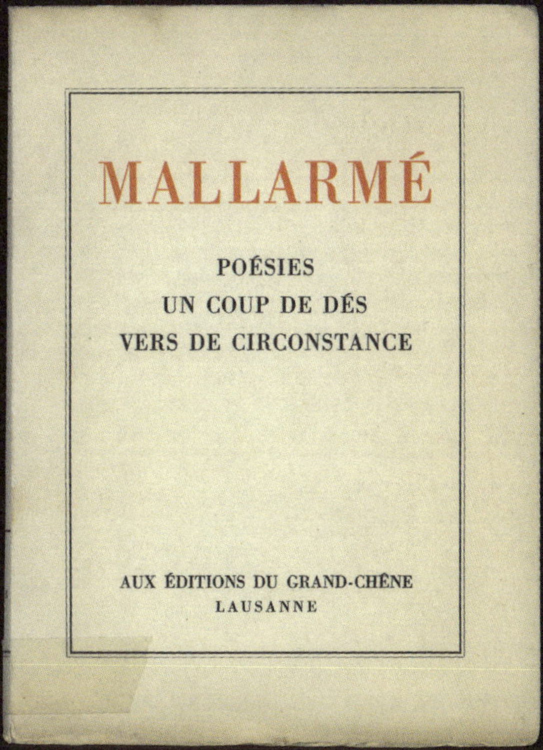

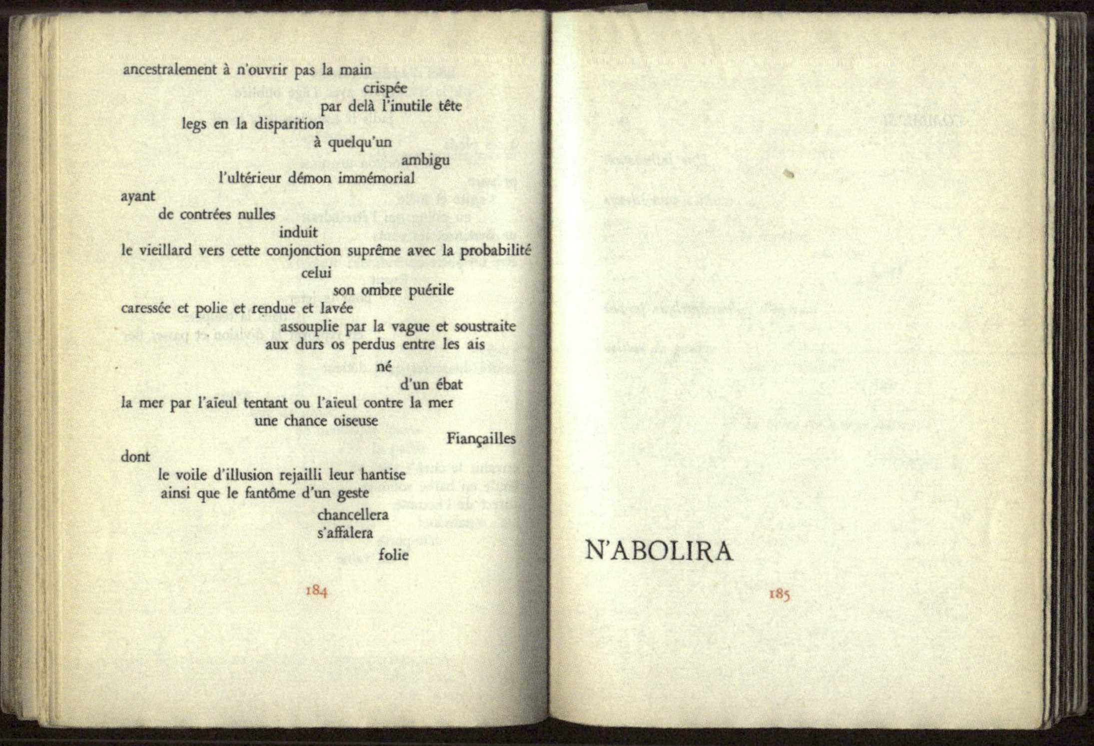

Robert Greer Cohn
Mallarmé's Un Coup de Dés*: an exegesis*
New Haven: Yale French Studies, 1949

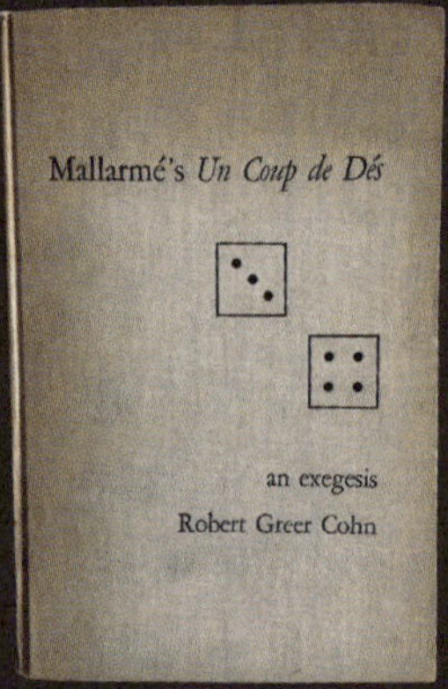

In this exegesis, R. G. Cohn collects evidence for the connection between *UN COUP DE DÉS* and *LE LIVRE*. They led him to the opinion—and numerous essays on the fiftieth anniversary of Mallarmé's death supported this opinion—"that the *UN COUP DE DÉS* more or less represents the famous BOOK... Tangible evidence exists that prove that the *COUP DE DÉS* is at least a fragment of Mallarmé's first view."

Mallarmé's words in his autobiographical letter to Verlaine of November 16, 1885, point also in this direction. He writes about his attempt "with the patience of an alchemist," to design the "BOOK... built up and thought through.... It will succeed, perhaps, not to create this work in its entirety... but to show an executed fragment of it..."

The back pocket of the book includes a facsimile of *UN COUP DE DÉS JAMAIS N'ABOLIRA LE HASARD*.

Stéphane Mallarmé
UN COUP DE DÉS JAMAIS N'ABOLIRA LE HASARD
With an English translation by Daisy Aldan
New York: Tiber Press, 1956
260 x 180 mm
Offset, thread binding

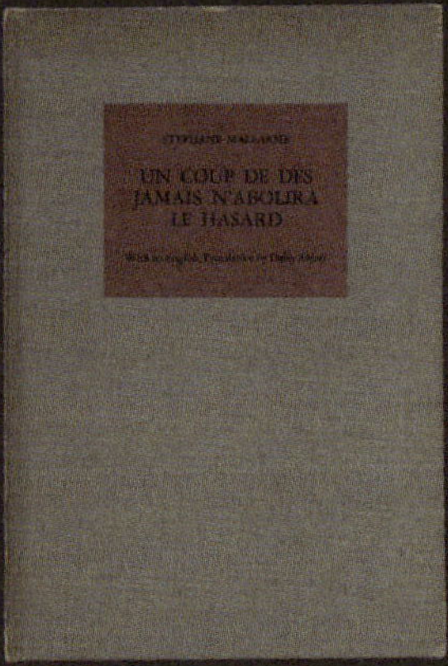

This first published translation of *UN COUP DE DÉS* into English has been authorized by Gallimard and the heirs of Mallarmé.

Daisy Aldan

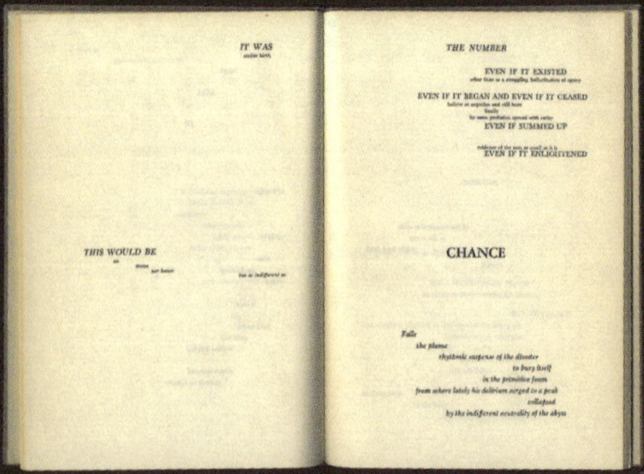

Stéphane Mallarmé, Andre Masson
UN COUP DE DÉS JAMAIS N'ABOLIRA LE HASARD
Paris: Amateurs du Livre et de l'Estampe Moderne, 1961
445 x 335 mm
In-folio, in sheets on Arches, folded cover fully lithographed, jacket and case decorated in brown and white
ed. 102

For this edition, surrealist painter André Masson (1896–1987) illustrated and rewrote, in his own handwriting, Mallarmé's text, following the 1914 Gallimard edition. The polychrome book, completely lithographed, constitutes a *livre de peintre*. Masson illustrated many books, usually limited editions.

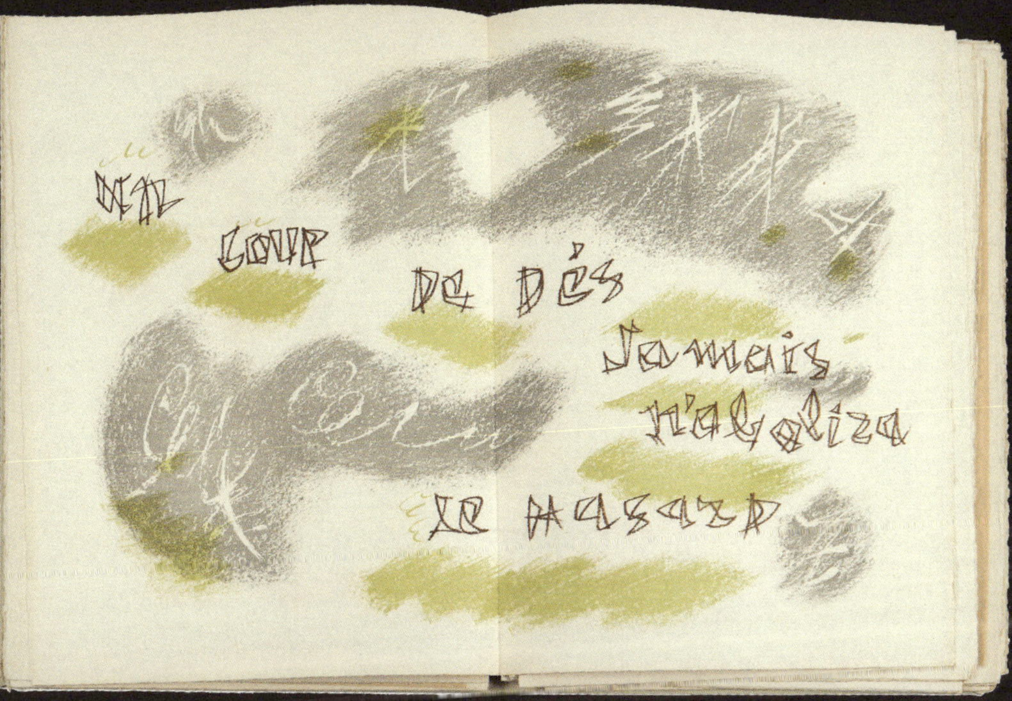

Stéphane Mallarmé, ed. G. Jean-Aubry
STÉPHANE MALLARMÉ ŒUVRES COMPLÈTES
with contributions by Henri Mondor
France: Bibliothèque de la Pléiade, 1965
110 x 180 mm, 1,660 pp.
Offset, thread binding

The Bibliothèque de la Pléiade is a French editorial collection, which was created in 1931 by Jacques Schiffrin, an independent young editor. Schiffrin wanted to provide the public with reference editions of the complete works of classic authors in a pocket format. André Gide brought Schiffrin's project to Gallimard, where it is still published today. The Pléiade has a strong emphasis on works that were originally written in French, though the collection also includes classics of world literature.

UN COUP DE DÉS is printed over twenty-one pages including only one blank page, of these twenty-one pages eighteen include pagination.

ES WAR

sternhaften Ursprungs

ES WÄRE

schlimmer

nicht

mehr oder weniger

ununterscheidbar doch gleichviel

DER ZAHL EINFALL

WÄRE ER
mehr als ein flüchtiges Trugbild im Sterben

OHNE ANFANG UND ENDE
werdend schon verneint und unwiderruflich wenn erschienen
endlich
aus einer Fülle erweitert in die Seltenheit
UMSCHRIEBEN

als offenbare Summe falls eine
BELEUCHTET

DER ZUFALL

Fällt
die Feder
ein rhythmisches Schwanken von Dunkel
unterzugehen
im Schaum der Herkunft
dem eben entsprang ihr Rausch zur Höhe
gestürzt
im identischen Gleichsinn der Gründe

Stéphane Mallarmé
Ein Würfelwurf
Olten and Freiburg: Walter-Verlag, 1966
237 x 145 mm, 136 pp.
Offset, thread binding
ed. 1,200

Bilingual in French and German throughout, *Ein Würfelwurf* features Mallarmé's "PREFACE", as well as *UN COUP DE DÉS* printed over twenty-four pages, unpaginated and including three blank pages.

The book also features a glossary, a scholarly essay by the translator Marie Louise Erlenmeyer, excerpts from Mallarmé's published writings and letters, and gathers excerpts from the reception history of the book by Paul Valéry, André Gide, Stefan George, Rainer Maria Rilke, James Joyce, Jean-Paul Sartre, Gottfried Benn, Gerda Zeltner-Neukomm, and Pierre Boulez.

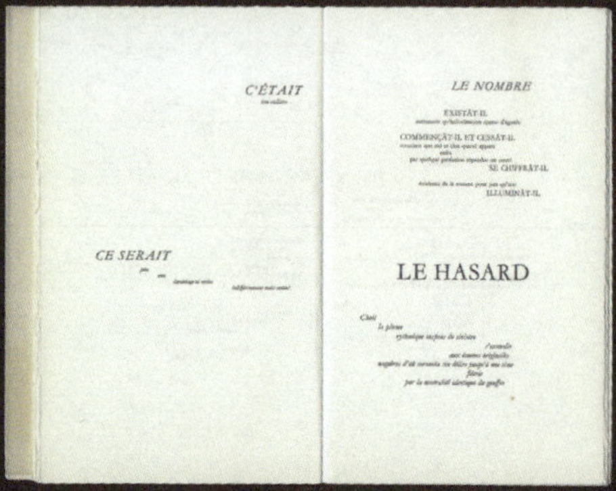

Robert Greer Cohn
Mallarmé's Masterwork: New Findings
The Hage, Paris: Mouton & Co., 1966
236 x 160 mm, 116 pp.

In this book, Robert Greer Cohn publishes facsimiles of the Lahure proofs of Mallarmé's *UN COUP DE DÉS JAMAIS N'ABOLIRA LE HASARD*, 1898, including three of four lithographs by Odilon Redon commissioned for this publication, and housed in Houghton Library, Harvard University.

Cohn proposes a close inspection of the Lahure proofs to support the thesis of a large-format version exceeding the dimensions of the NRF edition of *UN COUP DE DÉS*. Cohn notes: "The poet's intentions could only be shown in print since 'the type' is an integral part of the enterprise; in a sense he composed his poem on these sheets. Moreover, the text is modified in a few places, with indications in the poet's handwriting." (p. 78)

A digital folio of the of the Lahure proofs is available at: https://iiif.lib.harvard.edu/manifests/view/drs:434952194.

Stéphane Mallarmé, translation by Brian Coffey
DICE THROWN NEVER WILL ANNUL CHANCE, a translation of UN COUP DE DÉS JAMAIS N'ABOLIRA LE HASARD
Dublin: Dolmen Press Limited, 1967
230 x 153 mm
Offset, thread binding

The present translation follows the text and, thanks to Mr. Liam Miller, the typographical layout of the 1914 edition of the poem. A few turns of expression are due to Professor Cohn, who, very kindly, read the whole translation in manuscript, and was very encouraging to the translator. This is not, naturally, to claim Professor Cohn's approval of every part of the version in its present form.

Brian Coffey

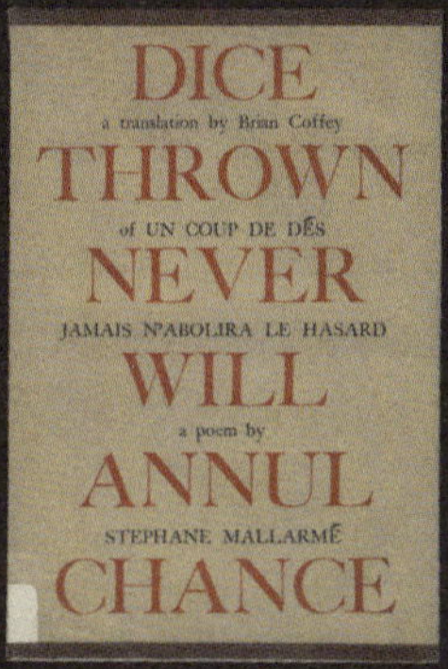

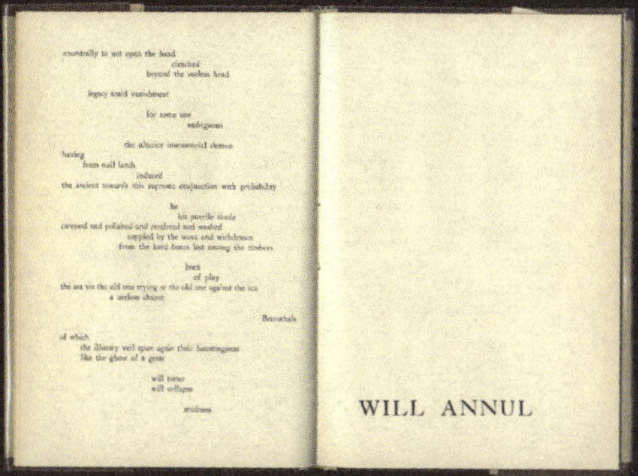

Stéphane Mallarmé
UN COUP DE DÉS JAMAIS N'ABOLIRA LE HASARD
Paris: Éditions Gallimard, 1969
230 x 190 mm, 30 pp.
Offset, thread binding

In 1969 Gallimard published a monographic pocket edition.

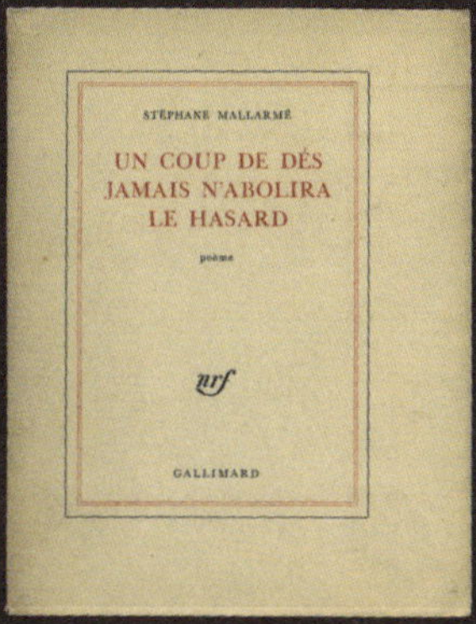

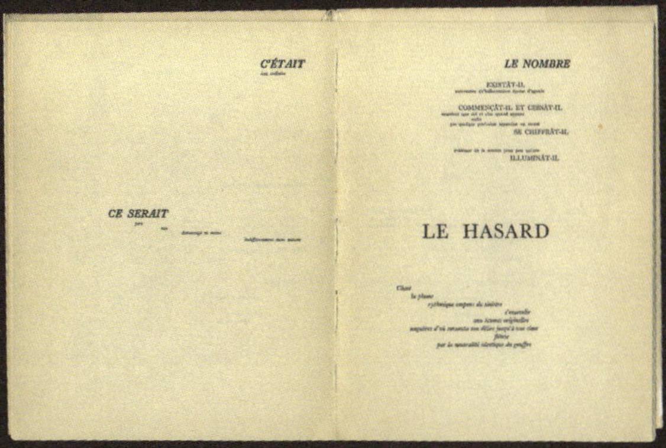

Stéphane Mallarmé

UN COUP DE DÉS JAMAIS N'ABOLIRA LE HASARD. POÈME

Geneva: Edwin, 1975

333 x 255 mm

Letterpress bound in cloth with original engravings

ed. 100

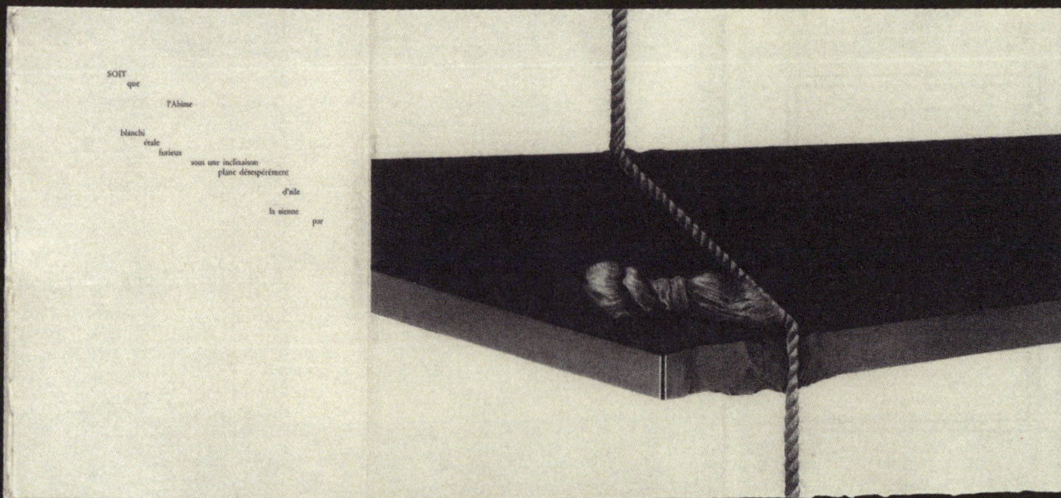

Stéphane Mallarmé
UN COUP DE DÉS...
Paris: Editions Baudouin, 1979
160 x 135 mm, 86 pp.
Offset, perfect binding

This pocket edition includes Mallarmé's *UN COUP DE DÉS* printed over twenty-three pages, without the "PREFACE," and also includes sixty-five blank pages for "NOTES."

An editorial note claims: "This 1914 edition is faithful and careful."

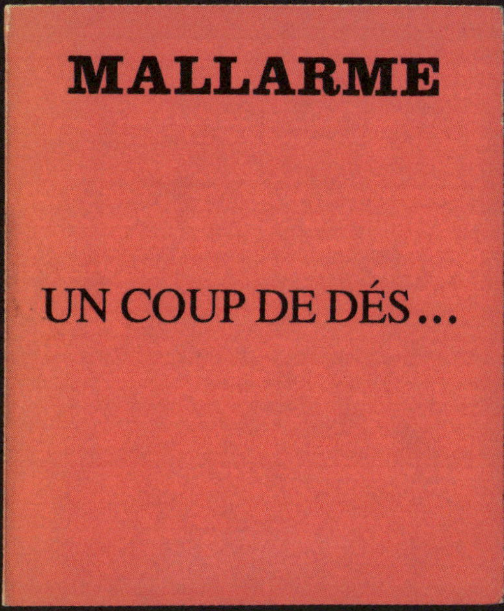

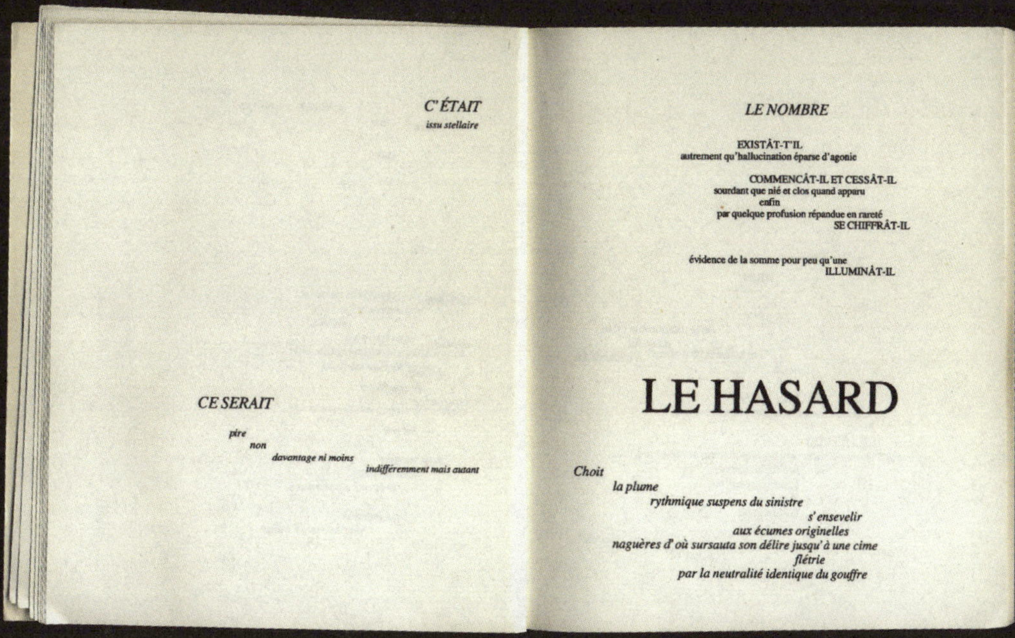

1:2

Stéphane Mallarmé, ed. Mitsou Ronat and Tibor Papp
UN COUP DE DÉS JAMAIS N'ABOLIRA LE HASARD
Paris: Change errant/d'atelier, 1980
380 x 285 mm, 24 pp.
Offset, two sets of folded and gathered folios, enclosed in a portfolio with four flaps

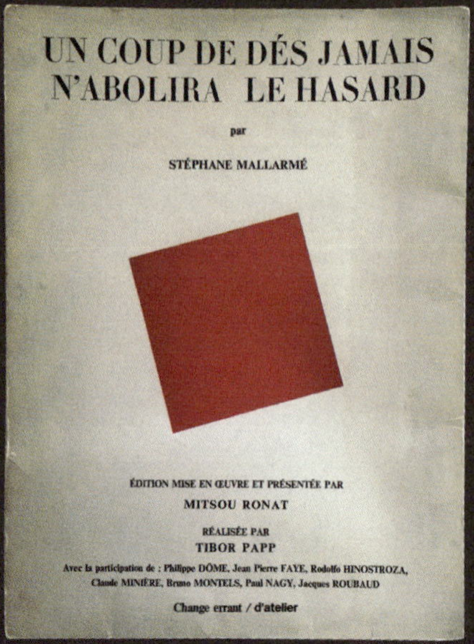

According to Mitsou Ronat, Cohn's publication of the large-format Lahure proofs convinced her to produce the first large double-page version of *UN COUP DE DÉS*, published by the Groupe d'Atelier, in collaboration with artist and typographer Tibor Papp.

In her book *The Book As Instrument: Stéphane Mallarmé, The Artist's Book, and the Transformation of Print Culture*, author Anna Sigrídur Arnar singles out Mitsou Ronat and Tibor Papp's edition of *UN COUP DE DÉS* for respecting Mallarmé's wishes, which she notes is "composed of six unbound folio leaves, each nestled within the other without a separate cover."

Stéphane Mallarmé, Wolfram Erber
Pastelle und Zeichnungen zu »Ein Würfelwurf«
Munich: Galerie Fred Jahn, 1980
270 x 210 mm
Offset, thread binding
ed. 300

The book features the German translation by Marie-Louise Erlenmeyer and is illustrated by Wolfram Erber.

Stéphane Mallarmé
A cast of dice never can annul chance
London: Tetrad, 1985
380 x 290 mm, 28 pp.
Offset with aquatint prints, unsewn, loosely laid in a folder
ed. 40

This collaboration between artist/publisher Ian Tyson and typographer Neil Crawford presents, in English, Stéphane Mallarmé's innovative poem *UN COUP DE DÉS JAMAIS N'ABOLIRA LE HASARD* (1897).

The work is accompanied by a series of rich black aquatints by Ian Tyson. These geometric abstracts complement the inconclusive mood of the poem, reversing its proportion of white to black, perhaps further to explore the idea of negative space between significant forms.

Collection: Victoria and Albert Museum, London

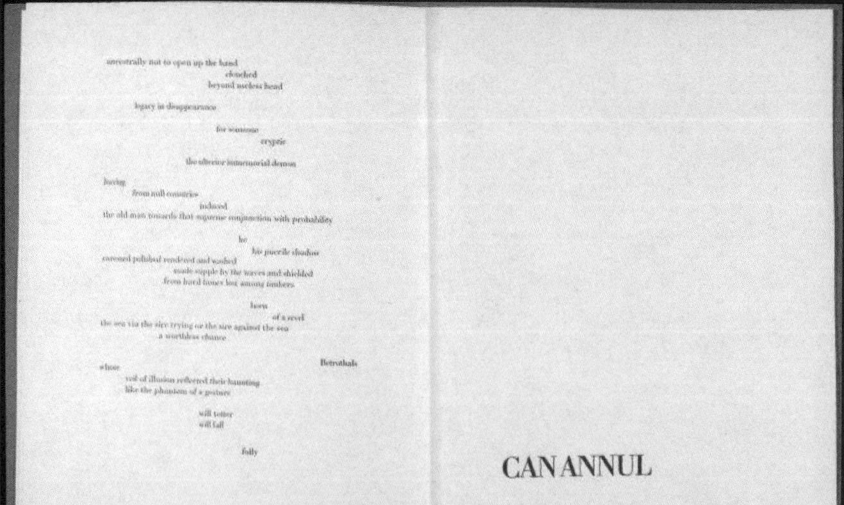

Stéphane Mallarmé, translation by Maurizio Cucchi
UN COUP DE DÉS JAMAIS N'ABOLIRA LE HASARD / UN COLPO DI DADI MAI ABOLIRÀ IL CASO
Verona: Edizioni Ampersand, 1987
325 x 260 mm, 70 pp.
Wood engravings and movable type, slipcased, paper bound, sewn
ed. 115

This letterpress edition of *UN COUP DE DÉS* hand-composed with Caslon types cast by Stephenson Blake, was printed by Alessandro Zanilla with the 1854 Stanhope hand press, assisted by Linda Samson-Talleur. The one hundred and fifteen copies of the print run are certified as follows: twenty-five, marked with Roman numerals, printed on Japan Gampi villum vat paper; ninety, marked with Arabic numerals, on Barcham Green English vat paper.

Colophon

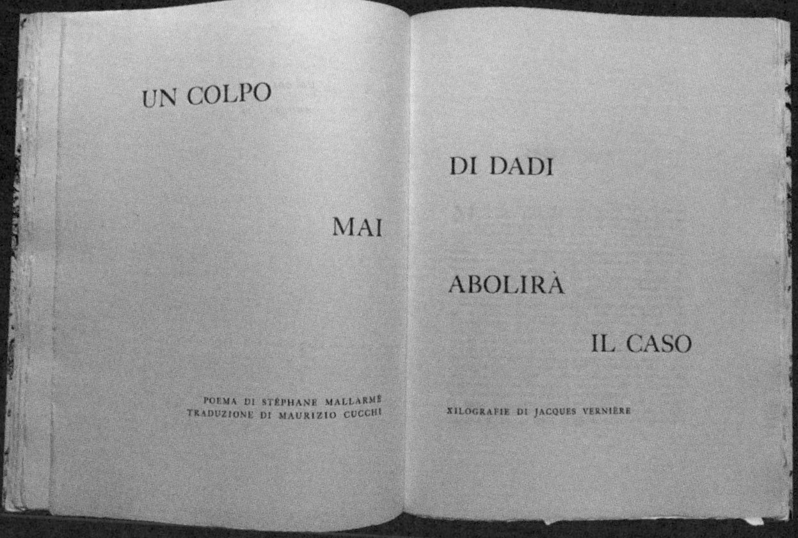

Stéphane Mallarmé, illustrated by Honorine Tepfer
UN COUP DE DÉS JAMAIS N'ABOLIRA LE HASARD: POÈME
1989
325 x 255 mm, 34 pp.
Offset, accordion fold with embossed paper cover
ed. 48

Stéphane Mallarmé, Ellsworth Kelly
UN COUP DE DÉS
New York: Limited Editions Club, 1992
430 x 314 mm
Full-page black lithographs printed on a fine ivory Rives paper, leather binding, black brushed-fabric covered portfolio
ed. 300

Although in no way mimetic, the lithograph exhibited expresses perhaps the descending movement of the text and the doomed ship.

A Throw of the Dice, UCI Libraries, 2003

In 1992, the Limited Editions Club (LEC) published *UN COUP DE DÉS* in the original French. Layout and typographical decisions were made after carefully consulting Mallarmé's original, hand-written proofs, which are now part of the Houghton Library at Harvard University. The publication features eleven original lithographs by Ellsworth Kelly and an English translation by Daisy Aldan.

An artist known for his meticulous attention to display settings, Kelly selected the poem (declining LEC director Sid Shiff's original suggestion that Kelly instead illustrate Walt Whitman's *Leaves of Grass*), and determined the placement of his prints within the publication.

Akzente Heft 2/April 1992. Zeitschrift für Literatur, herausgegeben von Michael Krüger Hanser, ed. Michael Krüger
Munich: Hanser, 1992
200 x 130 mm, 192 pp.
Offset, thread binding

Walter Höllerer and Hans Bender founded "Akzente" in 1953. Ingeborg Bachmann was an author from the very beginning, Hans Magnus Enzensberger made his debut here, Thomas Mann, Elias Canetti, Paul Celan and Nelly Sachs were represented with articles—the magazine became an institution. Michael Krüger edited the magazine from 1976 to 2014.

Hanser Literaturverlage

The April 1992 issue features a full (and paginated) reprint and translation of Mallarmé's UN COUP DE DÉS.

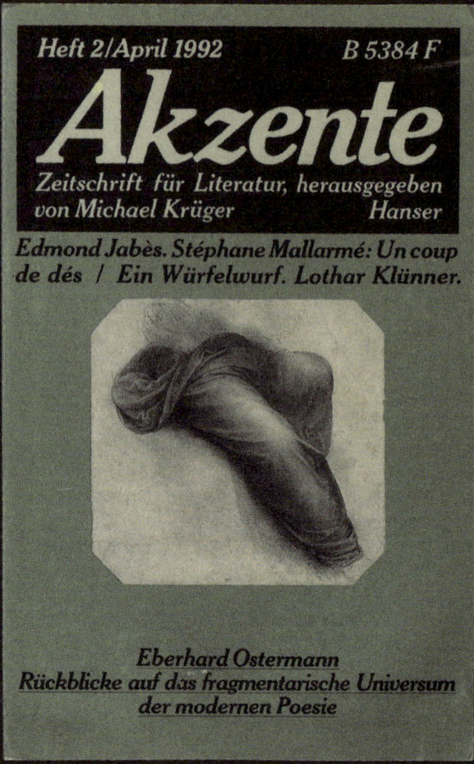

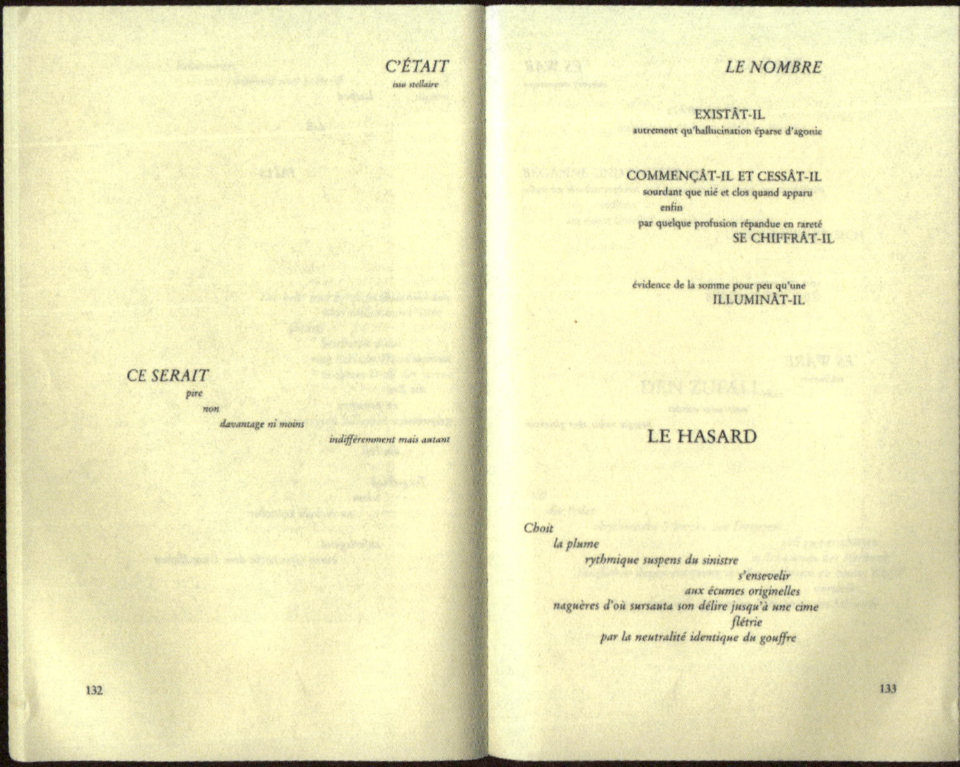

C'ÉTAIT
issu stellaire

CE SERAIT
pire
non
davantage ni moins
indifféremment mais autant

132

LE NOMBRE

EXISTÂT-IL
autrement qu'hallucination éparse d'agonie

COMMENÇÂT-IL ET CESSÂT-IL
sourdant que nié et clos quand apparu
enfin
par quelque profusion répandue en rareté
SE CHIFFRÂT-IL

évidence de la somme pour peu qu'une
ILLUMINÂT-IL

LE HASARD

Choit
la plume
rythmique suspens du sinistre
s'ensevelir
aux écumes originelles
naguères d'où sursauta son délire jusqu'à une cime
flétrie
par la neutralité identique du gouffre

133

Stéphane Mallarmé, ed. Klaus Detjen
UN COUP DE DÉS JAMAIS N'ABOLIRA LE HASARD. EIN WÜRFELWURF NIEMALS TILGT DEN ZUFALL
Göttingen: Steidl Verlag, 1995
310 x 235 mm
Offset, thread binding, hardcover and slipcase

This book is the second in the "Typographische Bibliothek" series, edited by Klaus Detjen, published from 1993 to 2005 by Steidl Verlag in Göttingen. According to critic Silvia Werfel, the book series "aims to offer the medium of typography a new and effective forum" in order to "re-interest readers in unfamiliar or long-forgotten forms of design". The bibliophilically designed volumes of the series each contain a variant of the text in reading typography as well as an artistic-interpretative part in staged typography. In addition to an epilogue, each volume also contains detailed notes by Detjen on the respective typographic design in the appendix.

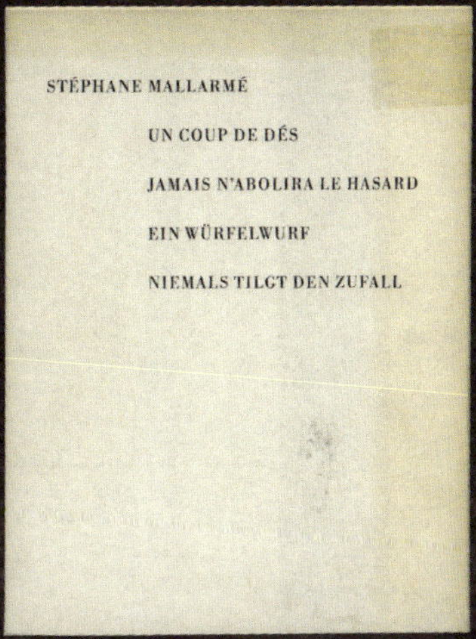

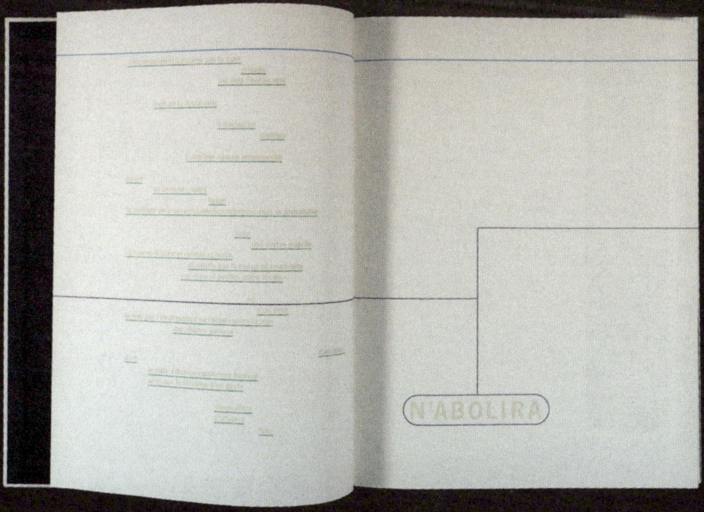

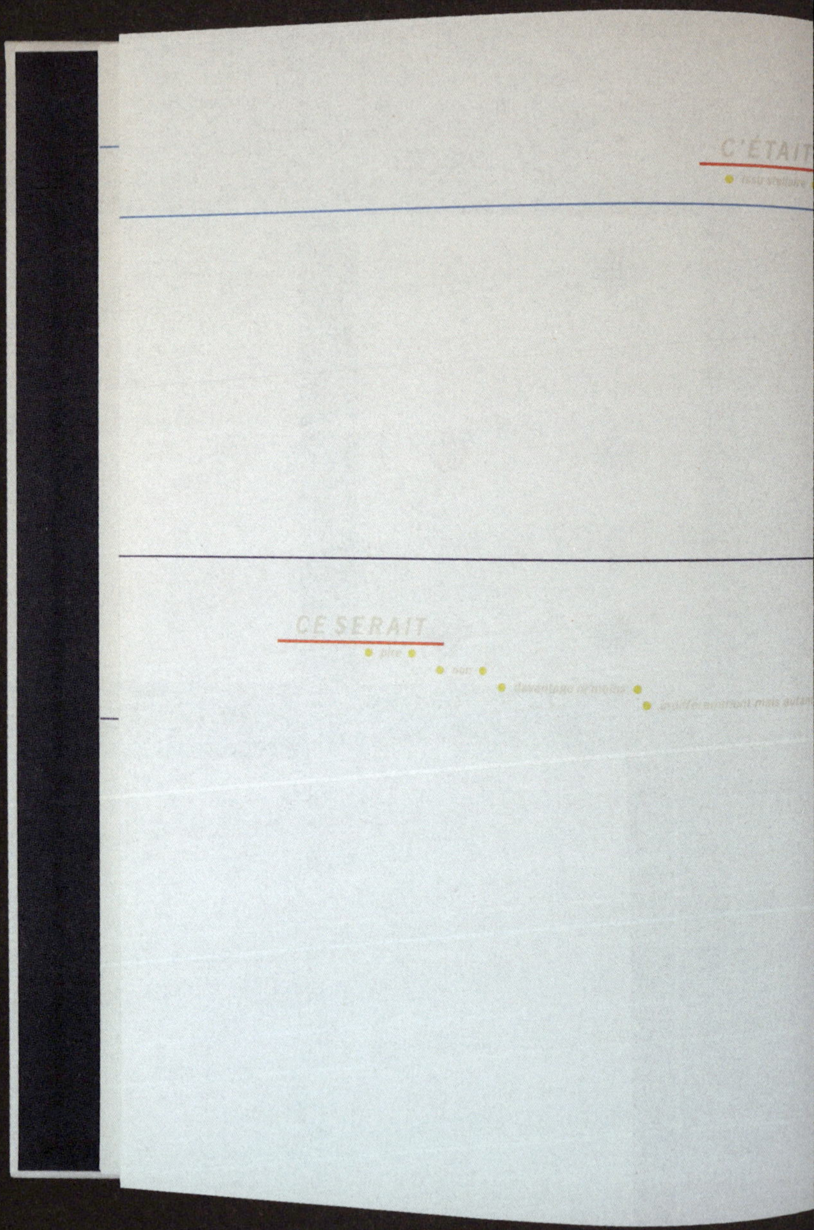
C'ÉTAIT
CE SERAIT

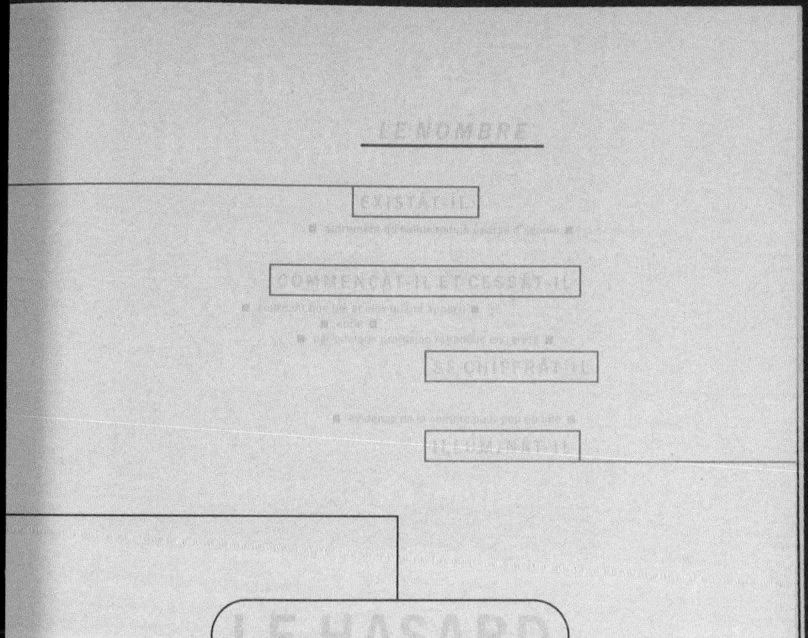

1:2

UN COUP DE DÉS JAMAIS N'ABOLIRA LE HASARD. EIN WÜRFELWURF NIEMALS TILGT DEN ZUFAL

Stéphane Mallarmé, Charles Chadwick
THE MEANING OF MALLLARMÉ.
A bilingual edition of his POÉSIES *and* UN COUP DE DÉS
Aberdeen: Scottish Cultural Press, 1996
195 x 130 mm, 180 pp.
Offset, thread binding

A literal rendering which simply reproduces the tortuous syntax, esoteric vocabulary and complex imagery of the original is of little help to the reader, and any attempt at a verse translation merely adds to the difficulties. It is for these reasons that this new bilingual version of Mallarmé's *Poésies* and UN COUP DE DÉS accompanies the French text with an expanded prose translation which aims above all at making the sense of the poems clear. As the title suggests, *The Meaning of Mallarmé* also includes an analysis of the poet's thought and technique and an assessment of his poetic achievement.

Scottish Cultural Press

Spreads of the French and English edition of the poem are interchanging throughout. As usual, the only blank page which is left intact, is the one verso to the phrase UN COUP DE DÉS, and facing *JAMAIS*.

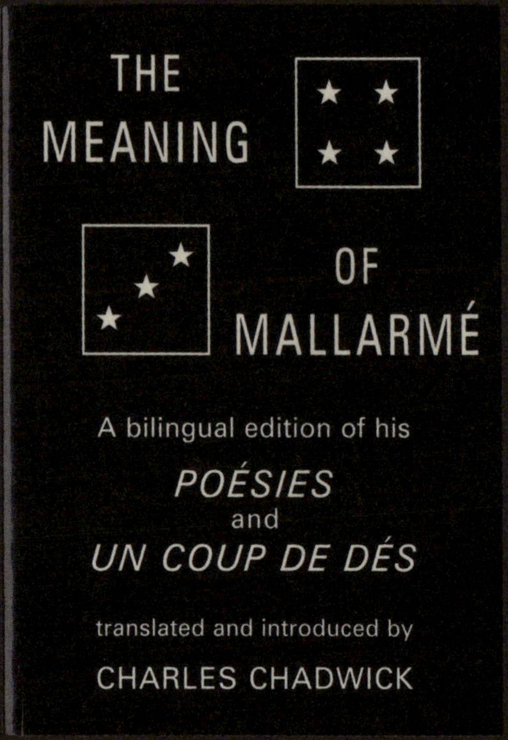

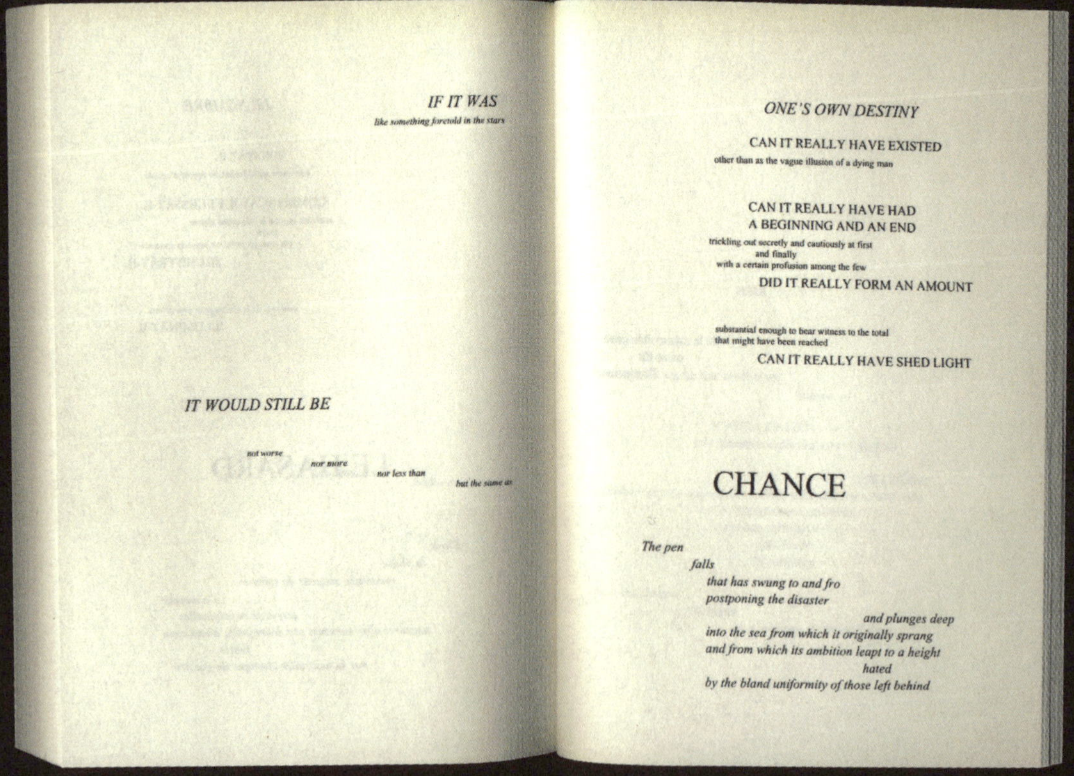

1:2

Stéphane Mallarmé, David Mus
*La Première édition d'*Un Coup de dés *par Stéphane Mallarmé*
Plombières-les-Dijon: Ulysse Fin de Siècle, 1996
241 x 167 mm, 20 pp.
Offset, thread binding
ed. 600

We present here what is, to our knowledge, the first facsimile edition. Photos from the National Library. Our facsimile and the introductory text appeared for the first time in the journal *Po&sie*, 58 (Paris, Éditions Belin, 1991).

David Mus

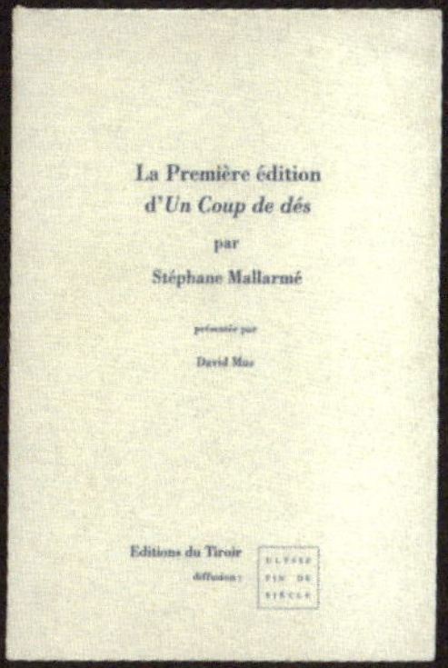

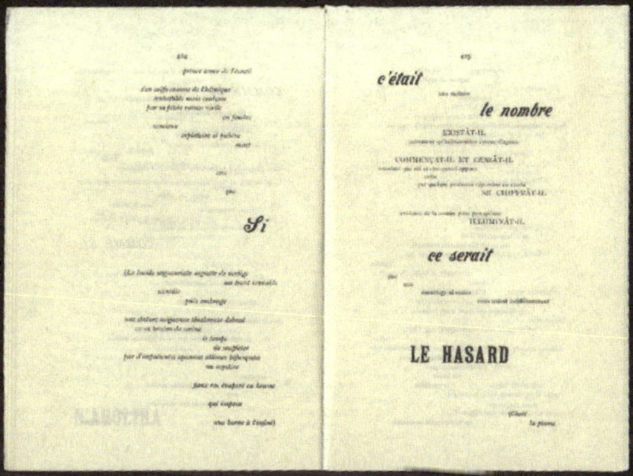

Stéphane Mallarmé, ed. Albert Dupont
UN COUP DE DÉS JAMAIS N'ABOLIRA LE HASARD / *Désir-hasard-dés: poème bloc poème*
Paris: L'Inéditeur, 1998
340 x 260 mm
Screen print on transparent polyester
ed. 41

Dupont faithfully reproduces Mitsou Ronat's edition on transparent vinyl sheets. A second section contains a verbal/visual accompainment. The vinyl sheets are housed in a wooden box.

Stéphane Mallarmé
Poésies et autres textes
Paris: Le Livre de Poche, 1998
175 x 111 mm, 374 pp.
Offset, thread binding

Stéphane Mallarmé
Poésies et autres textes
Paris: Le Livre de Poche, 2005
180 x 111 mm, 445 pp.
Offset, perfect binding

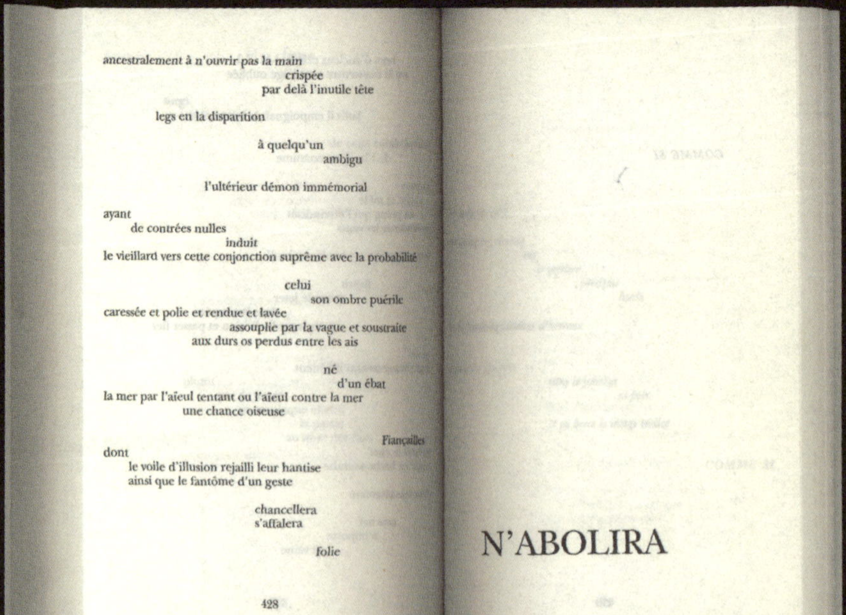

ancestralement à n'ouvrir pas la main
crispée
par delà l'inutile tête

legs en la disparition

à quelqu'un
ambigu

l'ultérieur démon immémorial

ayant
de contrées nulles
induit
le vieillard vers cette conjonction suprême avec la probabilité

celui
son ombre puérile
caressée et polie et rendue et lavée
assouplie par la vague et soustraite
aux durs os perdus entre les ais

né
d'un ébat
la mer par l'aïeul tentant ou l'aïeul contre la mer
une chance oiseuse

Fiançailles
dont
le voile d'illusion rejailli leur hantise
ainsi que le fantôme d'un geste

chancellera
s'affalera

folie

428

N'ABOLIRA

1:2

Stéphane Mallarmé
gitur Divigations UN COUP DE DÉS
Paris: Éditions Gallimard, 2003
180 x 110 mm, 528 pp.
Offset, perfect binding

According to the publisher, this edition is derived from *Bibliotheque de la Pléiade*. UN COUP DE DÉS is depicted over 22 pages (19 of these are paginated), including 2 blank pages. The "PREFACE" has been moved to an Annex.

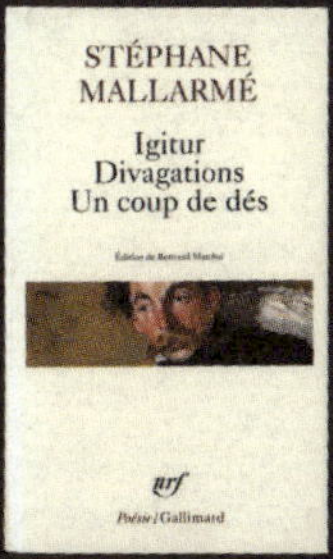

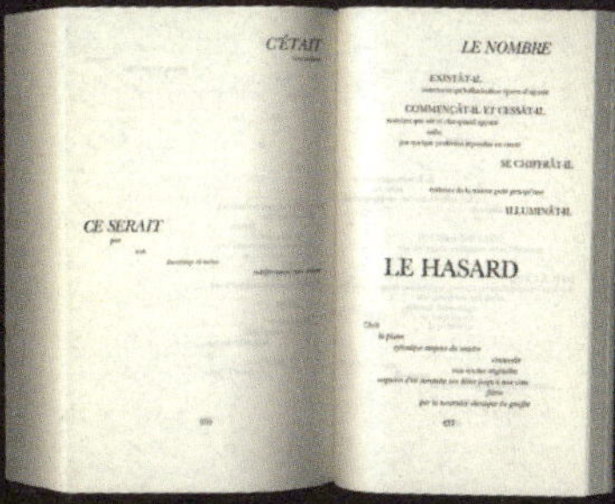

Stéphane Mallarmé
Collected Poems and Other Verse
Oxford: Oxford University Press, 2008
195 x 130 mm, 282 pp.
Offset, perfect binding, paperback

According to the publisher, "For the first time in any language, Mallarmé's *Poésies* (his major collection of verse) is printed in the last arrangement known to have been approved by the author. Prose poems, uncollected verse, and the unclassifiable UN COUP DE DÉS are also included. Original spelling, punctuation, and lineation have been preserved throughout." The publisher has added not so invisible para-text such as pagination to the poem.

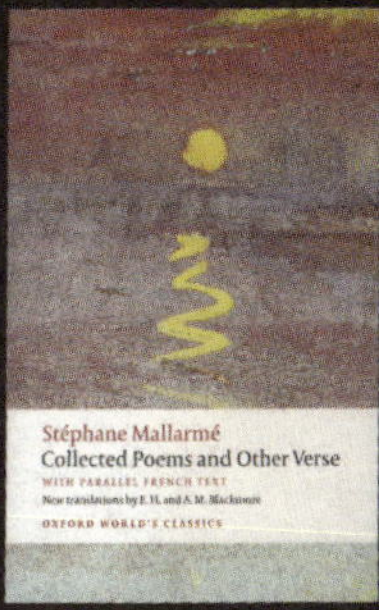

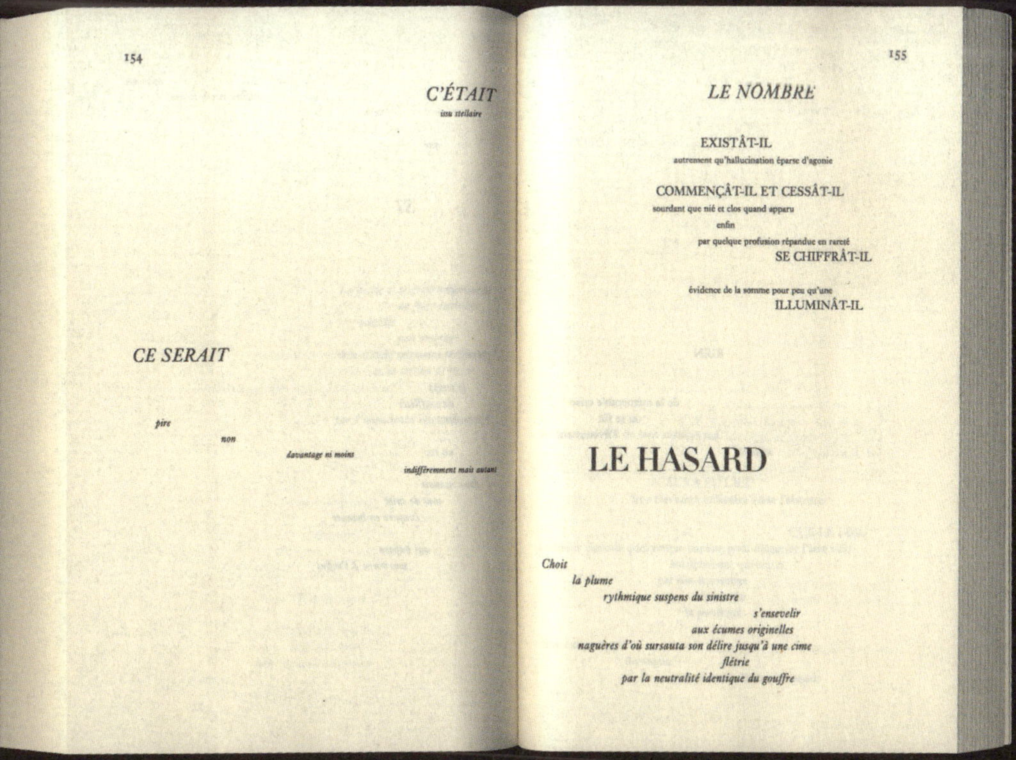

1:2

Denis Lavant
MALLARMÉ. UN COUP DE DÉS JAMAIS N'ABOLIRA LE HASARD
Paris: ÉDITIONS THÉLÈME, 2003
125 x 140 mm

A great specialist in Mallarmé, whose works he reads in a notable show, Denis Lavant offers here a new interpretation of the poet and his work.

ÉDITIONS THÉLÈME

1:2

Denis Lavant
MALLARMÈ UN COUP DE DÉS JAMAIS N'ABOLIRA LE HASARD
Paris: ÉDITIONS THÉLÈME, 2005
120 x 130 mm
CD with booklet

1:2

Stéphane Mallarmé, ed. Françoise Morel
Un coup de Dés jamais n'abolira le Hasard
Paris: La Table Ronde, 2007
320 x 240 mm, 200 pp.
Offset, slipcased, paper bound, sewn

This edition includes a facsimile of the *Cosmopolis* edition, a manuscript by Mallarmé in preparation for a monographic edition, hand-corrected print proofs of this (unrealized) edition by Ambroise Vollard, a newly typeset edition on occasion of this publication by La Table Ronde, and scholarly observations by the editor.

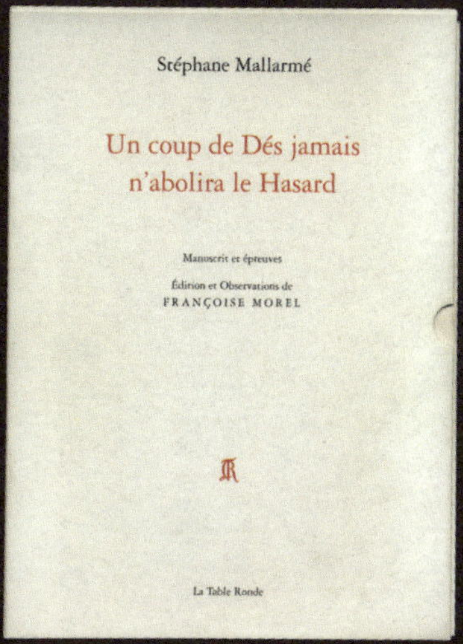

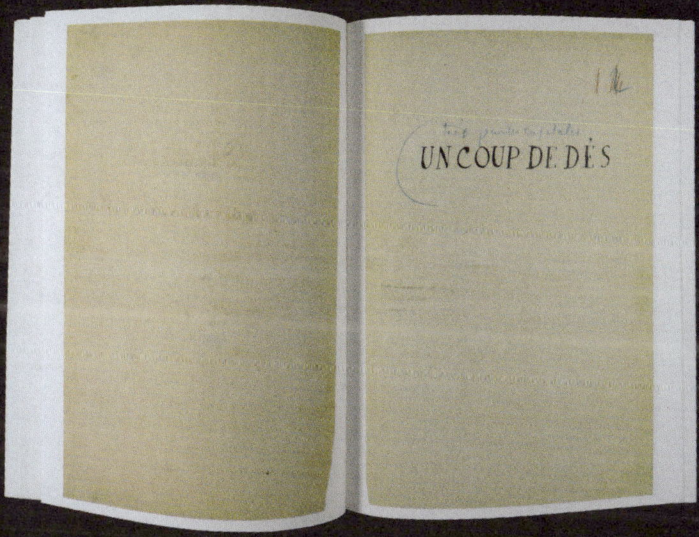

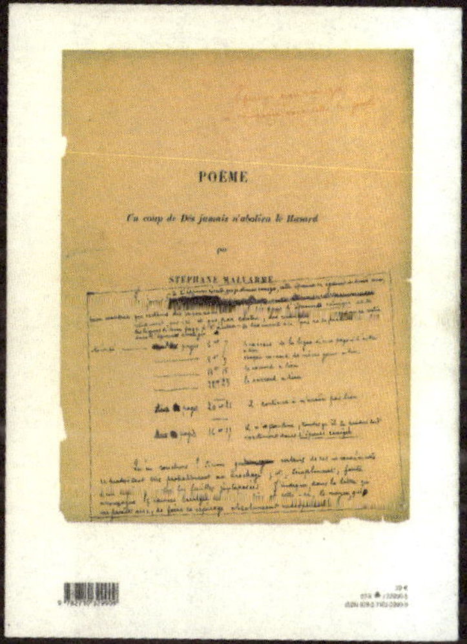

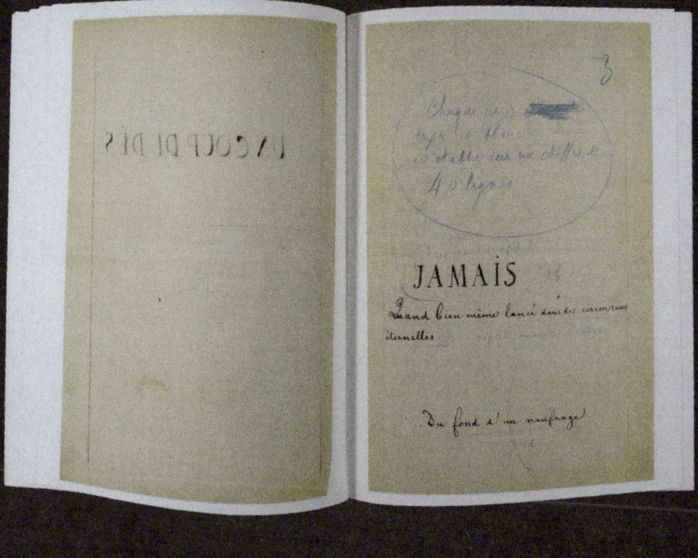

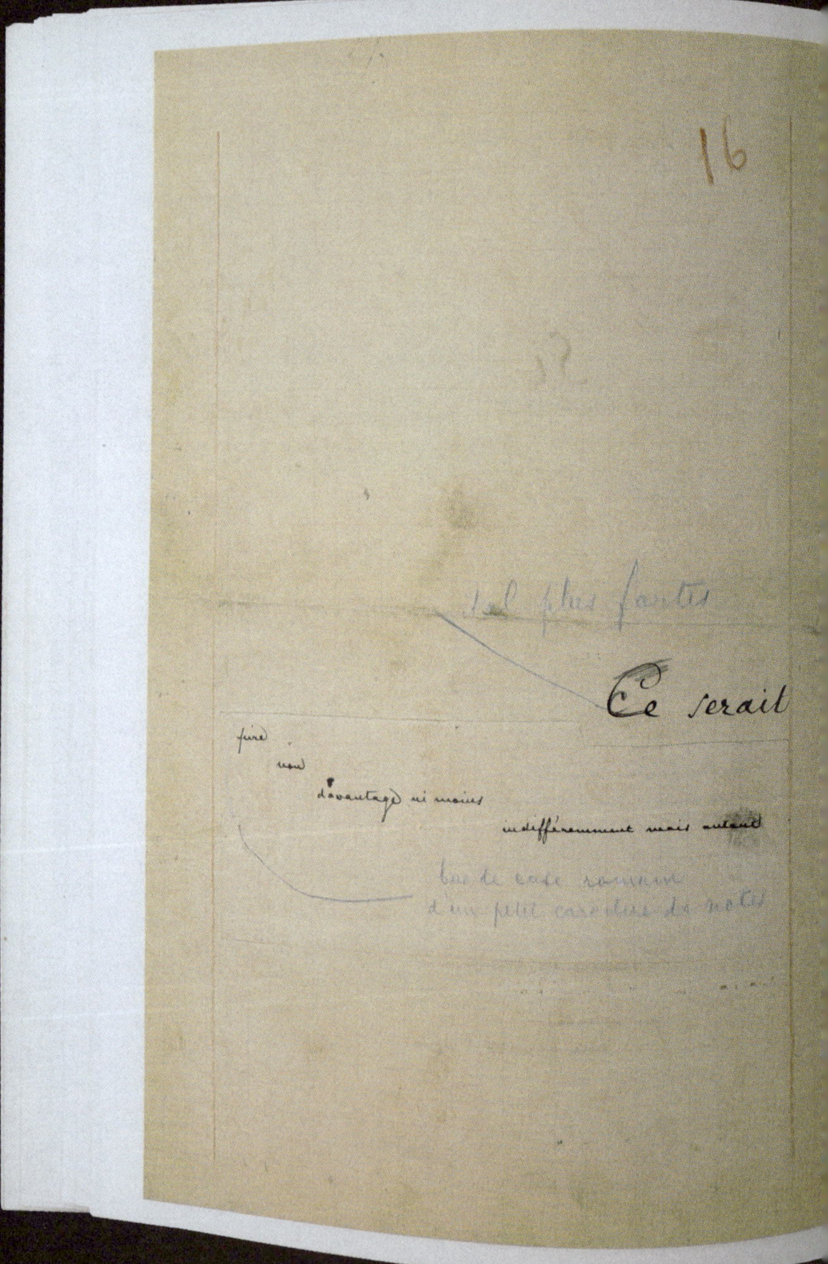

16

Ce serait

pire

non

davantage ni moins

indifféremment mais autant

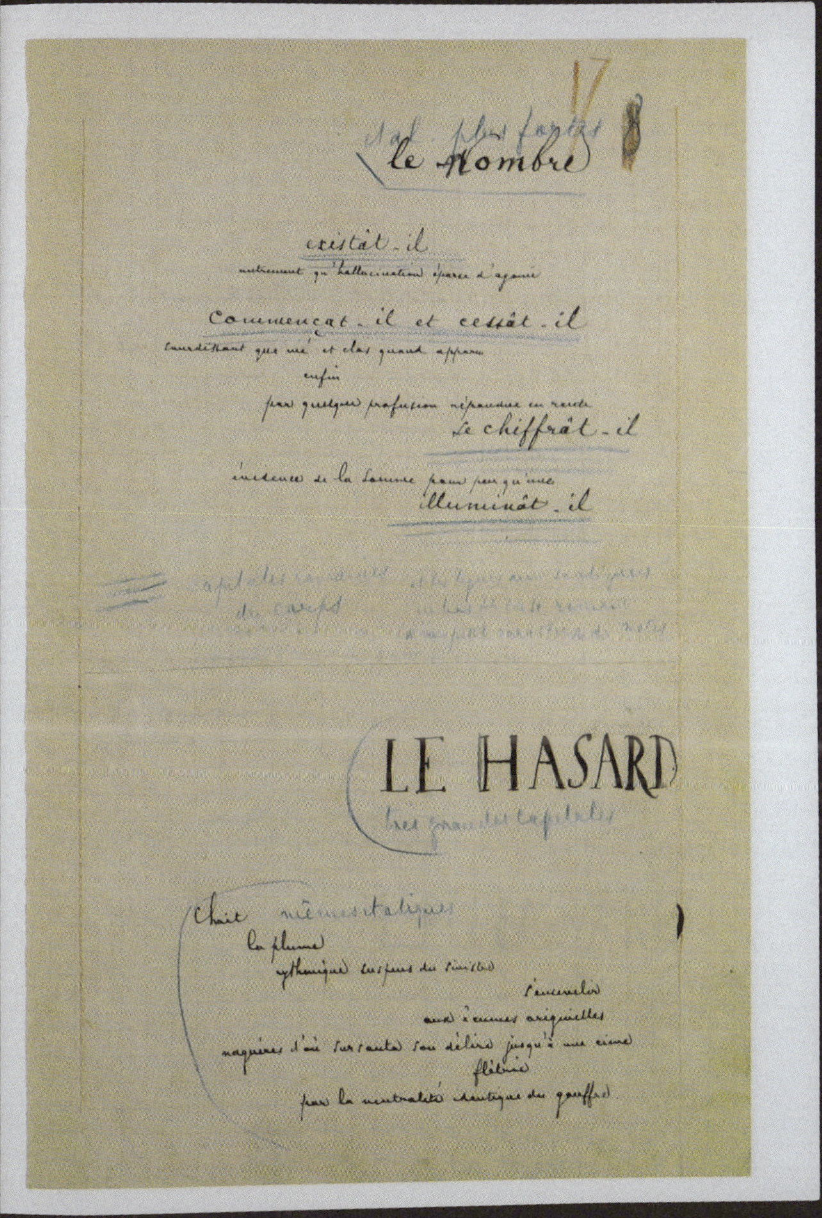

ital. plus fortes 17 8

le Nombre

existât-il

autrement qu'hallucination éparse d'agonie

commençât-il et cessât-il

sourdant que nié et clos quand apparu

enfin

par quelque profusion répandue en rareté

se chiffrât-il

évidence de la somme pour peu qu'une

illuminât-il

LE HASARD

très grandes capitales

Choit la plume

rythmique suspens du sinistre

s'ensevelir

aux écumes originelles

naguères d'où sursauta son délire jusqu'à une cime

flétrie

par la neutralité identique du gouffre

1:2

Stéphane Mallarmé
UN COUP DE DÉS JAMAIS N'ABOLIRA LE HASARD
رَمْيَةُ نَرْدٍ أبداً لَنْ تُبْطِلَ الزَّهْر
Paris: Ypsilon Éditeur, 2007
380 x 280 mm, 40 pp.
Offset, thread binding

The first Arabic translation, by the Moroccan poet Mohammed Bennis.

قَصِيدَة

رَمْيَةُ نَرْدٍ أبَداً لَنْ تُبْطِلَ الزَّهْر

بقلم

سْتِيفَانْ مَلاَرْمِي

ترجمة محمد بنّيس

ثلاثةُ رسُوم لأُودِيلُون رُودُون

PARIS
Ypsilon Éditeur
MMVII

UN COUP DE DÉS JAMAIS N'ABOLIRA LE HASARD
Paris: Ypsilon Éditeur, 2016
380 x 280 mm, 36 pp.
Offset, thread binding

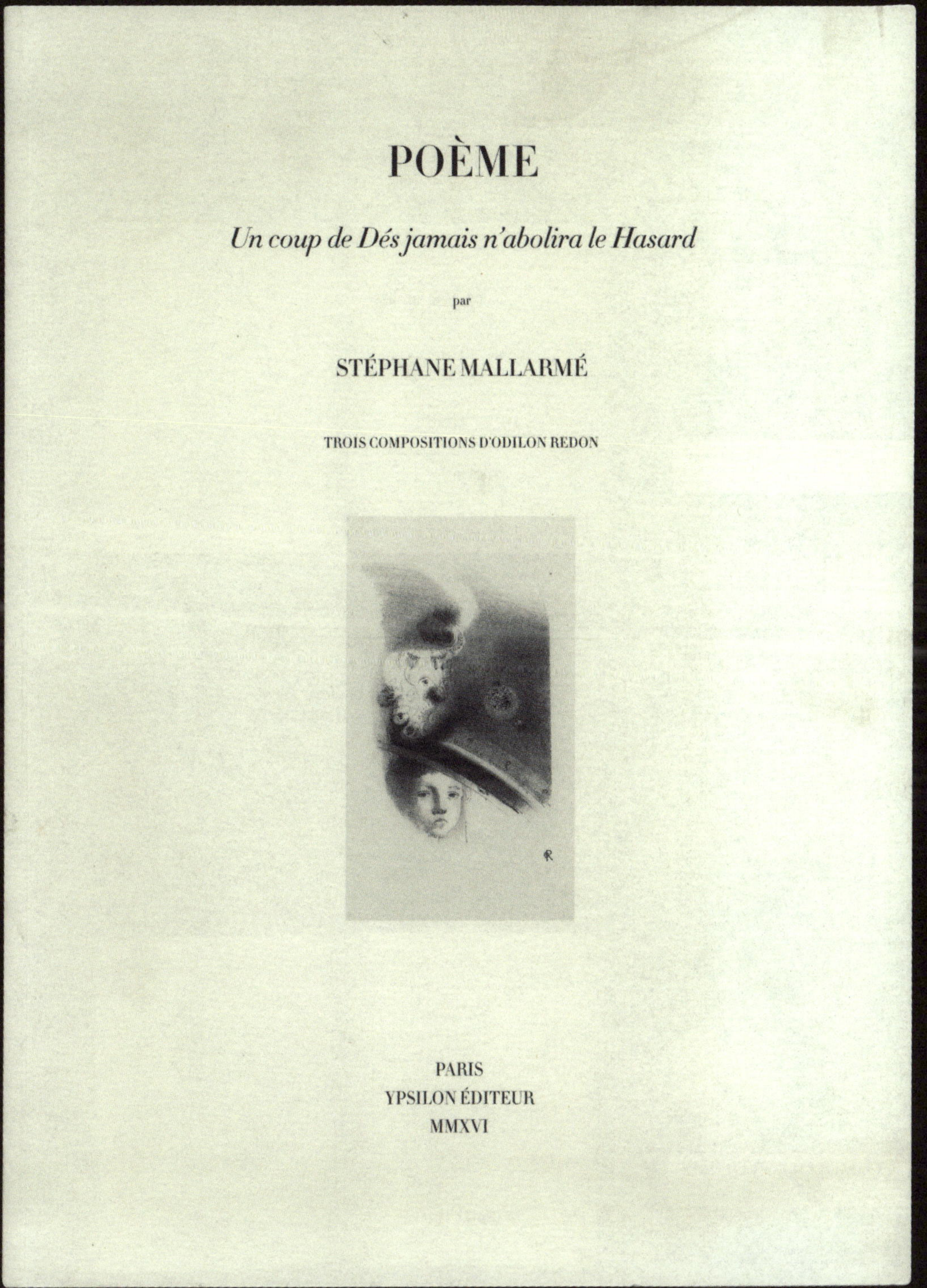

POÈME

Un coup de Dés jamais n'abolira le Hasard

par

STÉPHANE MALLARMÉ

TROIS COMPOSITIONS D'ODILON REDON

PARIS
YPSILON ÉDITEUR
MMXVI

Cosmopolis 6, ed. Fernand Ortmans
UN COUP DE DÉS JAMAIS N'ABOLIRA LE HASARD
Berlin: Nabu Press, 2010
189 x 246 mm, 930 pp.
POD, softcover

This volume is a reproduction of an original work published before 1932. (London: T. Fisher Unwin, New York: INTERNATIONAL NEWS COMPANY, 1897). The book may have occasional impefections that were either part of the original artefact or were introduced by the scanning process.

POD facsimile of *Cosmopolis* 6.

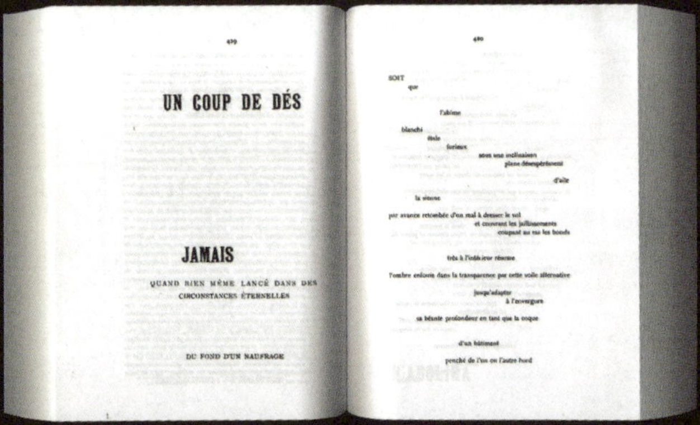

Cosmopolis 6, ed. Fernand Ortmans
UN COUP DE DÉS JAMAIS N'ABOLIRA LE HASARD
Berlin: Nabu Press, 2010
189 x 246 mm, 930 pp.
POD, softcover

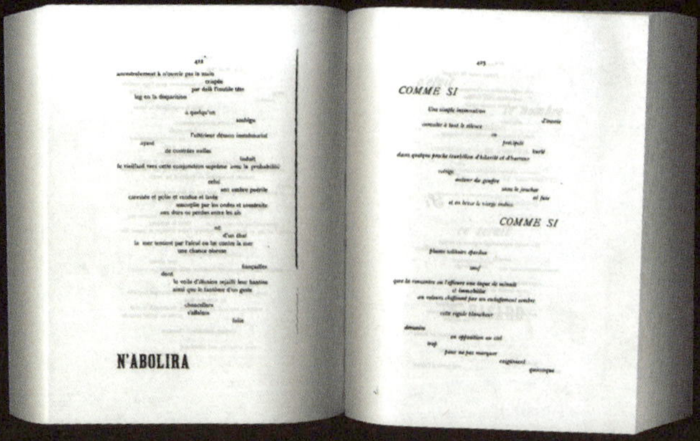

Stéphane Mallarmé
UN COUP DE DÉS JAMAIS N'ABOLIRA LE HASARD
Charlestown: Acme Bookbinding, 2010
246 x 190 mm, 36 pp.
POD, perfect binding, softcover

Stéphane Mallarmé
UN COUP DE DÉS JAMAIS N'ABOLIRA LE HASARD
India: SN Books World, 2020
135 x 206 mm, 40
POD, offset, stapled

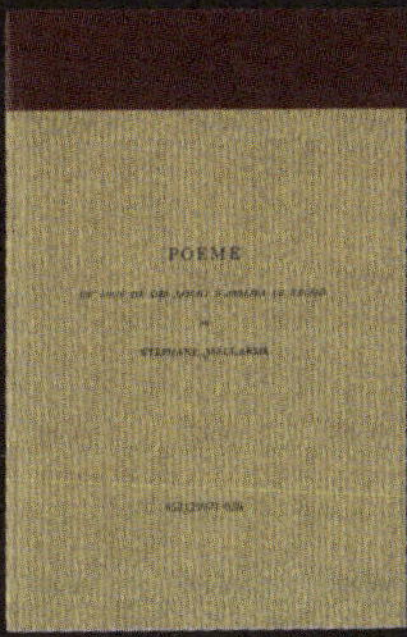

The numerous print-on-demand editons, that are circulating since roughly 2010, pull the text from online scans. This introduces an element of chance, regarding the way pages are scaled. That sometimes leads to text being printed relatively bigger, at the expense of surrounding white space, which is considered dispensable by the automated scanning devices that have been employed. As a result, lines which have been composed to continue over the spread, from a verso to a recto page, do not match anymore.

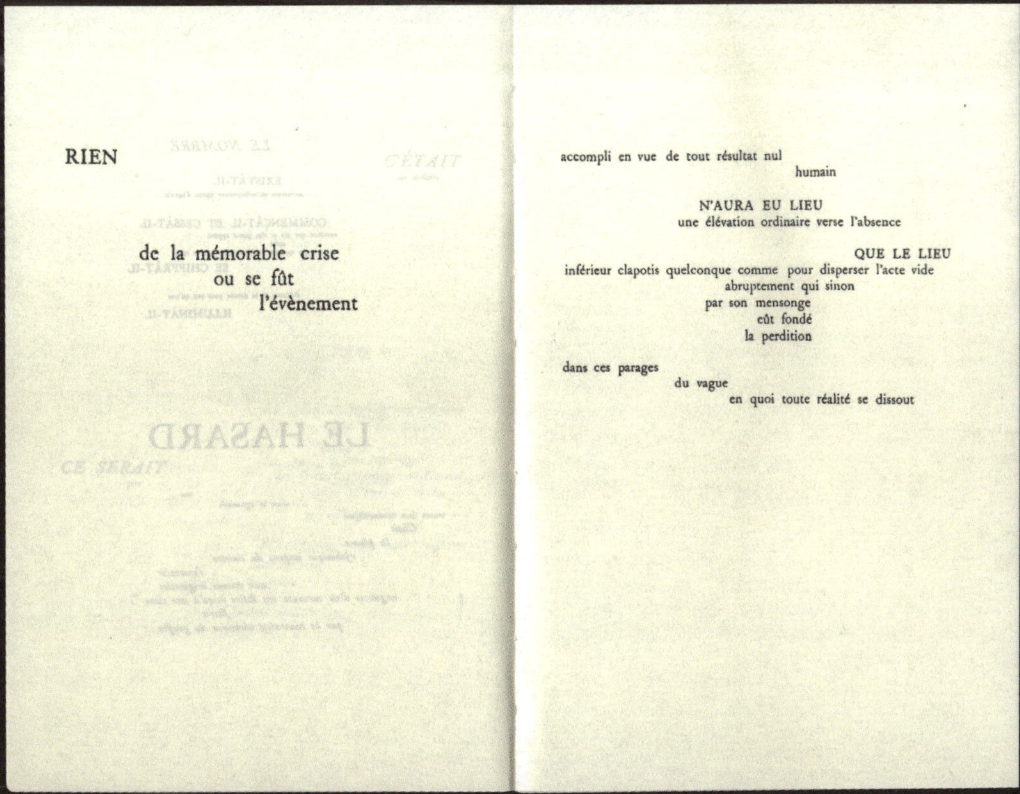

1:2

Quentin Meillassoux
The Number and The Siren, A Decipherment of Mallarmé's COUP DE DÉS
New York: Sequence Press, 2011; Farmouth, UK: Urbanomic, 2011
175 x 115 mm, 306 pp.
Offset, paperback

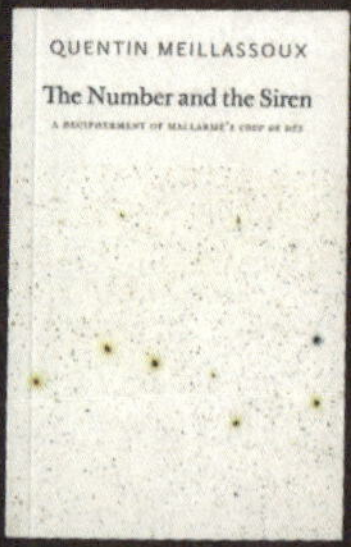

A meticulous literary study, a detective story à la Edgar Allan Poe, a treasure-hunt worthy of an adventure novel—such is the register in which can be deciphered the hidden secrets of a poem like no other. Quentin Meillassoux, author of *After Finitude*, continues his philosophical interrogation of the concepts of chance, contingency, infinity and eternity through a concentrated study of Mallarmé's poem *UN COUP DE DÉS*, patiently deciphering its enigmatic meaning on the basis of a dazzlingly simple and lucid insight with regard to Mallarmé's "unique Number."

[...] The volume contains the entire text of the *COUP DE DÉS* and three other poems, with new English translations.

Urbanomic x Sequence Press

The volume contains the entire text of the *UN COUP DE DÉS*, in French and English on eleven plates numbered I to XI. The "PREFACE" and following two blank pages are not reproduced.

Quentin Meillassoux
Die Zahl und die Sirene
Zurich: diaphanes, 2013
135 x 210 mm, 240 pp.
Offset, paperback

Let us come straight to the point: This book proposes to bring to light a procedure of encryption housed within Stéphane Mallarmé's Coup de dés. This procedure, once deciphered, allows the precise determination of the 'unique Number' enigmatically evoked in the poem. We thus claim: a) that Mallarmé's poem is coded; b) that the ability to read this code is a condition of the true comprehension of the Coup de dés, since it elucidates one of its essential components, namely the nature of the Number.

Quentin Meillasoux

The volume contains the entire text of the *UN COUP DE DÉS*, in French and German on eleven plates numbered I to XI. The "PREFACE" and following two blank pages are not reproduced.

Stéphane Mallarmé
UN COUP DE DÉS JAMAIS N'ABOLIRA LE HASARD
Conflans: L'Atelier, 2013
325 x 252 mm

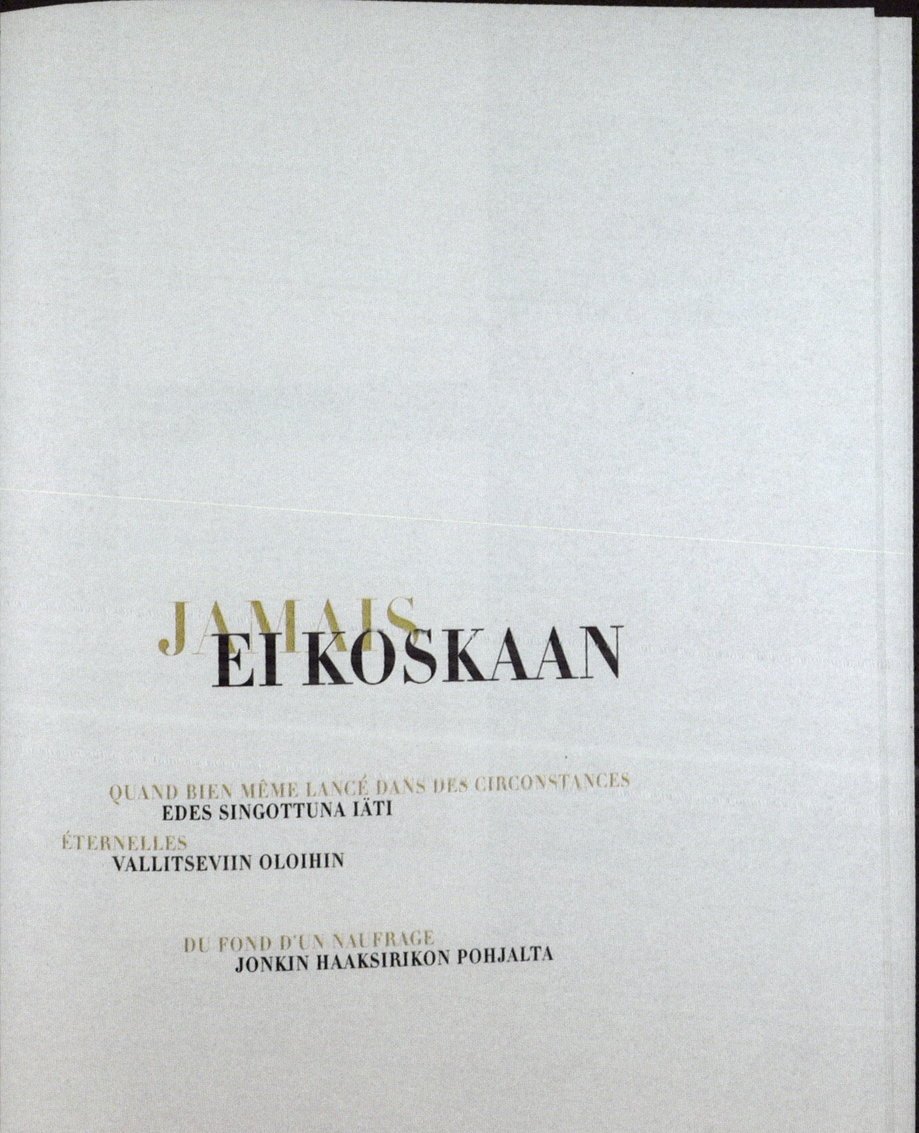

JAMAIS
EI KOSKAAN

QUAND BIEN MÊME LANCÉ DANS DES CIRCONSTANCES
EDES SINGOTTUNA IÄTI
ÉTERNELLES
VALLITSEVIIN OLOIHIN

DU FOND D'UN NAUFRAGE
JONKIN HAAKSIRIKON POHJALTA

— II —

1:2

NOPANHEITTO EI KOSKAAN TUHOA SATTUMAA, UN COUP DE DÉS JAMAIS N'ABOLIRA LE HASARD (POÉME)

Stéphane Mallarmé

NOPANHEITTO EI KOSKAAN TUHOA SATTUMAA, UN COUP DE DÉS JAMAIS N'ABOLIRA LE HASARD (POÉME)

Helsinki: Sémiosquare, 2014

330 x 250 mm, 30 pp.

Offset, thread binding

ed. 400

Now, a hundred years later, you have that poem in your hand translated by Helena Sinervo, in size and typography according to Mallarmé's goals. The original French text is projected onto the background of the Finnish poem. Helena Sinervo writes about Mallarmé: "With the help of typography, he created an audible visuality and polyphony for the eyes and rolled fragments of sentences across the opening like lottery cubes. The theme of the work, 'The roll of the dice never destroys Chance' sounds like ink played on brass in this symphony of well-considered chance."

Sémiosquare

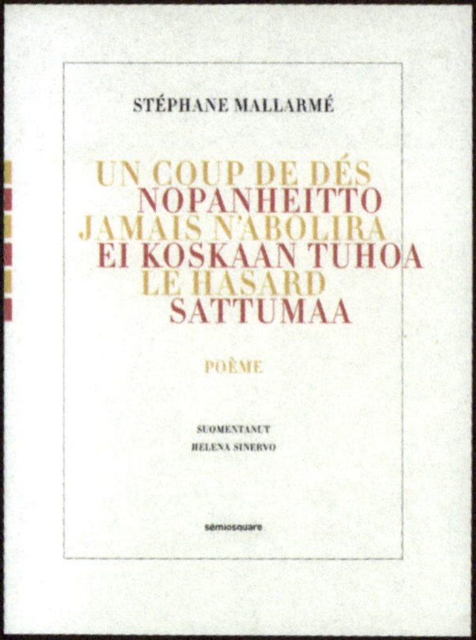

Stéphane Mallarmé, Jeff Clark, Robert Bononno
A Roll of the Dice: Will Never Will Never Abolish Chance
Seattle: Wave Books, 2015
275 x 185 mm, 54 pp.
Offset, hardcover

A translation by Robert Bononno and book designer Jeff Clark of one of Stéphane Mallarmé's most well-known and visually complex poems into contemporary English language and design. The book is composed in an elaborate set of type and photography to both honor the original and be an object of delight. Includes the original preface by Mallarmé. Bilingual edition.

Stéphane Mallarmé
UN COUP DE DÉS JAMAIS N'ABOLIRA LE HASARD
Paris: Mazeto Square, 2016
210 x 145 mm
Offset, stapled

The collection *Ab initio* sets out in search of ancient texts, sometimes forgotten, to rediscover them as on the first day, endeavoring to situate them in their time to better understand the importance they still have for ours. Historical speeches, political analyses, testimonies, essays, but also short stories, short stories, poems and other curiosities... this is, in a way, what is on the menu.

The publisher's desire is to participate in raising awareness of the importance of the universal heritage of works in the public domain. In this sense, each book is presented in a paper version, sold at a fair price, which considers the economy in which it is part, but also in an electronic version, made freely available to all.

Mazeto Square

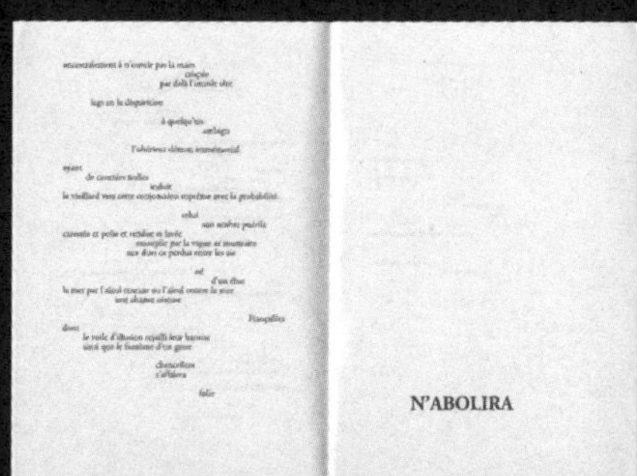

Stéphane Mallarmé, ed. Francisco Estrada
Un lance de dados jamás abolirá el azar
Jalisco: El Quinqué Amarillo Publicaciones, 2016
170 x 250 mm, 126 pp.
Offset, sewn binding

A peculiarity of *Un lance de dados jamás abolirá el azar* is that it is not an edition with the translation and the original text on the opposite page but has separate text streams. At the end of the Spanish translation, before UN COUP DE DÉS JAMAIS N'ABOLIRA LE HASARD starts, we find a series of notes (thirteen), explaining the choices for a particular word instead of another (such as *lance* itself, which was translated as *tiro* or *tirada*), but without going into the numerous earlier versions that have been made. Another special feature of the book is that it is available for free download online.

Samuel Bernal is the author of the prologue as well as the translator; in addition to his introductory text, this edition contains two more. The first is by the poet and essayist Luis Vicente de Aguinaga, who gives a historical review of the poem, focusing on its translations into Spanish. The second is a commentary on the poem by the poet Ángel Ortuño.

Stéphane Mallarmé
UN COUP DE DÉS *Un Tiro de Dados*
Mexico City: Ediciones el tucán de Virginia, 2017
235 x 177 mm, 108
Offset, perfect binding

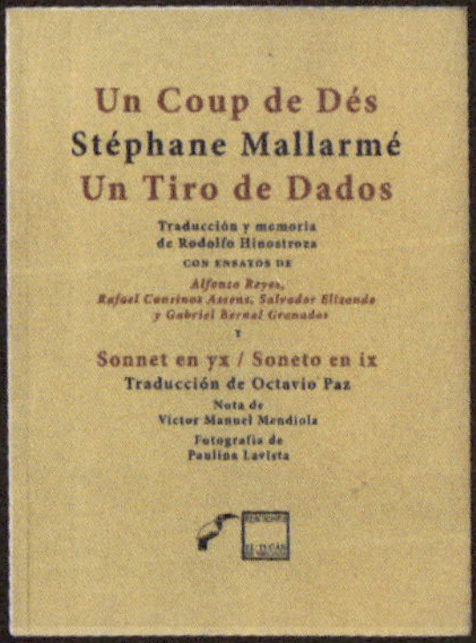

We could very well say that it was a destiny that Hinostroza translated "A throw of dice will never abolish chance". In this appropriation of Mallarmé's poem, the Peruvian poet explains himself and explains the explosion of freedom and enthusiasm of the sixties—it was the incredible moment of the "signs in rotation" that Octavio Paz himself had acutely deciphered. In Mexico, the understanding of the French poet Mallarmé is a remote and essential experience. With this new edition we mainly want to remember Rodolfo Hinostroza and think, at the same time, of those who have allowed us to read "the most beautiful poem in the world."

Stéphane Mallarmé, Nicolas Guyot
POÉME: UN COUP DE DÉS JAMAIS N'ABOLIRA LE HASARD par STÉPHANE MALLARMÉ
2019
200 × 150 mm
ed. 76

Hervé Di Rosa
UN COUP DE DÉS JAMAIS N'ABOLIRA LE HASARD
Dijon: Virgile LeGrand, 2021
205 × 245 mm, 36 pp.
Offset and engraved woodcuts and linocuts, casebound, cloth-covered hardboard
ed. 15

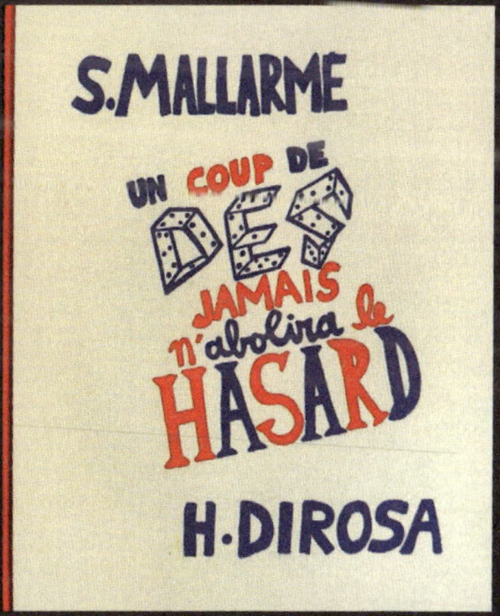

COMME SI

Une insinuation

au silence

dans quelque proche

voltige

simple

enroulée avec ironie
ou
le mystère
précipité
hurlé

tourbillon d'hilarité et d'horreur

autour du gouffre
sans le joncher
ni fuir

et en berce le vierge indice

COMME SI

Chapter Two
Editions of *UN COUP DE DÉS* attributed to other authors

Camille Soula
La poésie et la pensée de Stéphane Mallarmé. UN COUP DE DÉS
Paris: Le Bon Plaisir, 1931
290 x 230 mm, 48 pp.
Offset, thread binding
ed. 330

Camille Soula (1888–1963), a physician and a physiologist by profession, studied in depth the works of Stéphane Mallarmé and he wrote several publications on this subject. He confronted himself during decades with UN COUP DE DÉS JAMAIS N'ABOLIRA LE HASARD, analysing it and approaching it from different viewpoints, which he calls ideological, syntactic, literal analysis. In fact Camille Soula rewrites and formulates this poem with his own words.

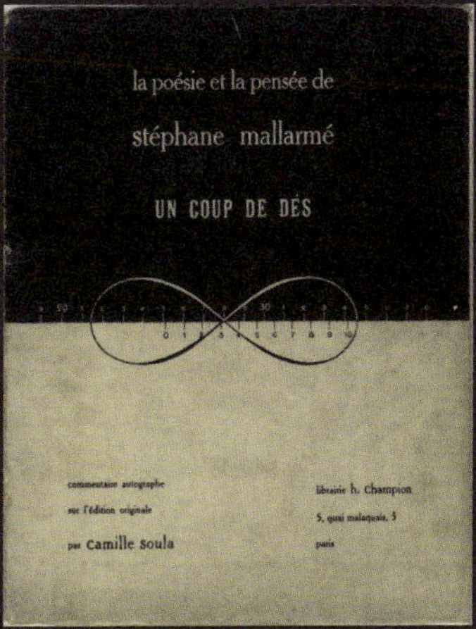

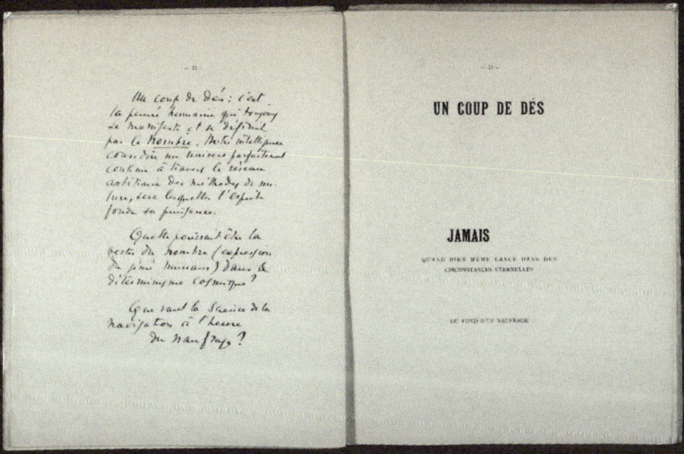

... même si cette foi humaine dans la vertu du nombre avait une justification métaphysique:

1° si la notion de nombre était autre chose qu'une superstition (<u>existât-il</u>)

2° si elle apparaissait autrement qu'une absurdité psychologique (<u>commençât-il et cessât-il</u>)

3° si on pouvait la considérer comme suffisamment justifiée par les propriétés arithmétiques qui en réalité découlent de sa convention même: raisonnement par récurrence. (<u>se chiffrât-il</u>)

4° si enfin elle nous était imposée par la perception même de l'univers (<u>illuminât-il</u>)

l'usage efficace ne nous en demeurerait pas moins interdit, puisque son rôle serait soustrait à notre contrôle.

Le nombre eût-il une vertu, comme ses lois nous sont fermées, la pensée humaine n'en resterait pas moins livrée au Hasard qui est la mesure de notre ignorance.

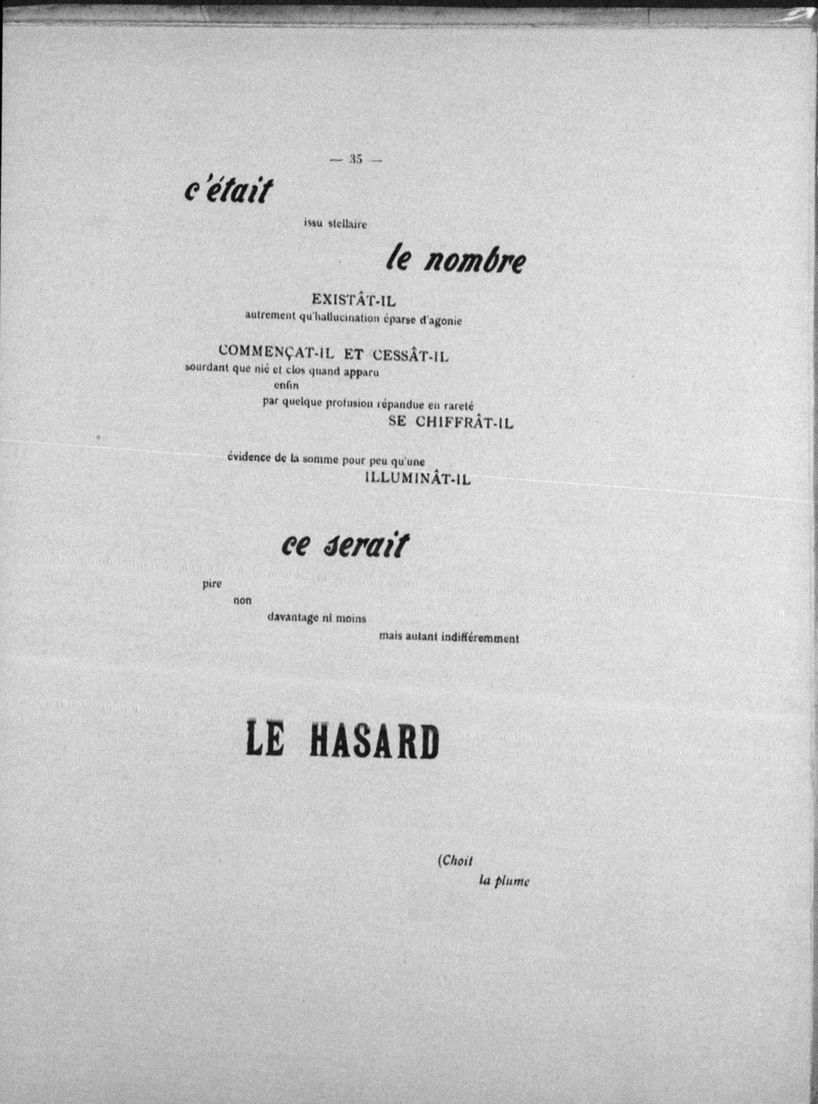

— 35 —

c'était

issu stellaire

le nombre

EXISTÂT-IL
autrement qu'hallucination éparse d'agonie

COMMENÇAT-IL ET CESSÂT-IL
sourdant que nié et clos quand apparu
enfin
par quelque profusion répandue en rareté
SE CHIFFRÂT-IL

évidence de la somme pour peu qu'une
ILLUMINÂT-IL

ce serait

pire
non
davantage ni moins
mais autant indifféremment

LE HASARD

(Choit
la plume

1:2

Ernest Fraenkel
LES DESSINS TRANS-CONSCIENTS DE STÉPHANE MALLARMÉ. À propos de la typographie de UN COUP DE DÉS.
Paris: Librairie Nizet, 1960
240 x 160 mm, 44 pp.

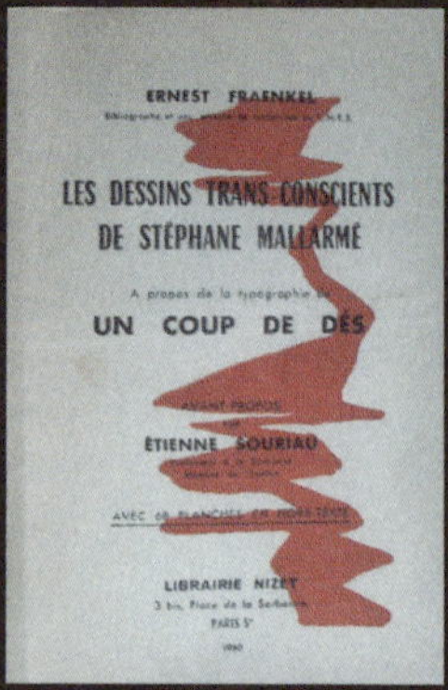

Ernest Fraenkel's 1960 *LES DESSINS TRANS-CONSCIENTS DE STÉPHANE MALLARMÉ. À propos de la typographie de UN COUP DE DÉS*, or *The trans-conscious drawings of Stéphane Mallarmé. A propos the typography of 'A Roll of the Dice'* is a graphic improvisation on Mallarmé's *UN COUP DE DÉS JAMAIS N'ABOLIRA LE HASARD* (1897, 1914), which Fraenkel developed starting in 1952. Proceeding by the abstraction of the text, he reveals the coded forms in the structures of the layout of the poem and brings out a multitude of graphic figures in blocks, trapezoids, spots, or dots to visualize what he calls Mallarmé's "abstract imagery" or "plastic text." Fraenkel's work played a decisive role in understanding the tradition of the contemporary artist's book.

Fraenkel's (1960) edition is an early manifestation, which still figures as a hybrid between a text attributed to Mallarmé and something of its own. Even though it claims to be a scholarly engagements of comparative literature, the interpretative drawings that go with the text are clearly primary information and engage in the writing of a palimpsest.

Ernest Fraenkel ed. Schuldt
Die unsichtbaren Zeichnungen Stéphane Mallarmés
Wien: EDITION PER PROCURA, 1998
240 x 160 mm
Offset, slipcase with booklet (Swiss binding) and posters

Newly published and with an essay "No Stuff for a Picture" by Schuldt. Folder with 9 large-format sheets with colored drawings and a fourty-seven-page accompanying book.

Images on following page and spread: scale 1:1

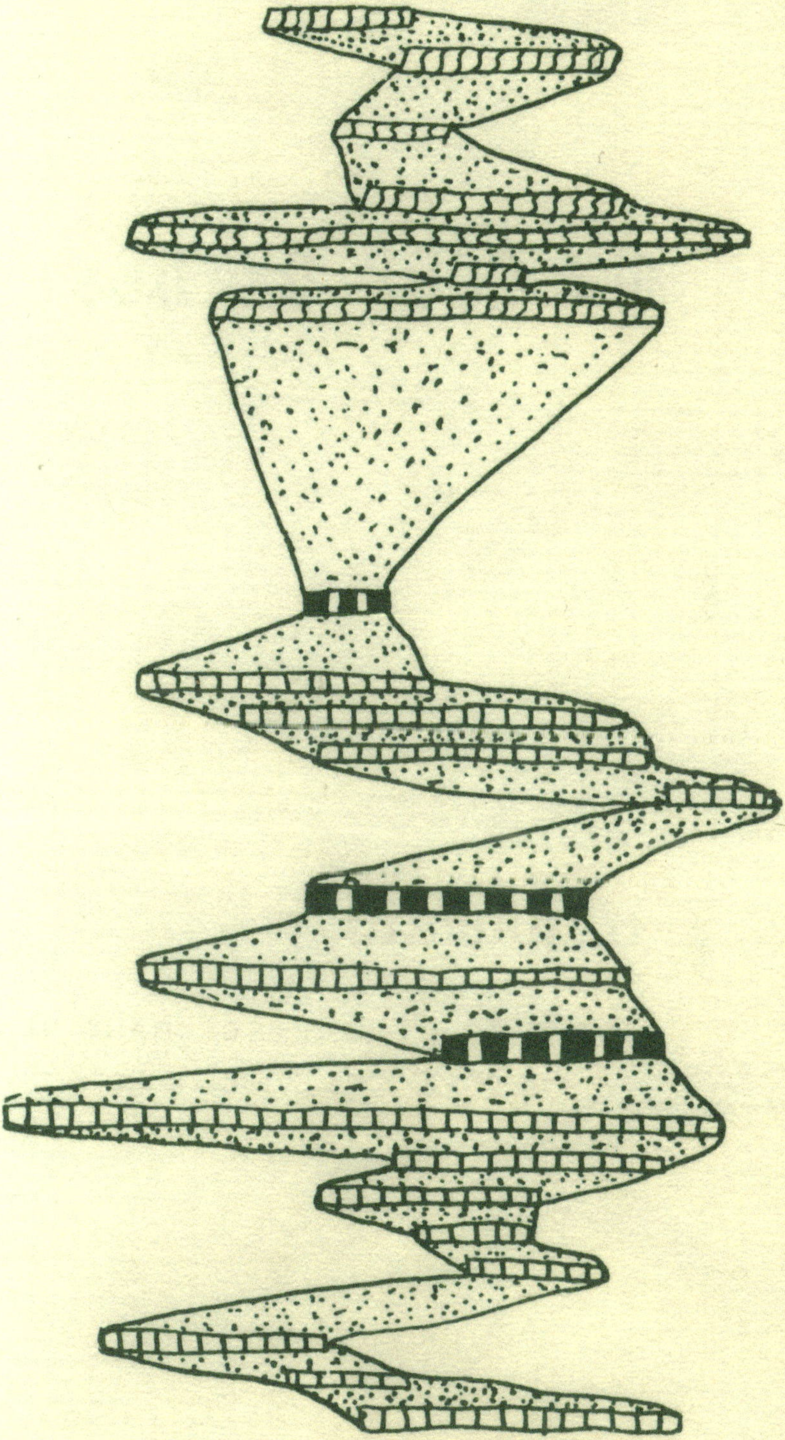

UN COUP DE DÉS

JAMAIS

QUAND BIEN MÊME LANCÉ DANS DES
CIRCONSTANCES ÉTERNELLES

DU FOND D'UN NAUFRAGE

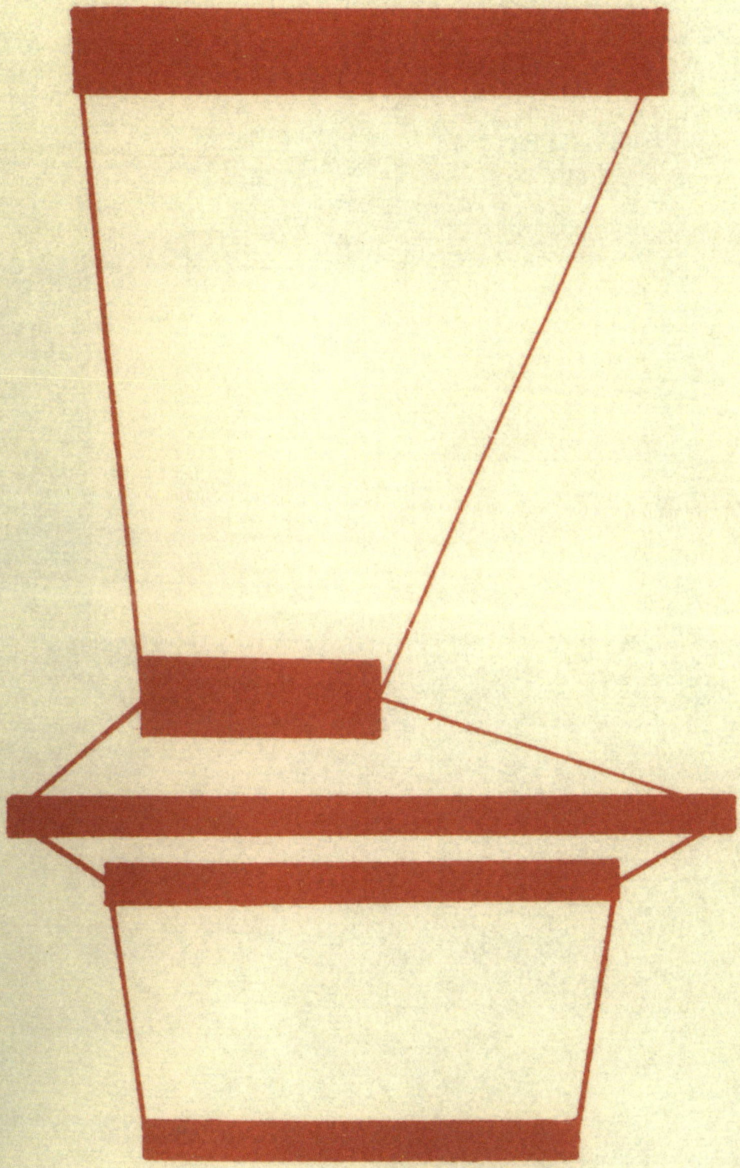

ed. André Dalmas and Marcelle Fonfreide
LE NOUVEAU COMMERCE Cahier 12
Paris: LE NOUVEAU COMMERCE, 1968
240 x 180 mm, 144 pp.
Offset, perfect binding
ed. 50

These two texts, which everyone will find strangely seductive, are the work of an IBM computer 360. The computer has been given memory, vocabulary and syntax. Then the machine's throw of the dice abolishes chance.

LE NOUVEAU COMMERCE

The featured piece is not published monographically but has one chapter in the revue, much like the first publication of UN COUP DE DÉS in *Cosmopolis*.

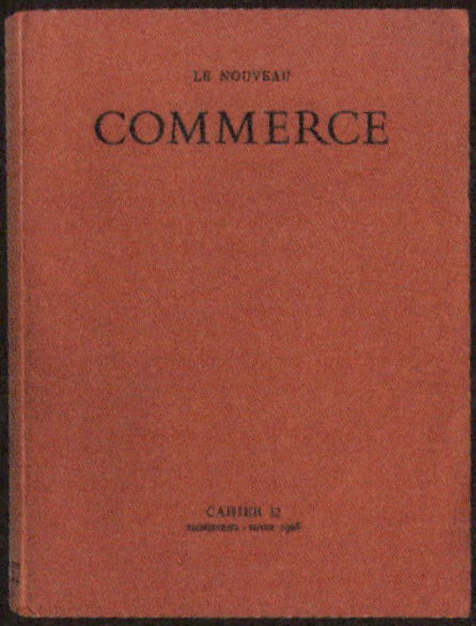

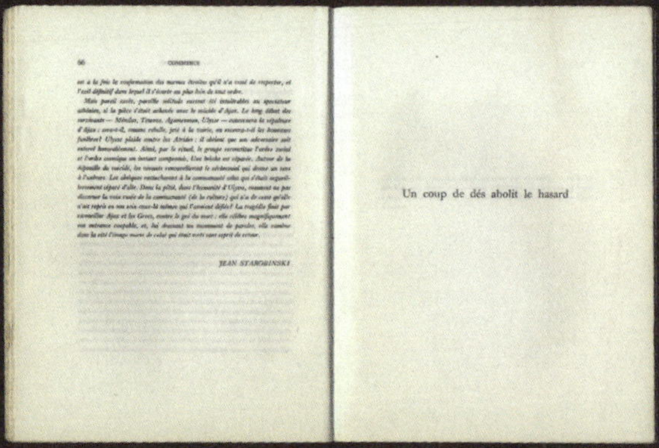

JCT 1 a MeTrica n'ABOOlira is modeled after Stéphane Mallarmé's *UN COUP DE DÉS JAMAIS N'ABOLIRA LE HASARD* in the edition Gallimard published posthumously in 1914. All the words are overprinted by colored bars in a way that corresponds directly to the typographic layout used by Mallarmé to articulate the text. The strips are arranged horizontally of different width and length and of orange and blue color. The lines, which were designated by Mallarmé to be set in italics, are overprinted by parallelograms.

The cover with title "JCT 1" in black rests on an orange background. The introductory pages feature a detoured comic book followed by the title page printed in black and orange.
It appeared as the first issue of the *JCT* series and went almost unnoticed, in great contrast to Broodthaers's *UN COUP DE DÉS*, even though it features striking similarities and preceded it.

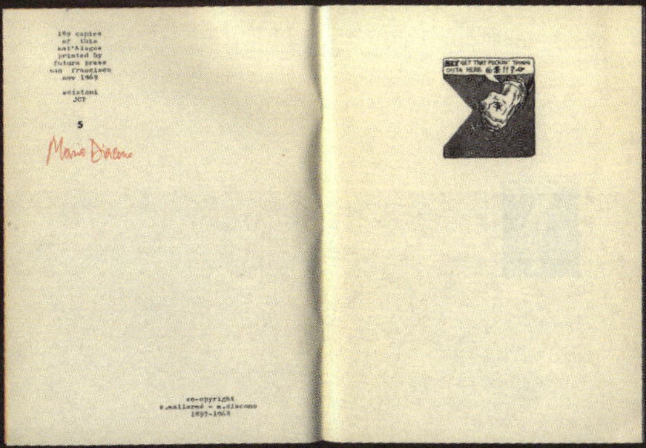

1:2

JCT 1 a MeTrica n'ABOOlirA

Marcel Broodthaers
UN COUP DE DÉS JAMAIS N'ABOLIRA LE HASARD (IMAGE)
Antwerp: Wide White Space, 1969; Cologne: Galerie Michael Werner, 1969
325 x 250 mm, 32 pp.
Offset, threadbound
ed. 300

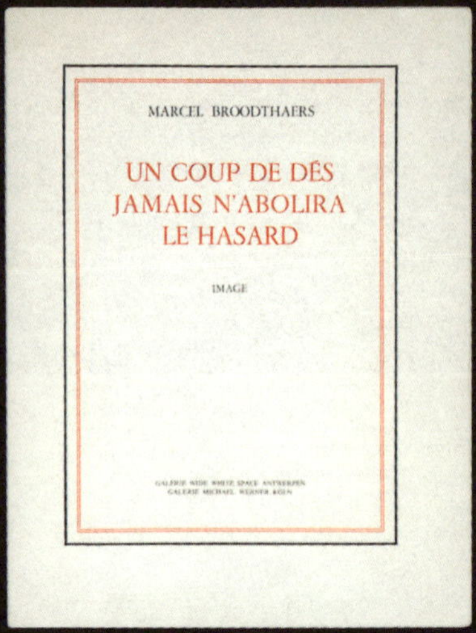

"Why? Without doubt, I once encountered Magritte, long ago, and he invited me to contemplate this poem. So, I forgot it; I contemplated it... today, I make this Image. I say farewell. A long period of life.
Farewell to all, to the men of letters that are deceased.
The dead artists.
New! New? Perhaps. Excepted. A Constellation."

Marcel Broodthaers, *Open Letter*, Antwerp, December 2, 1969, part of and distributed throughout *Exposition littéraire autour de Mallarmé*

UN COUP DE DÉS JAMAIS N'ABOLIRA LE HASARD (IMAGE) is a close copy of the 1914 edition of the French symbolist poet Stéphane Mallarmé's poem of the same name but with all the words overprinted by black bars, in a way that corresponds directly to the typographic layout used by Mallarmé to articulate the text. The edition numbers echo the editions of the 1914 NRF edition, with three hundred being the print run of the paper edition. For the "PREFACE," which is attributed to Mallarmé, Broodthaers carried out a transcription of the Mallarmé text. The "PREFACE" now features the entire poem written as a block of text, all in lowercase letters, with each line separated by a slash (/).

For the edition on translucent paper, Broodthaers "split" the recto and verso of the page onto separate sheets, which has hence sixty-four pages. The translucent edition also comes with two sheets of white card cut to the size of the book, which can be used as a reading background.

The aluminum edition features twelve plates, the first one being blank.

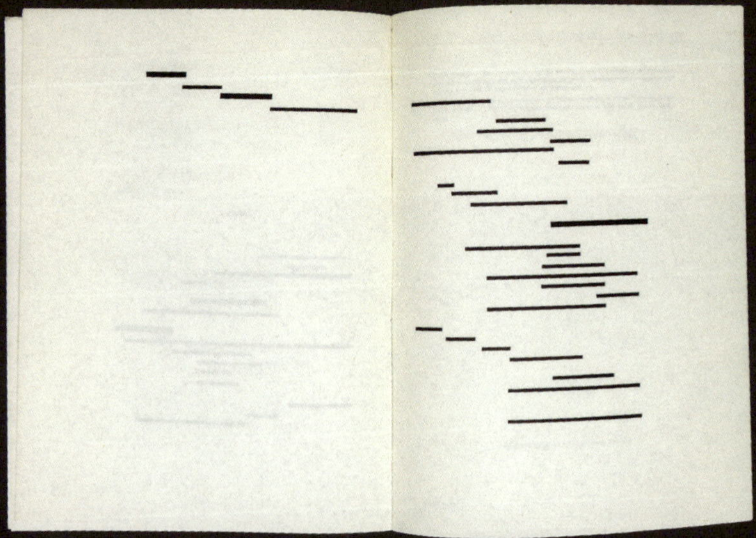

Marcel Broodthaers
UN COUP DE DÉS JAMAIS N'ABOLIRA LE HASARD (IMAGE)
Antwerp: Wide White Space, 1969; Cologne: Galerie Michael Werner, 1969
325 x 250 mm, 64 pp.
Offset on transparent paper
ed. 90

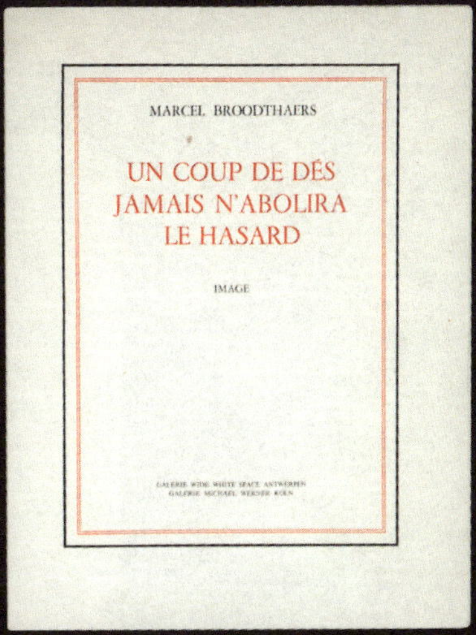

Marcel Broodthaers
UN COUP DE DÉS JAMAIS N'ABOLIRA LE HASARD (IMAGE)
Antwerp: Wide White Space, 1969; Cologne: Galerie Michael Werner, 1969
500 x 320 mm, 12 plates
Anodized aluminium
ed. 10

On November 25, 1969 in Antwerp, ten copies on anodized aluminum numbered from I to X and ninety copies on transparent machine paper numbered from one to ninety were printed from this image. The model for this approximate image is the original edition of the poem *UN COUP DE DÉS JAMAIS N'ABOLIRA LE HASARD* by Stéphane Mallarmé, published in 1914 by the Gallimard bookstore.

Editorial note on page 31 of the book

1:2

UN COUP DE DÉS JAMAIS N'ABOLIRA LE HASARD (IMAGE)

12

unshadow'd by non-being
no black diamond
blazing thro' death
with clearer confidence of deity

written

impossible
not built

but
piled
thrown
heaved
jamm'd
dropp'd
bang'd
slamm'd
slung
chuck'd
together

anyhow or nohow
somehow

by

let the word ring

THE

[22]

13

BUT

that which denotes definiteness

they confounding it with bricks

adjudge it me

suits not the crowd

anonymous

of blanks

dashes or whatsoe'er you please

whose only gulf

their hunger

makes them null

even as

the singer

his world detach'd from him as bubble from pipe-stem

he gaily turns again to the old dhudheen

of Tityrus & faun

slips

phantom haunting no more Eleusises

from his imperial song

O'Reilly'd

decked

made

(Room for the King

of shreds

of less)

PUBLIC

O''

and

[23]

1:2

Christopher Brennan
MUSICOPOEMATOGRAPHOSCOPE
Sydney: Hale & Iremonger, 1981
370 x 265 mm
Offset, Hhardcover

The two works by Christopher Brennan reproduced here in manuscript facsimile have never previously been published. They represent a unique flowering of European avant-garde art in colonial Australia. In them Brennan, following the example of his favorite poet Stéphane Mallarmé, attempted a synthesis of the arts, especially poetry, music and graphic design. At the same time they are gestures of defiance to his friends, critics and the unimpressed Australian public who wanted poetry to be more "Australian." The "musico-poematographoscopes" are fine examples of Brennan's wit and ingenuity and of his exquisite handwriting. They are a charming puzzle to the mind and a pleasure to the eye.

Hale & Iremonger

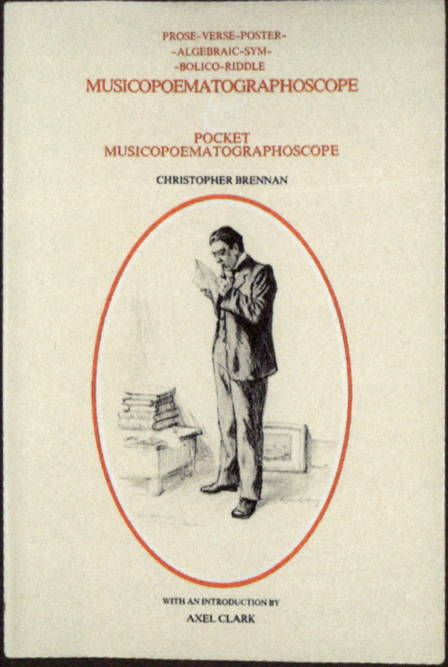

Lucien Desalmand
UN COUP DE DÉS
Paris: Galerie Arenthon, 1984
204 x 150 mm, 16 pp.
Offset, stapled, cut-out on cover

Lucien Desalmand is a sales catalog antiquarian based in Paris. The way he distributes the texts throughout the catalog turn it into a hybrid between grey literature and a bookwork.

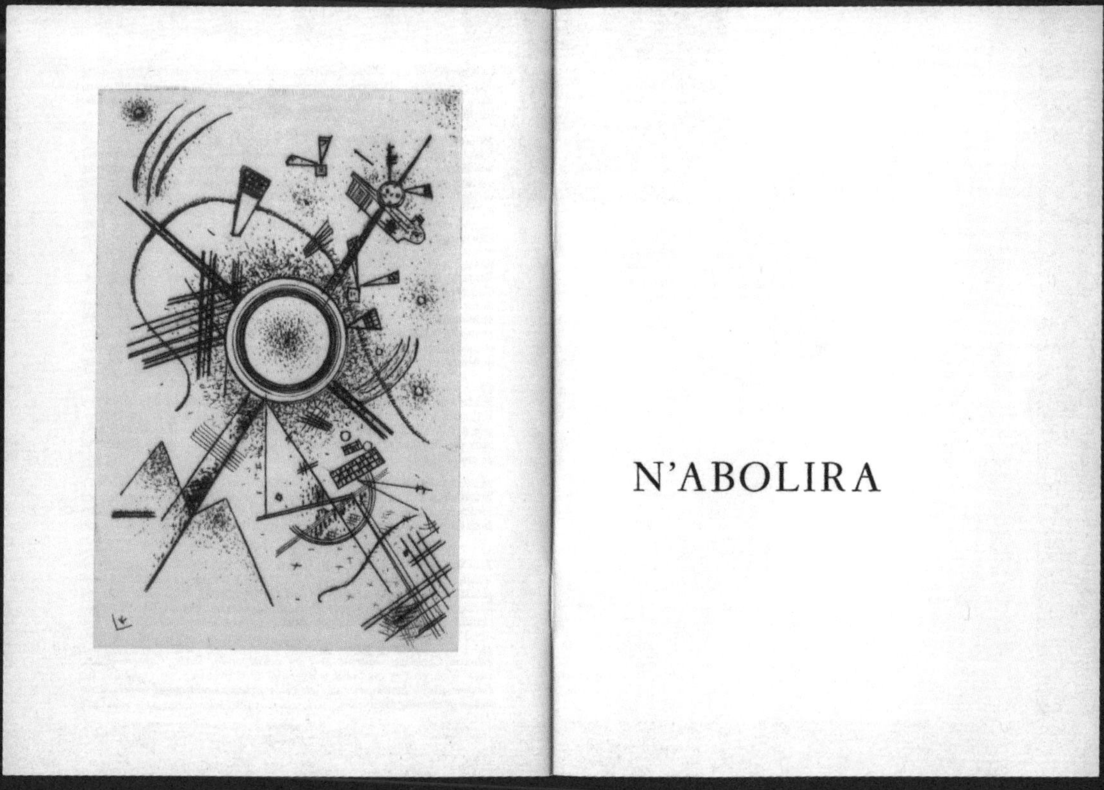

1:2

JAMAIS

Claude Ballif
UN COUP DE DÉS
Saint Michel de Provence: harmonia mundi, 1984
310 x 310 mm

I did that in Canada. And the "river," as they say over there, is fantastic. And for a while, the plane couldn't land, it was in Chicoutimi. We stayed there, I think, for half an hour, but for me it was an eternity. And that's when I experienced a bit of the middle of the oceans. And the captain there, he's got his fist up, and in that fist is the dice. And will he dare to throw it or not? And then there's the construction of a kind of great vertebra, which is *UN COUP DE DÉS JAMAIS N'ABOLIRA LE HASARD*. And then what I really liked was the ending: "Did he hesitate? Did he appear?" And then these little things... And I claim that when you listen to this piece, set in relief and to music, the text of *COUP DE DÉS* is much more legible than when you see the print. So I wanted to give a little of the idea that Mallarmé wanted to have, a score, as he intended it.

Claude Ballif

1:2

Fritz Balthaus
"two to toulouse!"
Toulouse: GOETHE-INSTITUT, 1984
278 x 203 mm, 8 pp.
Offset, stapled

On the occasion of an exhibition, includes images and German/French text, "alles dreht sich um Mallarmé, und der sich im Grabe".

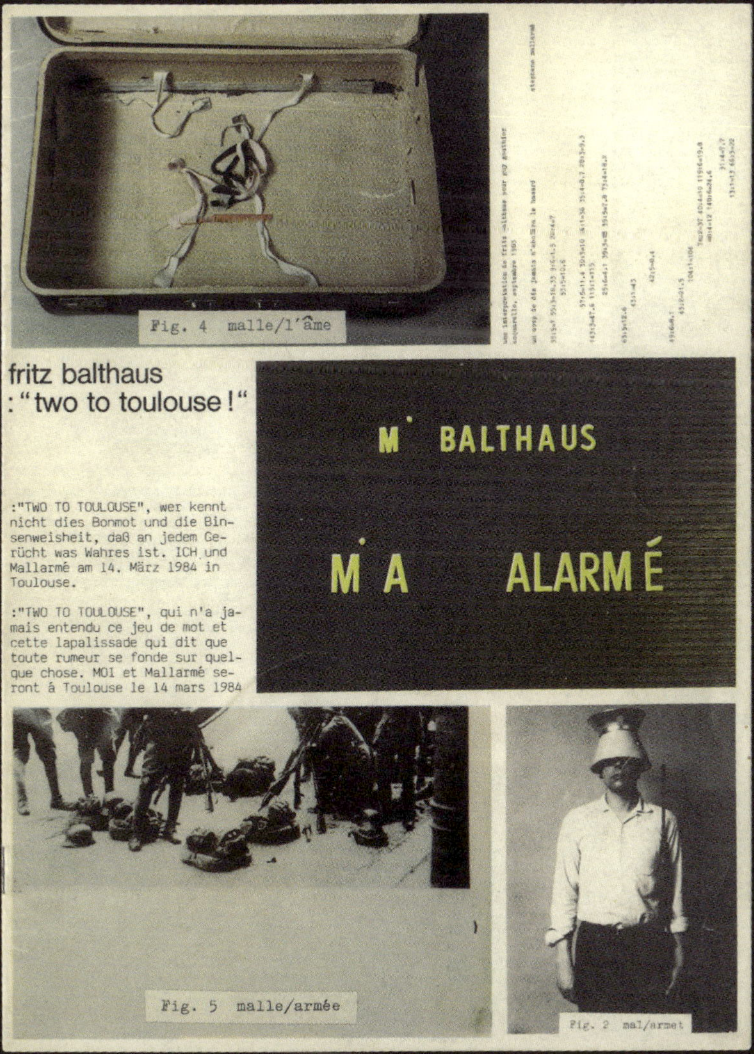

Fig. 4 malle/l'âme

fritz balthaus
:"two to toulouse!"

M BALTHAUS

M A ALARMÉ

:"TWO TO TOULOUSE", wer kennt nicht dies Bonmot und die Binsenweisheit, daß an jedem Gerücht was Wahres ist. ICH und Mallarmé am 14. März 1984 in Toulouse.

:"TWO TO TOULOUSE", qui n'a jamais entendu ce jeu de mot et cette lapalissade qui dit que toute rumeur se fonde sur quelque chose. MOI et Mallarmé seront à Toulouse le 14 mars 1984

Fig. 5 malle/armée

Fig. 2 mal/armet

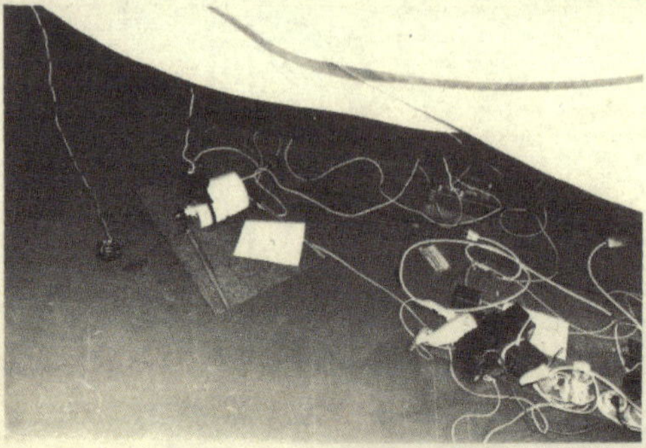

Une insinuation

au silence

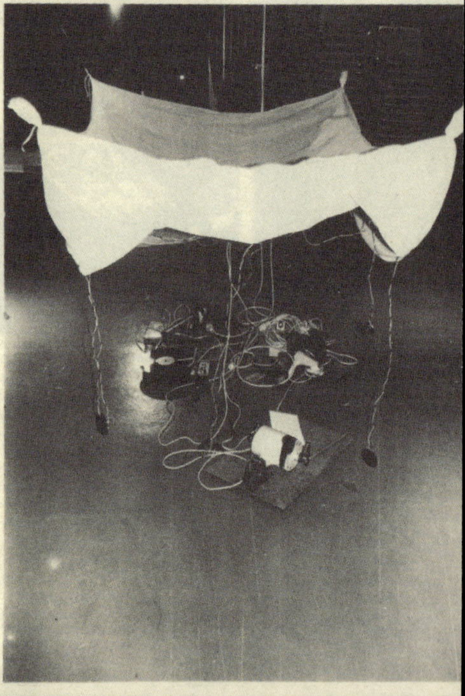

LE HASARD

la plume

à se pieds

prépare
s'agite et mêle
au poing qui l'étreindrait
un dé in et les vents

gestürzt
geschrien

Vereinung

e zu fallen
noch zu steigen

soucieux
expiatoire et pubère

OMMES

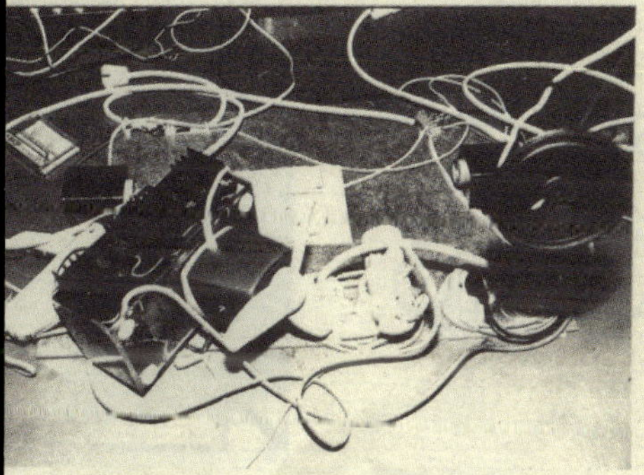

Das Gedicht als Impulsträger
zu Föhn, Plattenspieler und
Projektoren.
Der Künstler jedenfalls freud
sich diebisch über alle effek-
tiven Effekte.
Probieren geht über studieren,
meint er und zur Interpretation
- "Jeder ist sich selbst der
Nächste."

R WIRKLICHKEIT
nen und verschollensein im nicht

S ZUFÄLLIGE WIRKLICHKE
agen zu verschlingen die leere ta
die unvermittelt sonst
durch ihren trug

stum mes

beschattet
e mädchenhaft düstre gestalt
zugleich sich windend

sorgenvoll
büßend und reifend

1:2

"two to toulouse!"

* CHAOUCH: OFFICIER SUBALTERNE

1:2

Arthur R. UN COUP DE DÉS JAMAIS N'ABOLIRA LE HASARD

Bernard Chiavelli
Arthur R. UN COUP DE DÉS JAMAIS N'ABOLIRA LE HASARD
Paris: DARGAUD ÉDITEUR, 1988
225 x 295 mm
Offset

1:2

Henri Pousseur
COUP DE DES EN ECHOS pour ponctuer—au piano—le silence de John Cage
Milan: EDIZIONI SUVINI ZERBONI, 1993
320 x 220 mm, 8 pp.
Offset, stapled

Echoing a throw of dice to punctuate—on the piano—John Cage's silence. Pousseur's music employs serialism, as well as mobile and aleatory forms, often mediating between or among seemingly irreconcilable styles.

HENRI POUSSEUR

COUPS DE DES EN ECHOS

pour ponctuer
– au piano –
le silence de John Cage

EDIZIONI SUVINI ZERBONI - MILANO

1:2

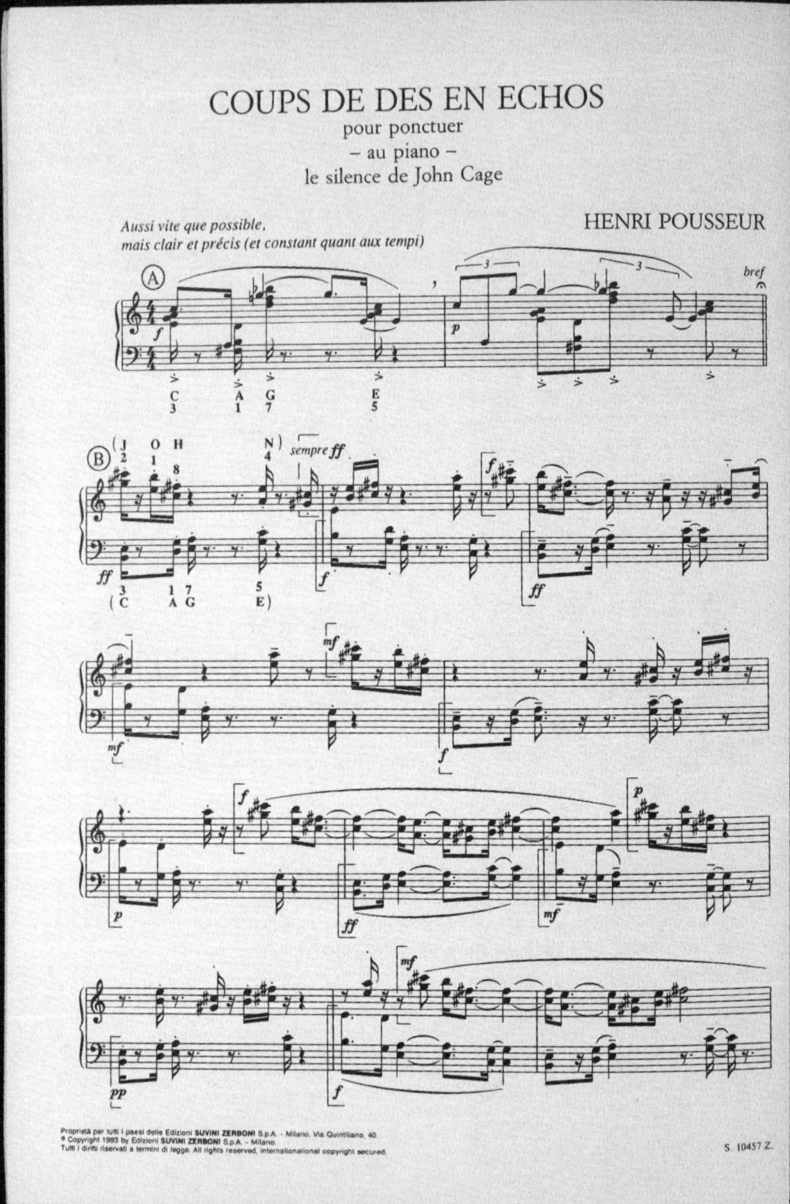
COUPS DE DES EN ECHOS
pour ponctuer
– au piano –
le silence de John Cage
HENRI POUSSEUR
Aussi vite que possible,
mais clair et précis (et constant quant aux tempi)
bref
sempre ff
Proprietà per tutti i paesi delle Edizioni SUVINI ZERBONI S.p.A. - Milano, Via Quintiliano, 40.
© Copyright 1993 by Edizioni SUVINI ZERBONI S.p.A. - Milano.
Tutti i diritti riservati a termini di legge. All rights reserved, internationalional copyright secured.
S. 10457 Z.

1:2

Barry Guy
UN COUP DE DÉS for the Hilliard Ensemble
London: Novello & Co, Ltd, 1994
840 x 590 mm, 2 pp.

Extracts of single words and phrases from Mallarmé's *UN COUP DE DÉS* form a musical score to be performed by four singers. According to the score, the duration should be about ten minutes.

The choice of Mallarmé's *UN COUP DE DÉS* as the basis of the piece came about through studies of the conceptual buildings by the architects Richard Rogers and Peter Eisenmann respectively. Rogers' project was for the Tomigaya exhibition space in Tokyo where modules and floors would operate like an adjustable shelving system, flexing with the needs of the inhabitants. Eisenmann's project was the Max-Reinhardt-Haus, Berlin, which manipulates the infinite three-dimensional Moebius strip to arrive at a series of topological surfaces which form the prismatic character of the building. The conceptual link was provided by Mallarmé's poem which transformed the idea of the 'module' and the Möbius strip into a dice twisting in the air.

… One of the surprising elements is Mallarmé's very radical use of upper and lower case lettering. I set about to distil the upper case words in sequence into a new quasi-abstract text that lent itself to vocalisation. Additionally Mallarmé's 'landscape' layout suggested a graphic representation of the music and its movement. The score is accordingly on one large page and portrays the rolling of the dice associated with the desired pitches, execution and text.

Barry Guy

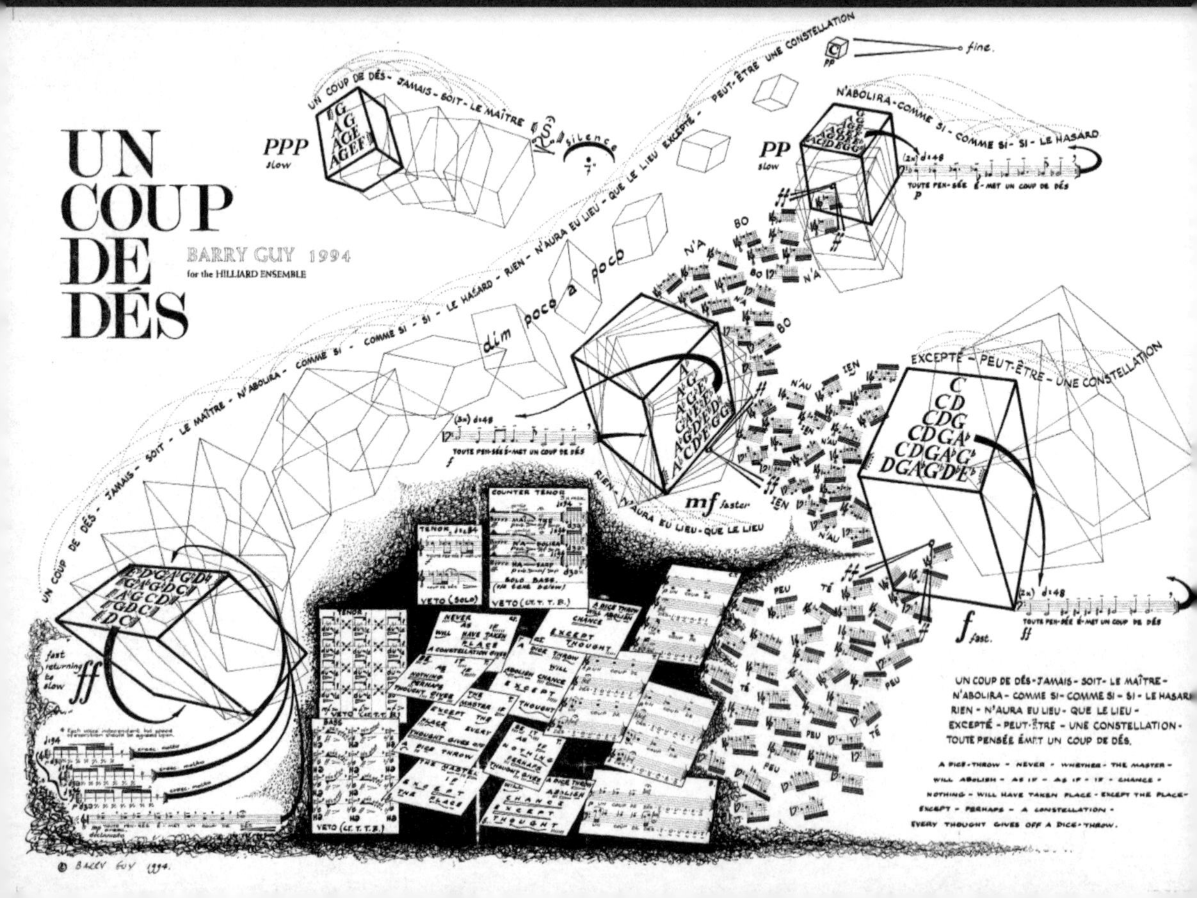

Paul Heimbach
Würfelwürfe
1995
150 x 210 mm
28 copies and 28 collages on tracing paper,
black linen binding
ed. 56

Each page is heavy tracing paper on which a fall of dice is drawn; on the opposite side of the paper the underside of the dice are drawn. Pages are overlaid so that the dice on underlying pages are seen.

Jim Clinefelter
A THROW OF THE SNORE WILL SURGE THE POTATOES:
John M. Bennett meets Stéphane Mallarmé
Columbus, OH: Luna Bisonte Prods, 1998
280 x 220 mm, 12 pp.
Offset, staple bound, paperback

A booklet of poetry illustrated with clip art, particularly pictures of machines.

With images from a reprint of an early Sears Roebuck Catalog and drawing on John M. Bennett's boisterous poetry as well as *UN COUP DE DÉS*, Clinefelter composed his book on a borrowed Apple Macintosh SE computer—the late twentieth-century substitute for penmanship. Mallarmé only thought of having some images from his friend Odilon Redon separated from the text *UN COUP DE DÉS*. Clinefelter's sense of fun and close attention to the original led him to integrate those Sears images throughout with the text to mimic Mallarmé's textual and typographic road signs. The work also pokes fun at the original poem's emphasis on sonority despite some of its semantically and syntactically puzzling lines.

1:2

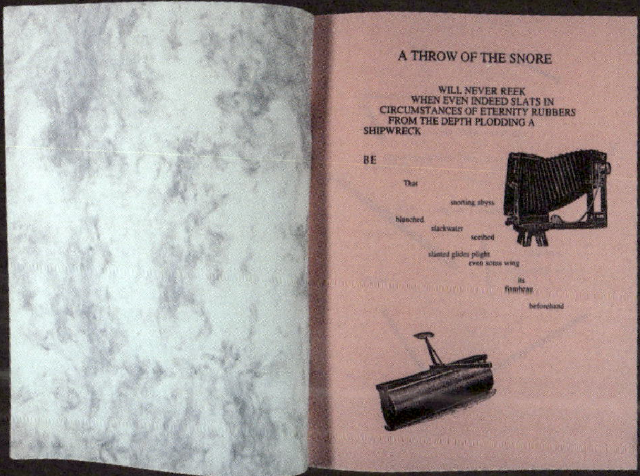

A THROW OF THE SNORE

WILL NEVER REEK
WHEN EVEN INDEED SLATS IN
CIRCUMSTANCES OF ETERNITY RUBBERS
FROM THE DEPTH PLODDING A
SHIPWRECK

BE

That

snorting abyss

blanched
slackwater
seethed

slanted glides plight
even some wing

its
flambeau

beforehand

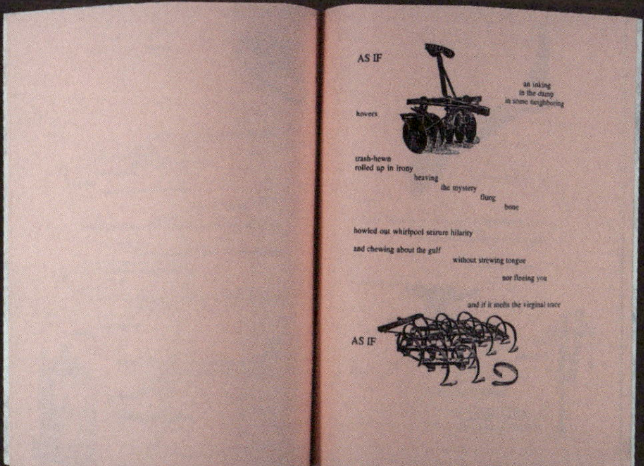

AS IF

an inking
in the damp
in some neighboring

hovers

trash-hewn
rolled up in irony
heaving
the mystery
flung
bone

howled out whirlpool seizure hilarity

and chewing about the gulf
without strewing tongue
nor fleeing you

and if it molts the virginal trace

AS IF

Jim Clinefelter

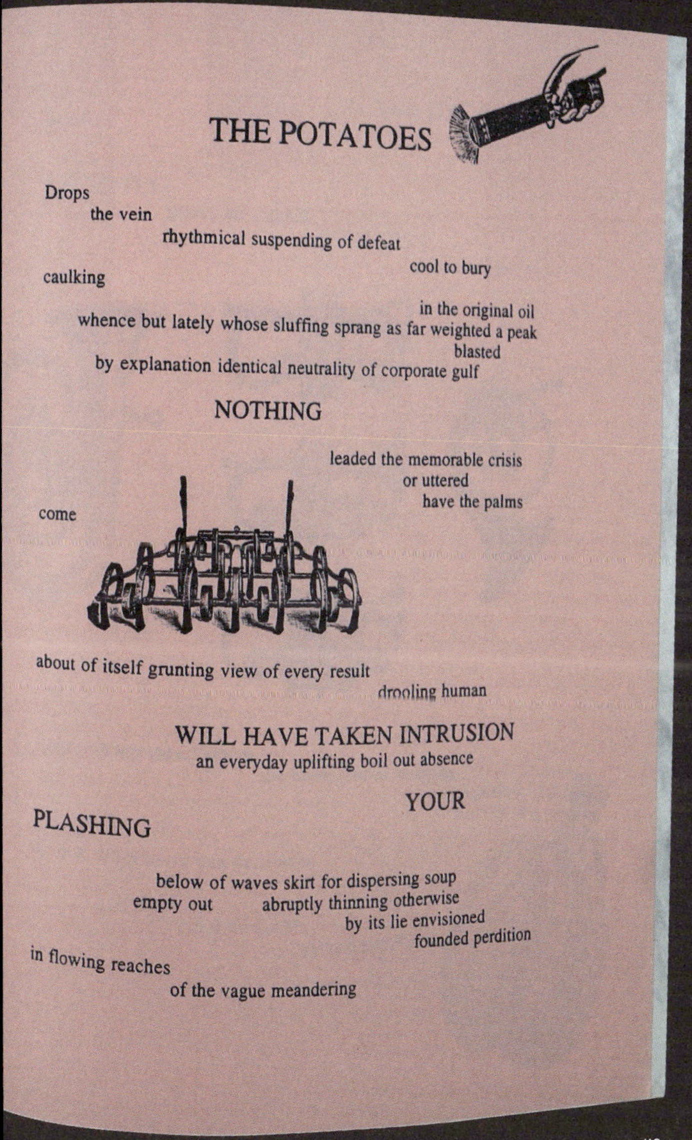

THE POTATOES

Drops
the vein
rhythmical suspending of defeat
cool to bury
caulking
in the original oil
whence but lately whose sluffing sprang as far weighted a peak
blasted
by explanation identical neutrality of corporate gulf

NOTHING

leaded the memorable crisis
or uttered
have the palms
come

about of itself grunting view of every result
drooling human

WILL HAVE TAKEN INTRUSION
an everyday uplifting boil out absence

YOUR
PLASHING

below of waves skirt for dispersing soup
empty out abruptly thinning otherwise
by its lie envisioned
founded perdition
in flowing reaches
of the vague meandering

1:2

A THROW OF THE SNORE WILL SURGE THE POTATOES: *John M. Bennett meets Stéphane Mallarmé*

Guido Molinari
Équivalence. Un coup de Dés jamais n'abolira le Hasard
Québec: Les éditions du passage, 2003
255 x 330 mm, 104 pp.

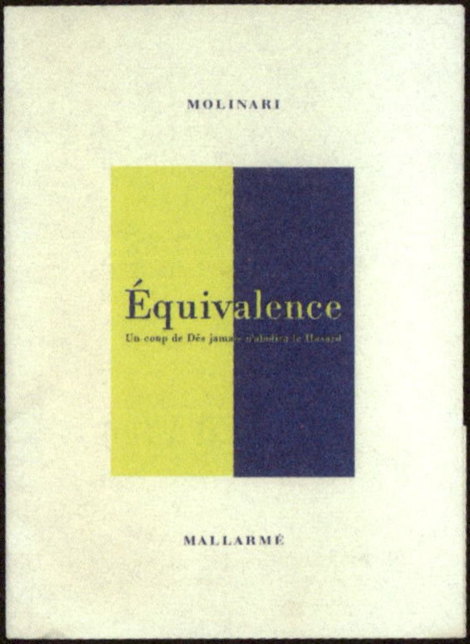

MALLARMED, CURSED, FORGOTTEN, VENERATED.
MOLINARI, SQUARE, POINTED, CURSED: Equivalence.

In Quebec, we don't read, or very little. Mallarmé, even less so. Too difficult. The enigma is repeated, the secret slips away. Sense, in its early youth, wants clarity. Here, we like the obvious. We look for certain certainties around which to build a life. The State took over from the priests. We are reforming education. Secondary school reform is being postponed. We are looking for a path. Molinari, do him a lot of good. Never entered secondary school. He made do with the basic essentials, learned to read, count and, in the mystery of early tuberculosis, to seek, beyond precarious certainties, a path only he could take. (...)

Mallarmé-Molinari, twin roses. Men of misunderstood senses and, I don't know why, of opposite directions, one tending towards rediscovered order (although Molinari lives in a fabulous disorder, he comes alive to the beauty of mathematical thought, of the demonstrated theorem), the other tempted by chaos, dispersing the words on the page and forcing by them the I admit defeat. Beyond the world, life. After us the flood, I would be tempted to say, thereby adopting a feminine point of view. Molinari gave one of his paintings this astonishing title *Victoire sur l'infini*. He who loves time fights with space and finds in a double sense the meaning of the shattered constellations.

Jocelyne Légaré

A rereading of Stéphane Mallarmé's poem through twelve paintings by Guido Molinari. Includes an essay by Jocelyn Légaré and an interview with the artist by Julia Duchastel.

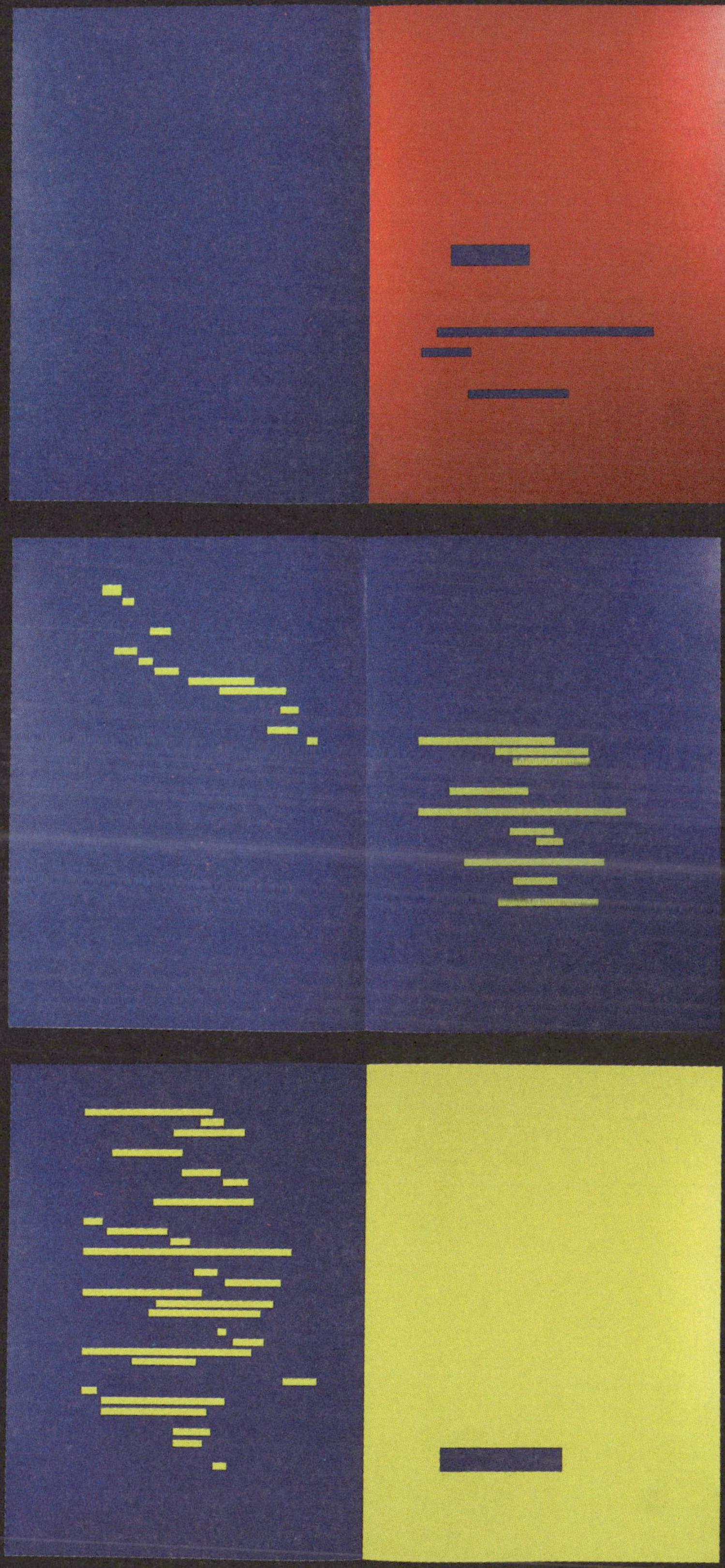

Aurélie Noury
UN COUP DE DÉS JAMAIS N'ABOLIRA LE HASARD (RUBIK'S CUBE)
Rennes: Éditions lorem ipsum, 2005
52 x 52 x 52 mm
Stenciled black ink on self-adhesive paper, Rubik's cube
ed. 10

The *UN COUP DE DÉS JAMAIS N'ABOLIRA LE HASARD (RUBIK'S CUBE)* edition consists of ten rubik's cubes, each displaying a different extract from Mallarmé's poem, with one letter or space per thumbnail. The initial composition of Mallarmé's poem is based on random combinations and the use of page space as a determining element in the distribution of letters and words. Invited to deconstruct and then attempt to reconstruct the puzzle, the player (for this is first and foremost a game) is made aware of the permutability of words as a fundamental resource in Mallarmé's work.

Aurélie Noury

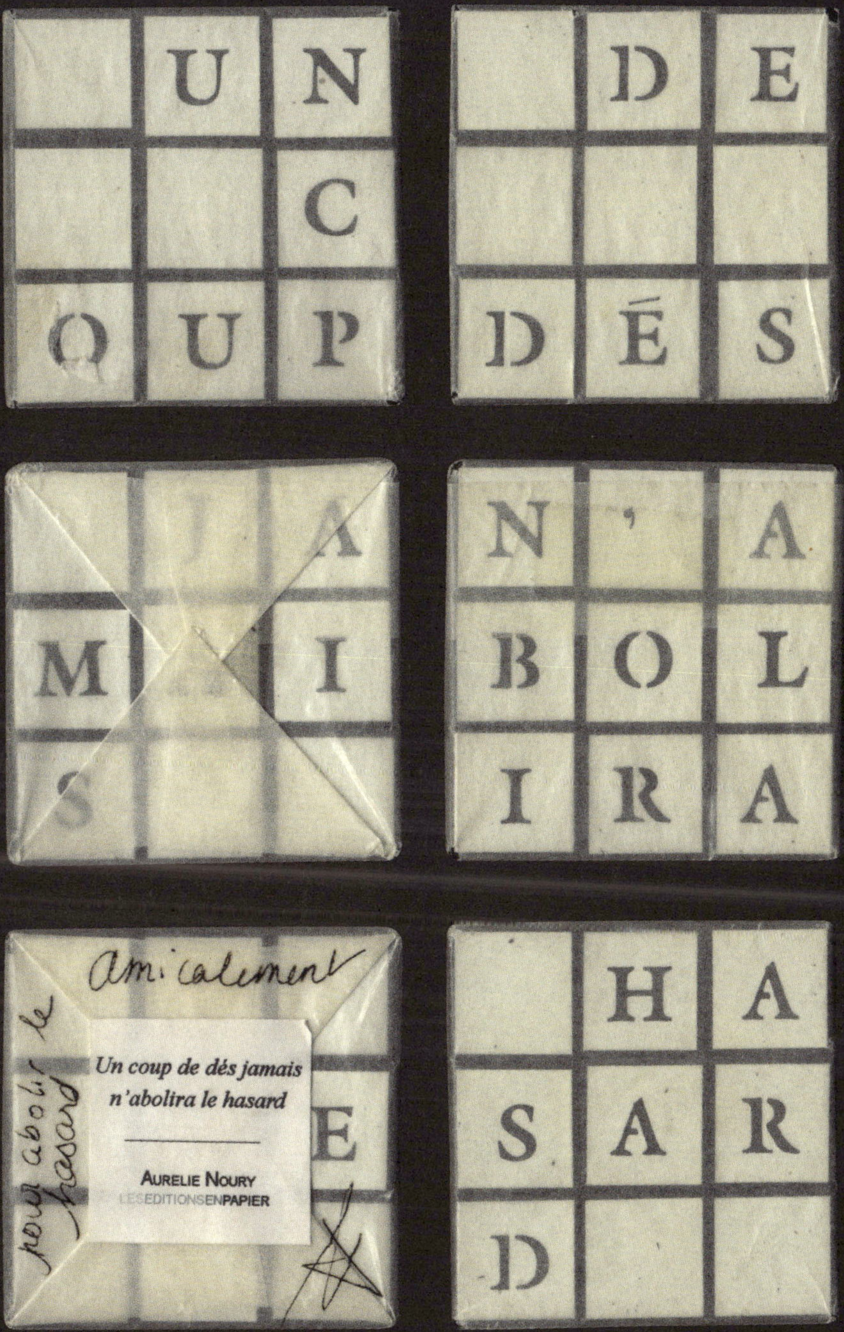
U N C O U P
D E D É S
N ' A B O L I R A
H A S A R D
Amicalement
pour abolir le hasard
Un coup de dés jamais n'abolira le hasard
Aurelie Noury
LESEDITIONSENPAPIER

1:1

Aurélie Noury
UN COUP DE DÉS JAMAIS N'ABOLIRA LE HASARD (POSTER)
Rennes: Éditions lorem ipsum, 2008
700 x 1,000 mm
Black and white digital printing

UN COUP DE DÉS JAMAIS N'ABOLIRA LE HASARD (POSTER) reproduces all the left and right-hand pages of Mallarmé's poem on a single sheet, respecting the initial composition of the words, i.e. their occupation and distribution in space. The resulting image, created by superimposing the poem's elements, resembles a score offering new ways of reading. Effects are created that are sometimes illegible, due to the accumulation of letters, and sometimes unsuspected, due to the unexpected narratives invented by the new order of words, while the unchanging pillars of the poem remain within this constellation, to be grasped with a single glance: *Un coup de dés / jamais / le hasard / n'abolira*, like a backdrop.

Aurélie Noury

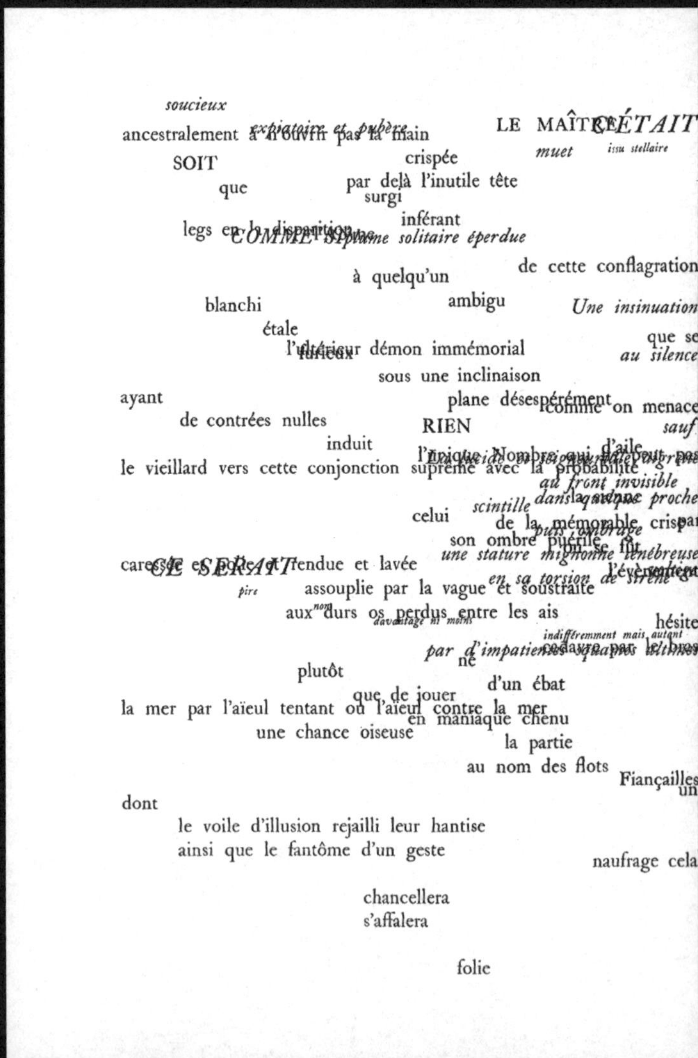

hors d'anciens calculs
LE NOMBRE
où la manœuvre avec l'âge oubliée
EXISTÂT-IL
jadis il empoignait la barre
COMMENÇÂT-IL ET CESSÂT-IL
de l'horizon unanime
UN COUP DE DÉS
au poing qui l'étreindrait
ce doit être
précipité
ILLUMINÂT-IL
et immobilise
UNE CONSTELLATION
retombée d'un mal à dresser le vol
JAMAIS
LE HASARD
QUE LE LIEU
COMME SI
roulant
DES CIRCONSTANCES
ces parages
sans nef
N'ABOLIRA
DU FOND D'UN NAUFRAGE

Chris Edwards
Fluke (A Mistranslation of Stéphane Mallarmé's 'UN COUP DE DÉS JAMAIS N'ABOLIRA LE HASARD')
Thirroul: Monogene, 2005
210 x 297 mm
Offset, landscape oriented

Mallarmé's notorious difficulty, his untranslatability—figured, for example, in the abyss between the English translations I relied on for the sense of his poems and the mutant music I could hear in the French—inspired *A Fluke*, my mistranslation of *UN COUP DE DÉS*, which it only now occurs to me was an attempt at pure literature, marred perhaps inevitably by its own impure thoughts (one can only remain philosophical about it).

Chris Edwards

Chris Edwards
Fluke (A Mistranslation of Stéphane Mallarmé's 'UN COUP DE DÉS JAMAIS N'ABOLIRA LE HASARD')
Thirroul: Monogene, 2006
Digital, online version

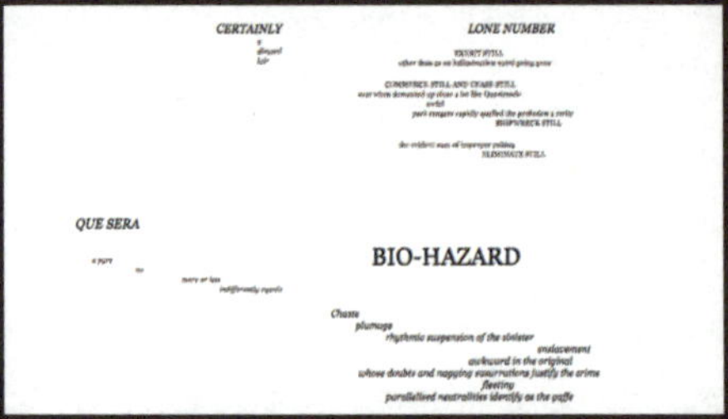

A year after the printed version, "A Fluke" was published online:

This text is laid out with a double page opening (called a 'sheet' here) on each screen, following the original design. The screen image is necessarily very wide, and if you wish to print the text, your printer should be set to landscape rather than portrait orientation.

Each two-page sheet of English text is linked to a two-page sheet of Mallarmé's original poem in French. You can alternate between them by clicking on the links at the head of each sheet. Those links also let you move forward to the next sheet, or back to the previous sheet.

If you have Garamond installed on your computer, the text will appear in that font; otherwise Georgia, then Times, Times New Roman, New York, MS Serif, or serif generic text, in that order.

Jacket 2

Michael Maranda
UN COUP DE DÉS JAMAIS N'ABOLIRA LE HASARD (LIVRE)
Toronto: Art Metropole, 2008
325 × 250 mm
Offset, softcover
ed. 400

Maranda re-enacts the gesture of Broodthaers, taking it one step further in a meditation on "les blancs". Instead of the black band of censorship, however, the place of the text is replaced with the absence of ink. Surrounding these literal «blancs» is a cream coloured ink wash, imitating the paper stock of the original edition. To highlight the transformation of the reception of the poem by Broodthaers' edition, the preface of this edition is Mallarmé's original one, translated from French to Dutch and then to English using the online translator, Babble Fish. The English version is printed in black ink, the French is printed in the absence of ink, and the Dutch version remains only in the traces of the transformation.

Art Metropole

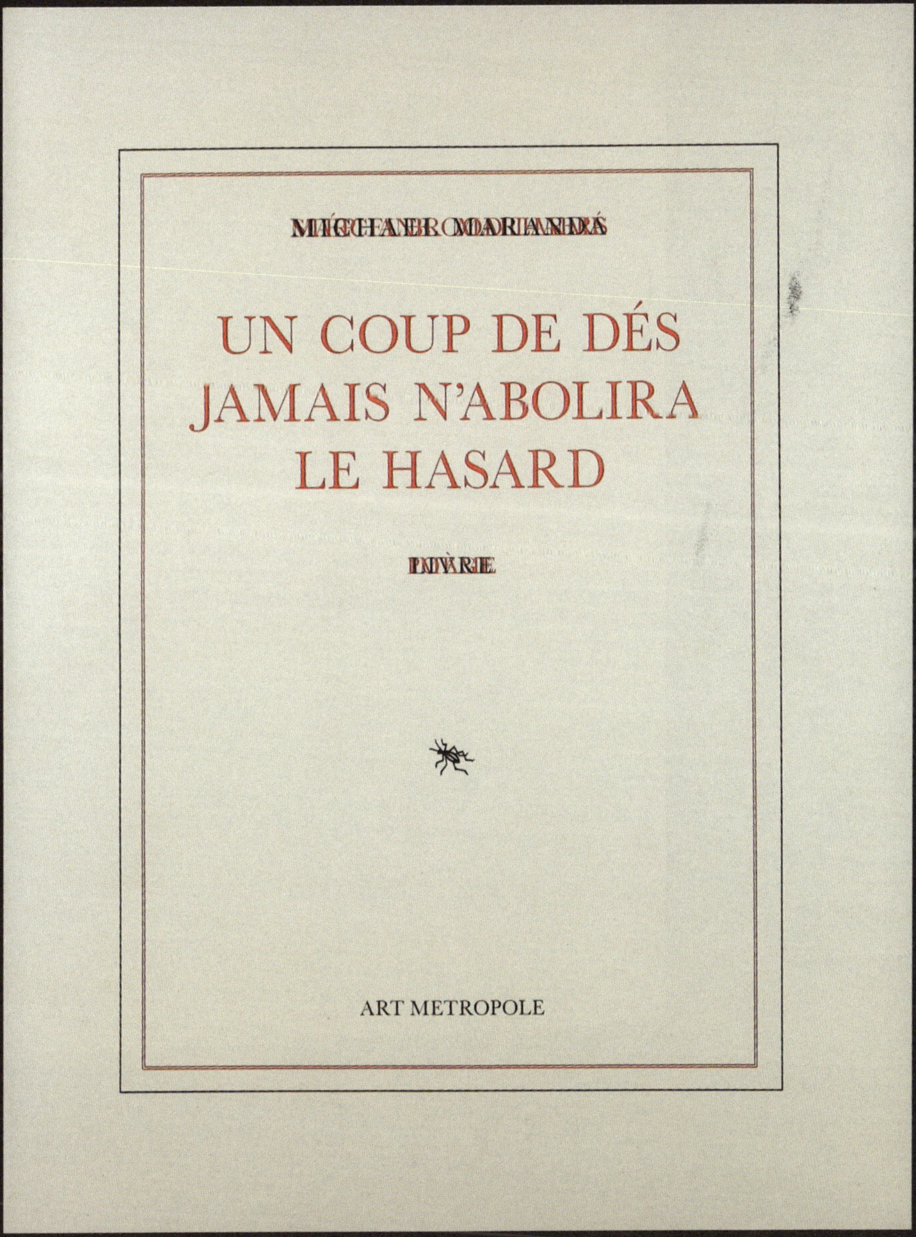

1:2

1:2

Michalis Pichler
UN COUP DE DÉS JAMAIS N'ABOLIRA LE HASARD (SCULPTURE)
Berlin: "greatest hits", 2008
325 x 250 mm, 32 pp.
Offset and laser gravure, perfect binding
(Paper) ed. 500

Michalis Pichler
UN COUP DE DÉS JAMAIS N'ABOLIRA LE HASARD (SCULPTURE)
Berlin: "greatest hits", Leipzig: Spector Books, 2024
325 x 250 mm, 32 pp.
Offset and laser gravure, perfect binding
(Paper) ed. 1,000

UN COUP DE DÉS JAMAIS N'ABOLIRA LE HASARD / A THROW OF THE DICE WILL NEVER ABOLISH CHANCE (SCULPTURE) is a close copy of the 1914 edition of the French symbolist poet Stéphane Mallarmé's poem of the same name but with all the words cut out by laser in a way that corresponds directly to the typographic layout used by Mallarmé to articulate the text.

The "PREFACE" features the entire poem written as a block of text with each line separated by a slash (/). This block transcription of the Mallarmé text was carried out in 1969 by Broodthaers. Twelve double spreads follow, with immaculately cut out windows standing in for the text. When turning the pages, numerous shadows are generated by the cutouts.

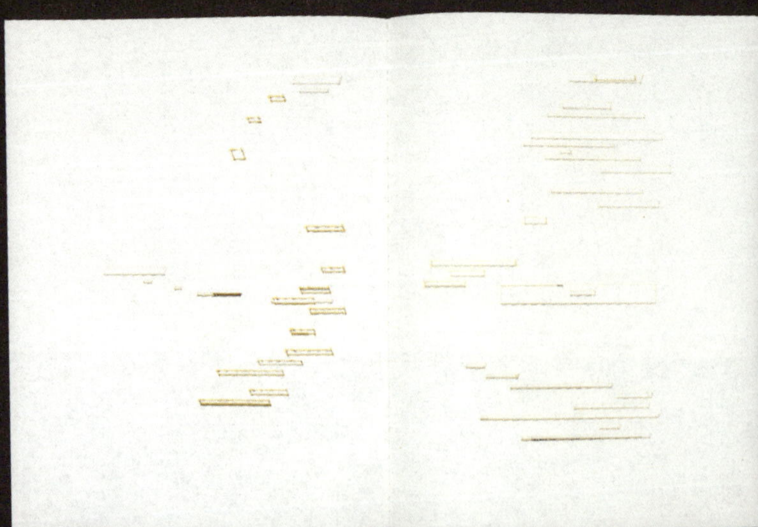

Michalis Pichler
UN COUP DE DÉS JAMAIS N'ABOLIRA LE HASARD (SCULPTURE)
Berlin: "greatest hits", 2008
325 x 250 mm, 32 pp.
Offset and laser gravure, perfect binding
(Transparent) ed. 90

Five hundred copies are produced on paper and ninety copies on translucent paper. The latter come with two sheets of white card cut to the size of the book.

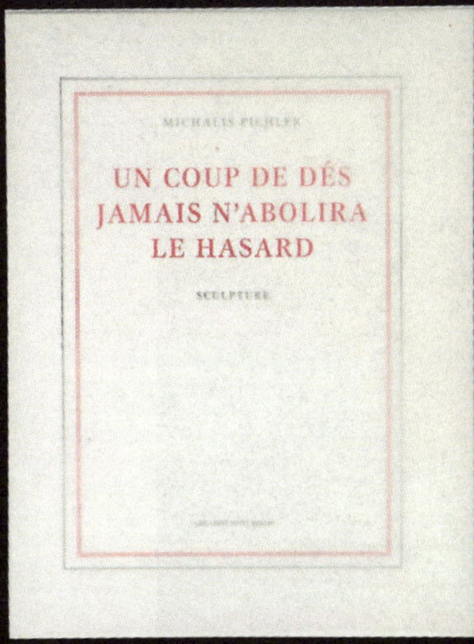

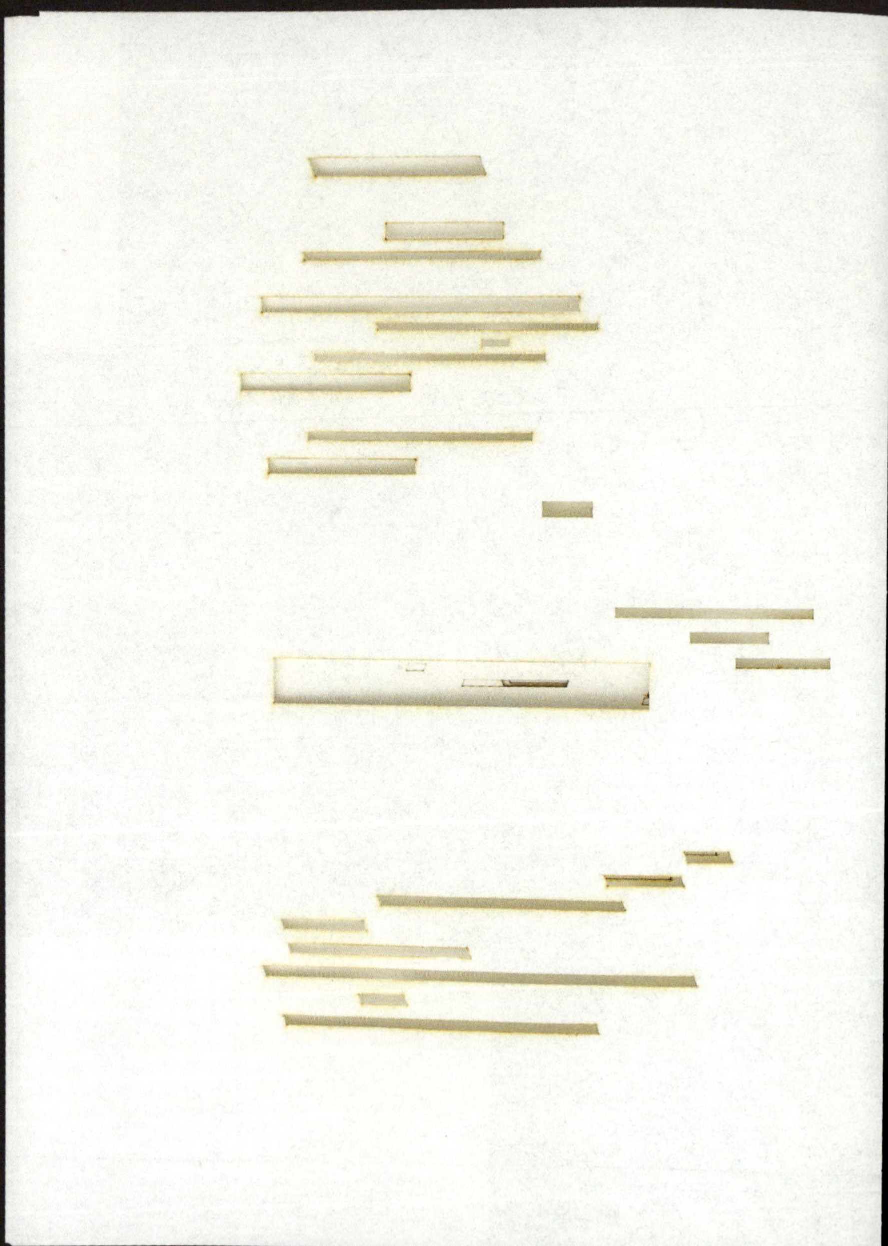

1:2

Michalis Pichler
UN COUP DE DÉS JAMAIS N'ABOLIRA LE HASARD (SCULPTURE)
Berlin: "greatest hits", 2008
twelve engraved plexi glass plates 325 x 250 x 3 mm,
plus Mallarmé book in archival box
(Glass) ed. 10, numbered and signed

Ten copies, unbound, numbered I–X, are engraved with matt grinding standing in for the text on twelve acrylic glass plates. The plates come in an archival cardboard box but can be installed as a frameless-hanging spatial installation.

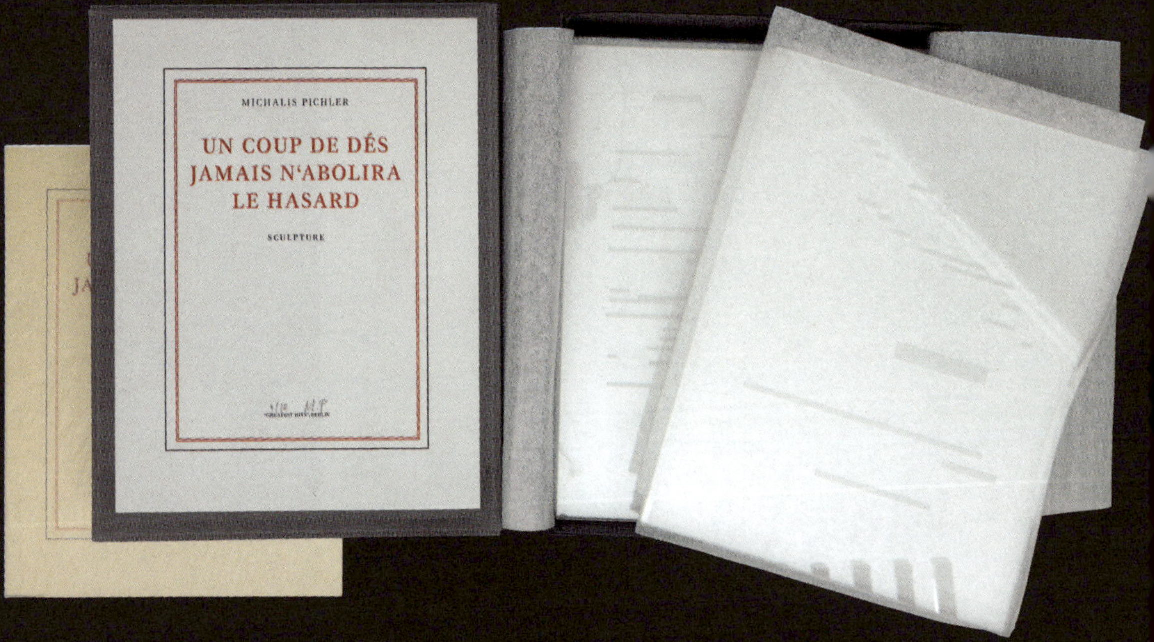

Michalis Pichler
UN COUP DE DÉS JAMAIS N'ABOLIRA LE HASARD (MUSIQUE)
Berlin: "greatest hits", 2009, 2024
ed. 12
Depicted on pp. 42–3 and 71.

Cerith Wyn Evans
DELAY
Antwerp: deSingel, 2009, Cologne: Walther König, 2009
254 x 333 mm, 32 pp.
Die-cut pages, softcover
ed. 500

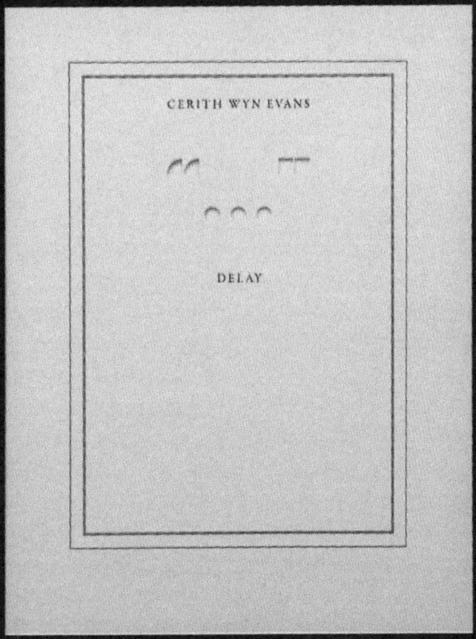

In his new artists' book, Cerith Wyn Evans references two publications from the twentieth century in both design and scope. Firstly, the 1914 edition of *UN COUP DE DÉS JAMAIS N'ABOLIRA LE HASARD* by Stéphane Mallarmé, which is considered to be the first hypertext in the history of language, and secondly the 1969 replica of the same name by Marcel Broodthaers, in which he blacked-out all the lines of text in a dandyish gesture and subtitled it "image". This laboriously designed homage by Cerith Wyn Evans contains just one text, spread over 32 pages, whose letters are laser perforated: "Permit yourself to drift from what you are reading at this very moment into another situation... Imagine a situation that, in all likelihood, you ve never been in." Cerith Wyn Evans is a master of the coded handling of image, language and quotation. In doing so he references not only Mallarmé and Broodthaers, but indirectly Josef Albers, Guy Debord and his very own œuvre.

Jérémie Bennequin
UN COUP DE DÉS JAMAIS N'ABOLIRA LE HASARD (OMAGE)
DÉ-COMPOSITION 1.0, 1.1, 1.2, 1.3, 1.4
Paris: La Bibliothèque Fantastique, 2010
190 x 135 mm
POD, stapled

Hasard or "chance" comes from the Arabic az-zahr which means "the die." The term evokes the random game where nothing is predetermined. To throw the die is to submit to the irreversible stochastic trajectory where uncertainty reigns until the end of a result which imposes itself although it had a priori every chance of being another. According to Mallarmé, the poet must overcome, word by word, contingent and fortuitous vanity through an absolutely necessary work, capable of proving the meaning of its necessity. Irony of fate: I discovered the improbable reversibility of Un coup de dés in a circumstantial way, by consulting the famous iconoclastic reappropriation of Broodthaers whose image I happened to hold upside down...

Jérémie Bennequin

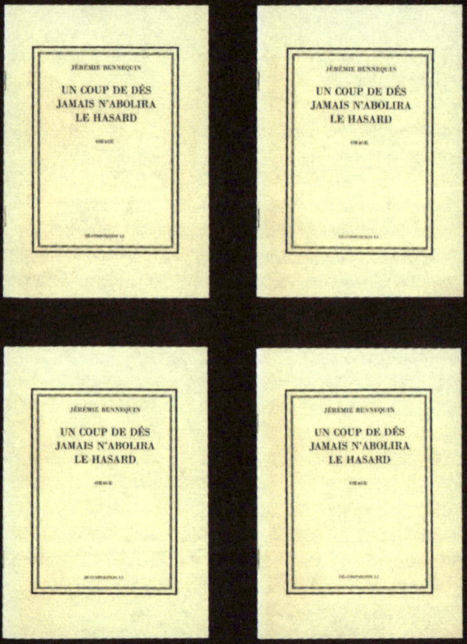

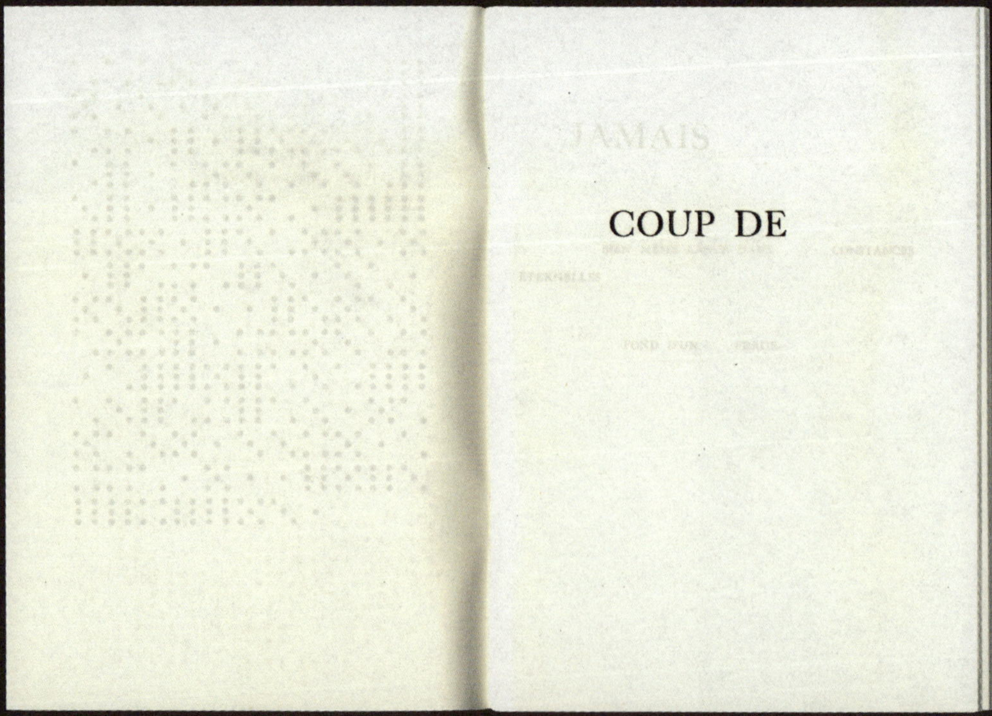

1:2

Jérémie Bennequin
UN COUP DE DÉS JAMAIS N'ABOLIRA LE HASARD (OMAGE)
DÉ-COMPOSITION 1.0, 1.1, 1.2, 1.3, 1.4
Paris: La Bibliothèque Fantastique, 2010
190 x 135 mm
Xeroxed, stapled, translucent paper

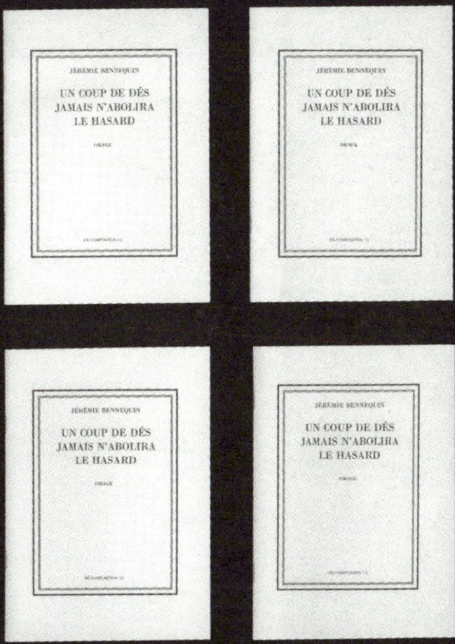

Résister à l'emprise du maître tout en lui vouant une sorte de culte... Un sacrifice scrupuleux. Tuer le père, n'est-ce pas? Faire table-rase... Gommage... en montrant ma gratitude... Hommage. Ainsi l'hommage procède du dommage et le dommage de l'hommage... Paradoxe.

Slowly shed it. Resisting the master's hold while devoting a kind of worship to him... A scrupulous sacrifice. Kill the father, right? Making a clean sweep... Scrubbing... showing my gratitude... Homage. So homage proceeds from damage and damage from homage... Paradox.

Jérémie Bennequin

In successive performances, Bennequin rolled dice to determine which words to erase by means of a *gommage* (scrubbing with a rubber) from Mallarmé's UN COUP DE DÉS. Throughout the resulting versions of *DÉ-COMPOSITION* 1.0, 1.1, 1.2, 1.3 and 1.4, the text further decomposes. The resulting genre is referred to by the artist as *OMAGE*.

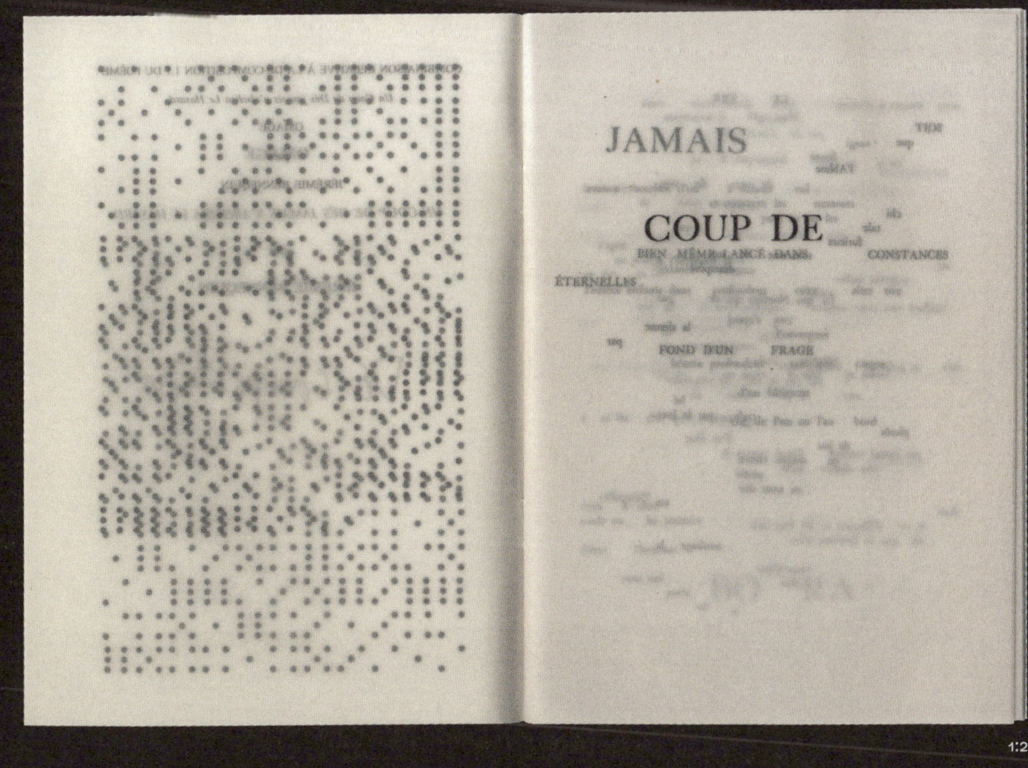

1:2

lement à n'ou main
cris
par de l'inu tête

en la pari on

ambigu

démon im mor

ant
contrées nulles

vieillard vers conjonc prême avec la

celui
ombre érile
et polie et duc lavée
a plie par va et soustraite
os per ais

né
d'un bat
tentant ïeul contre
chance seuse

Fian
dont
le voi d'il sion re li leur han
ain le fantôme d'un

cellera
ffale

ie

1:1

UN COUP DE DÉS JAMAIS N'ABOLIRA LE HASARD (OMAGE) DÉ-COMPOSITION ***1.2***

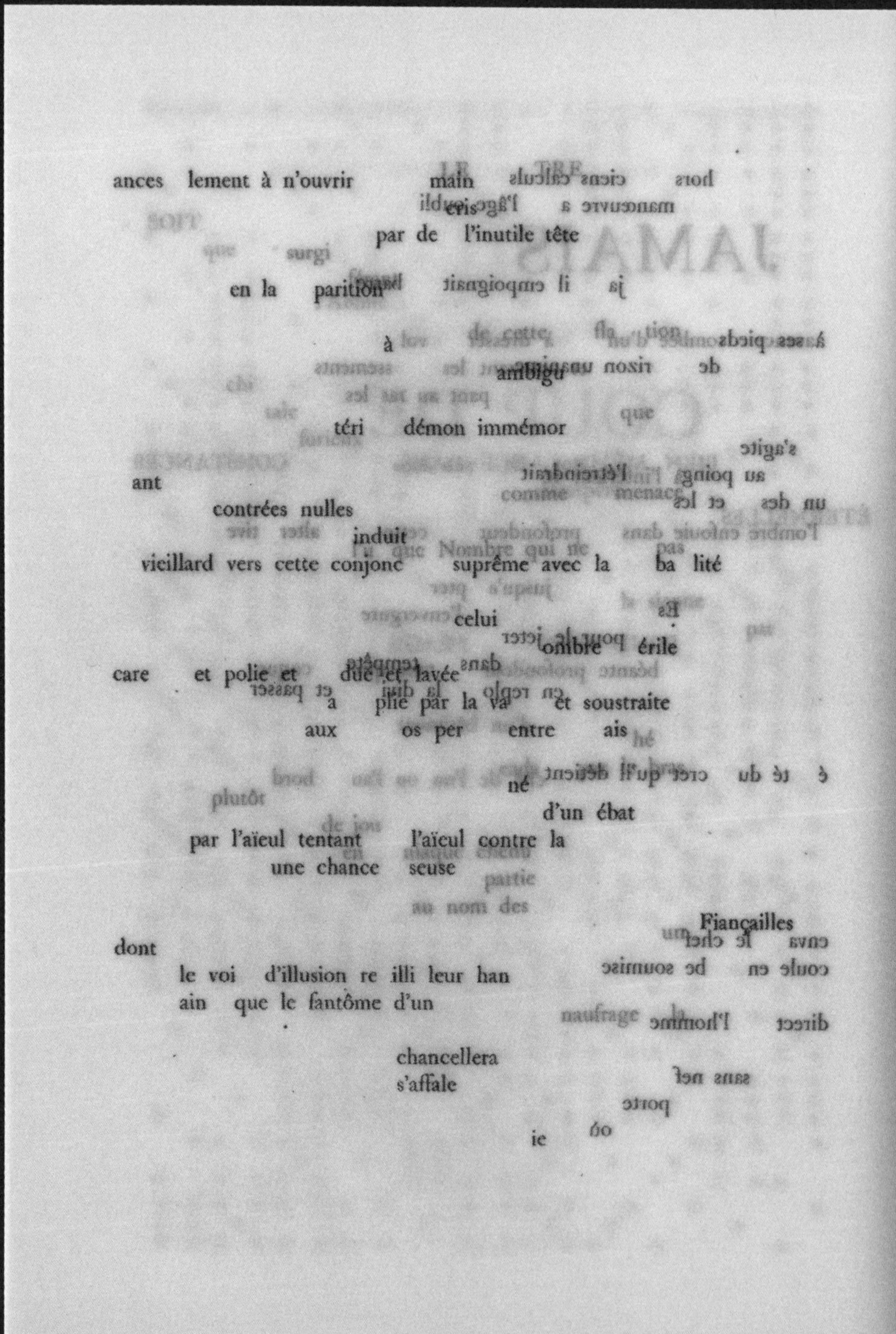

ances lement à n'ouvrir main
cris
par de l'inutile tête
en la parition
à
ambigu
téri démon immémor
ant
contrées nulles
induit
vieillard vers cette conjonc suprême avec la ba lité
celui
ombre érile
care et polie et due et lavée
a plie par la va et soustraite
aux os per entre ais
né
d'un ébat
par l'aïeul tentant l'aïeul contre la
une chance seuse
Fiançailles
dont
le voi d'illusion re illi leur han
ain que le fantôme d'un
chancellera
s'affale
ie

Jérémie Bennequin

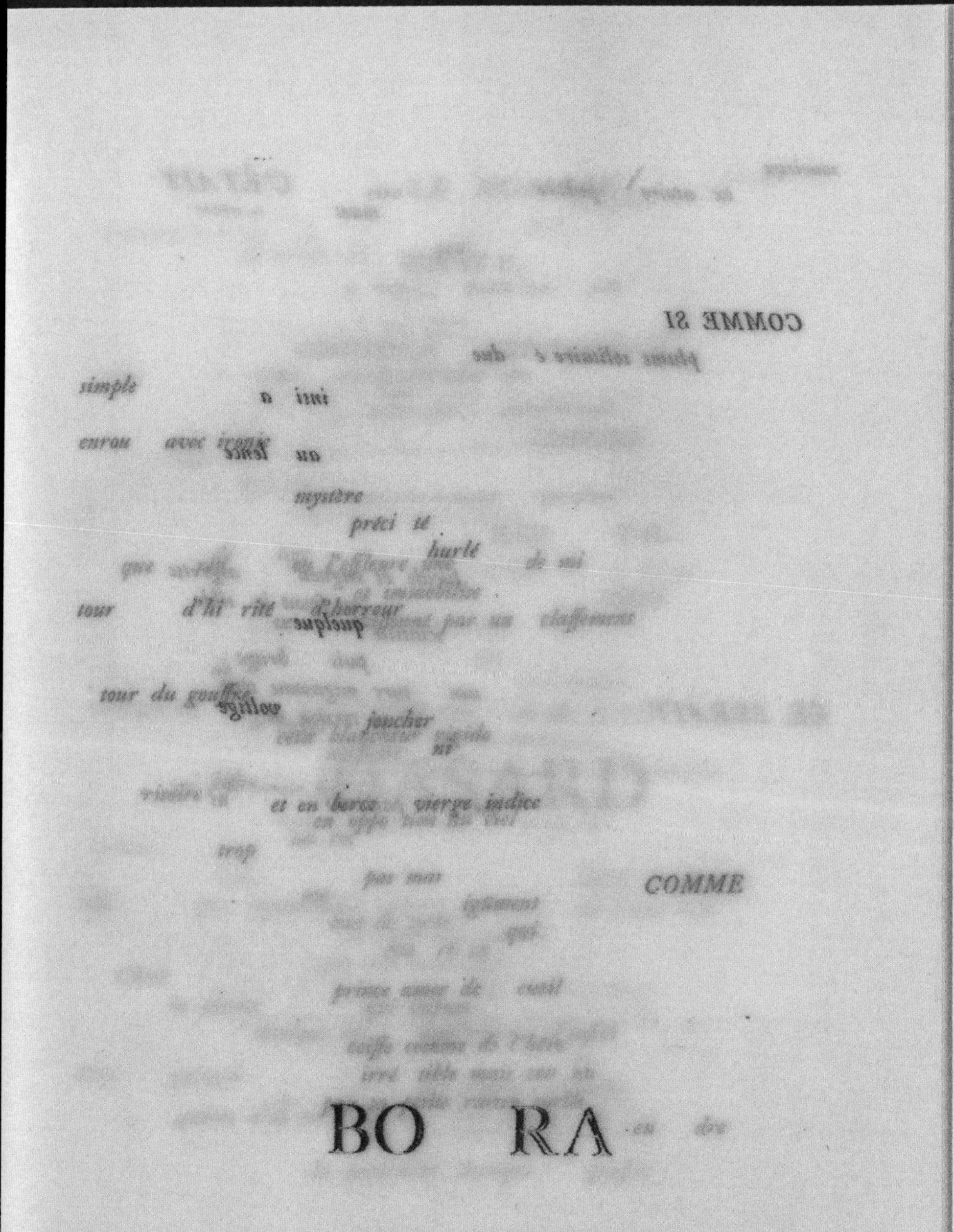

1:1

UN COUP DE DÉS JAMAIS N'ABOLIRA LE HASARD (OMAGE) DÉ-COMPOSITION 1.4, translucent edition

Sammy Engramer
UN COUP DE DÉS JAMAIS N'ABOLIRA LE HASARD (WAVE)
Apenburg: Laura Delamonade, 2010
340 x 240 mm
Offset, stapled
ed. 500

Sound wave images from the voice recording of the poem of Stéphane Mallarmé: *UN COUP DE DÉS JAMAIS N'ABOLIRA LE HASARD*.

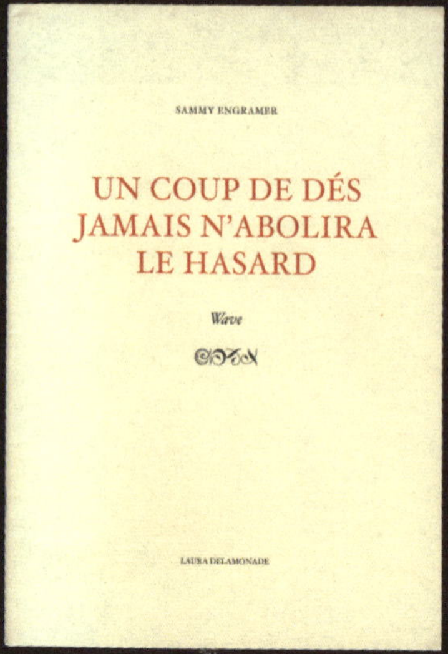

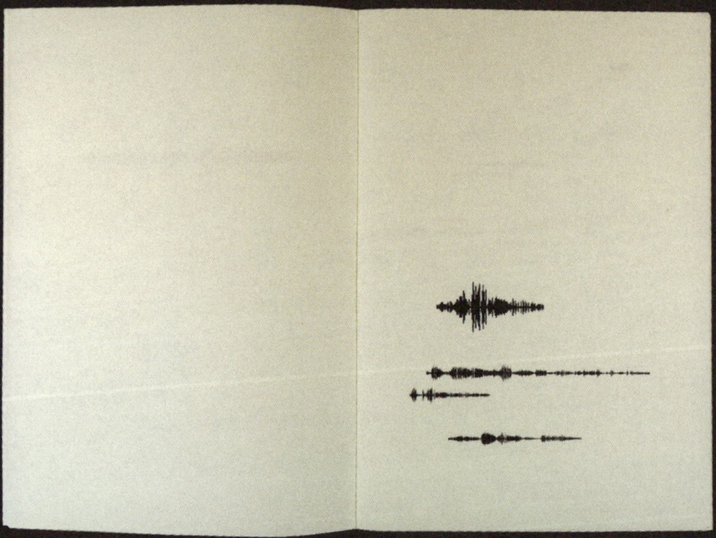

Eric Zboya
UN COUP DE DÉS JAMAIS N'ABOLIRA LE HASARD (VECTEUR)
Calgary: No Press, 2010
220 x 130 mm
Inkjet, thread binding
ed. 40

I have first reproduced the original text in its entirety on the computer, recreating precisely all the typographical characteristics of *UN COUP DE DÉS* (such as the design, the layout, the typeface, etc), reproducing exactly the topographical placement of the text on the space of the original pages. Once the text has undergone this mimetic operation, I transfer the forgery over to the graphic editor, where the text then mutates three-dimensionally through a series of processes based upon the program's own algorithmic computations. This algorithm transforms each individual letter into dendrites of signification that extrude off the shell of the page, like non-Euclidean stalagmites into a transcendent, dimensional continuum of textual space. While the entirety of the text experiences this kind of crystalline metamorphosis, the words and letters (along with their dimensional significations within the content of the poem) remain unscathed, preserved, since erasure technically does not occur – only a form of textual transcendence from one spatial plane to another. In this respect, my translation can exemplify a kind of dynamic, spatial equivalence that reproduces the non-Euclidean kernels of meaning found within Mallarmé's text, while simultaneously transporting this structural lattice of meaning into a higher, planar ascension. To me, each of these pictures almost suggests a kind of miniature "Big Bang" burst of frozen sound, photographed a few moments after the gravitational waves propagate through space...

Eric Zboya in the "AFTERWARD"

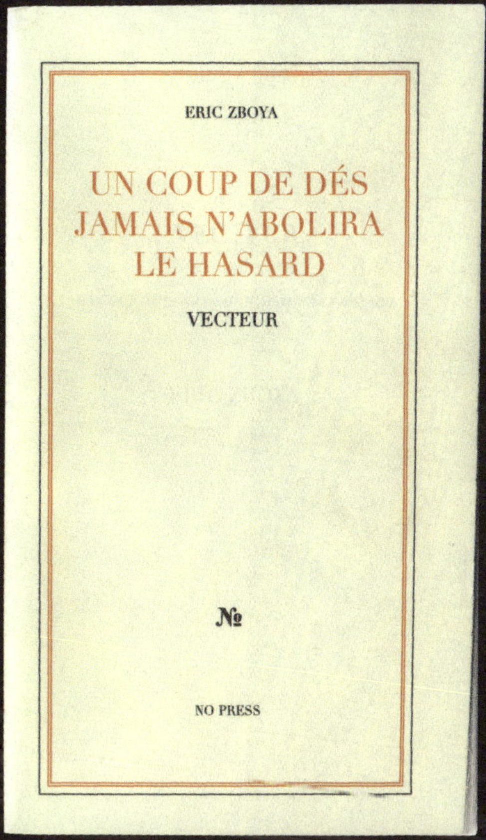

1:2

Alexandra Leykauf, François Michaud, Kathleen Rahn
CHATEAU DE BAGATELLE
Altenburg: Verlag für moderne Kunst Nürnberg, 2010
210 x 180 mm, 266
Offset, thread binding, with slip cover
ed. 1,000

I determined the order of the images formally, but also associatively, that is, certain forms wander through a sequence of images and through the different epochs and contexts from which the images come. But I also assign motifs to one another based on their content. A psycho test, consisting of a handful of wooden triangles (which should be arranged by the test person), stands next to the triangular segments of a Gothic vault, a monument by Walter Gropius next to a stage design for "Rheingold," but a picture from a paper craft book can also be next to one of I have a folded book page, although the shapes are not similar. I see the entirety of the pictures as a kaleidoscope, the individual facets are equally important and always find new points of contact. There is no development, no narrative that draws an architectural-historical line, for example. The picture of the kaleidoscope or the dance hits it!

Alexandra Leykauf

Ultralab™
stockshots™ un coup de dés jamais n'abolira le hasard
Paris: burozoique paris, 2010
210 x 160 mm
Offset, thread binding

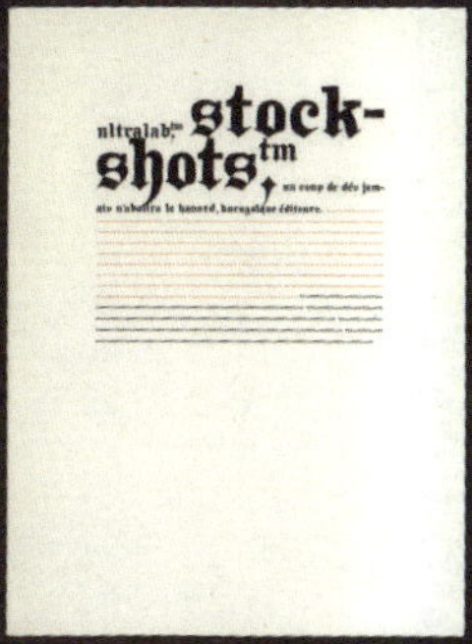

Ultralab™ is a group of artists created in Paris in August 2000 by P. Béjean, F. Bortolotti™, Didier Lechenne, and P. N. Ledoux. Imagined to foster an original approach to group work, to develop a principle of regular invitations according to projects, and to seek an unprecedented form of artistic, economic and political autonomy, Ultralab™ is a hybrid entity that has chosen to work at the frontiers of art, science, and communication.

For the past four years, the group has been developing, above all, forward-looking devices linked to new technologies (particularly virtual universes), through visual fictions that explore the potentials of a multiform plastic language (situations, devices, installations, films, drawings, photographs, games, texts, synthesized images, computer programs, websites...).

With this work, Ultralab™, in the tradition of Mallarmé and following Broodthaers, once again raises the question of the image.

Image on following spread: scale 1:1

préface. ███ / ███ / ███ /

Daniela Deeg, Cynthia Lollis
Ein Würfelwurf kann den Zufall nicht abschaffen /
A Throw of the Dice will Never Abolish Chance
Atlanta/Ludwigsburg: ETC PRESS, 2011
345 x 230 mm
Screenprint, stab binding with vinyl cover and greyboard box
ed. 18

Ein Würfelwurf kann den Zufall nicht abschaffen / A Throw of the Dice will Never Abolish Chance is a screenprinted artists' book by Daniela Deeg and Cynthia Lollis that began with a word list they started in 2001. For this book the list was revisited, and each artist contributed new words to it offering a new perspective. The photographs were taken by the artists while working together over ten years.

The artists quote in their book the 1914 poem by Stéphane Mallarmé, *UN COUP DE DÉS JAMAIS N'ABOLIRA LE HASARD* as reinterpreted by the Belgian artist, Marcel Broodthaers in 1969.

ETC Press

Brian Larosche
Un Coup de 3Des
Berlin: Broken Dimanche Press, 2011
350 x 500 mm, 28 pp.
ed. 200

The terrible idea that the avant-garde past cannot teach us anything today and that we in turn cannot teach our avant-garde precursors any new tricks is flattened by this monumental (it is indeed very big) edition by Brian Larosche, a beautiful, playful edition to the family of books.

There is an imperative today for books to know themselves as it were, to be sure of their place in the world: proud, assertive, bold, daring; for bibliophiles and lovers of poetry Mallarmé is an almost messianic figure and his *UN COUP DE DÉS* is a monument of modernity, the poetic, the visual, the book as space and opportunity, a whole host of 20th century poetic, visual and philosophical highways run out from its cascading lines, and they have yet to reach their termini. As a publisher it is a dream to produce an edition of *UN COUP DE DÉS*. But not only that—we're still on the highway—to do so with the vision of a certain Brian Larosche, the irreverent, incessant book sorcerer is nothing but exhilarating. Because if James Cameron can do it, books can do it too. Mallarmé made it clear that books can own space, that they revel in it, that words draw pictures in the mind but also on the page itself; we open a book and walk into it, Larosche has built a new layer to the puzzle of the sailor and the swirling miasma of the throwing of the dice, he has rendered it in 3D no less and by doing so invites us, the reader, to actively don the glasses and enter the ring of this classic poetic bookwork.

Rodney Graham
Poème: "Au Tatoueur"
Brussels: GEVEART ÉDITIONS, 2011
320 x 250 mm, 16 pp.
Offset
ed. 250

The poem "Au Tatoueur" is a French version of the poem "To the Tattooist" written and designed by Rodney Graham using the Didot typeface. The poem addresses tattoo artists and describes a proposed tattoo depicting Popeye battling a giant squid. The layout of the poem is inspired by Mallarmé's typographic innovations in *UN COUP DE DÉS JAMAIS N'ABOLIRA LE HASARD*.

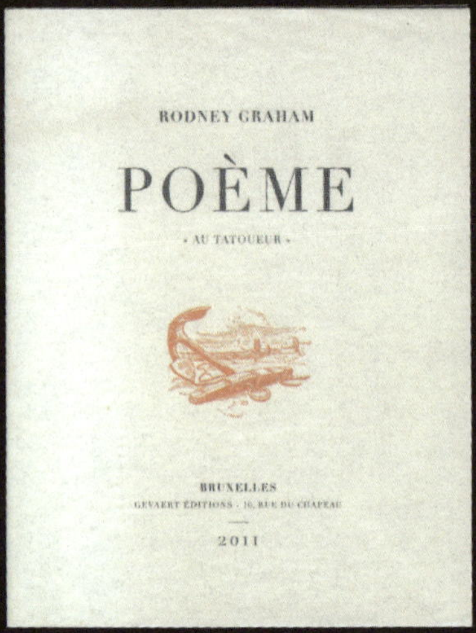

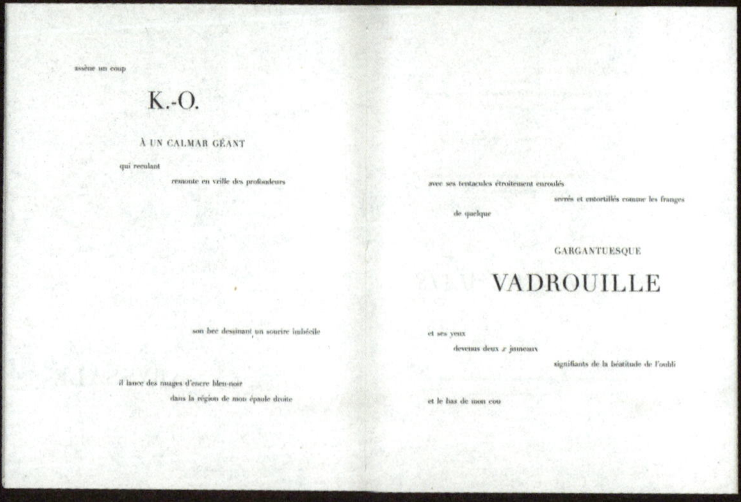

January 5–31, 2012
with contributions by Craig Dworkin, Kenneth Goldsmith, Jonathan Monk, Michalis Pichler
Berlin: "greatest hits", 2012
210 x 175 mm, 20 pp.
Xeroxed, spiral binding
ed. 400

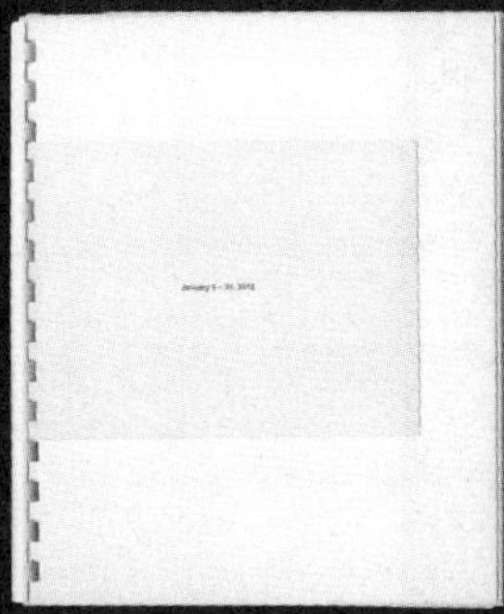

In 1969 Seth Siegelaub organized an exhibition (and publication) with the title *January 5 – 31, 1969*, one of the first exhibition projects of conceptual art, with the participation of Robert Barry, Douglas Huebler, Joseph Kosuth, and Lawrence Weiner. Back then there was already talk about a so-called linguistic turn that had been taking place in the visual arts and that consequently led to idea art. These artistic/poetic strategies have been reused and radicalized since the turn of the millennium. *January 5 – 31, 2012* gathers some of these positions. Like in the preceding book, every contributor has four pages (a list of works, two depictions, and a statement page). The piece on page fifteen reads *Un texte imprimé jamais n'abolira l'image*.

ed. Antoine Lefebvre
Pirate Box
Brooklyn: La Bibliothèque Fantastique, 2012
220 x 160 mm
Inkjet, stapled, available for download at
http://labibliothequefantas.free.fr/index.php?/pirate/

La Bibliothèque Fantastique is an artist's books virtual publisher. Our books are free and downloadable from the internet so that you can print them at home. Most of our books are exclusive productions. The others are reeditions of works who are free of any kind of rights. The purpose of LBF is to offer a view on books expressed by books themselves. Its works are made of excerpts of other works, with pages, sentences and words met in a stroke of good fortune.

La Bibliothèque Fantastique

This box is composed of eighteen unauthorized copies of well-known artists' books made by Lawrence Weiner, Marcel Broodthaers, Roland Topor, Sol LeWitt, Claude Closky, Michael Clegg, Hanne Darboven, Eric Watier, and Martin Guttman. Unlike most of the books included in the box, Broodthaers's UN COUP DE DÉS actually not reproduced in facsimile, but was apparently reengineered for this bootleg series.

Most of the titles reproduced in *Pirate box* are not free of copyright. Next to the download links, the publisher added the following statement: "The goal of this collection is to present hard to find artists books to make them accessible to everyone. If you own the copyrights please contact us, and we will take them off."

Image on following spread: scale 1:1

Marcel Broodthaers, ed. Maryam Sachs and Wilfried Dickhoff
album. Un Coup de Dés
Berlin: Éditions Moon Rainbow GmbH, 2012
297 x 420 mm, 42 pp.
Offset on transparent paper, silk-screen on cardboard, crystal-clear slipcase
ed. 500

Facsimile edition of an unpublished artist's book by Marcel Broodthaers from 1968 referring to Stéphane Mallarmé's poem UN COUP DE DÉS JAMAIS N'ABOLIRA LE HASARD.

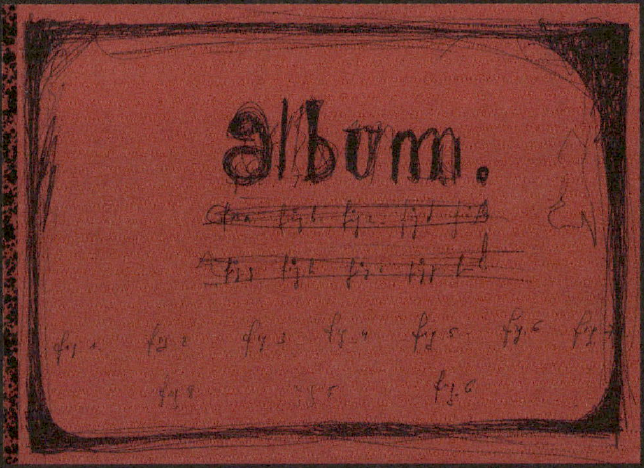

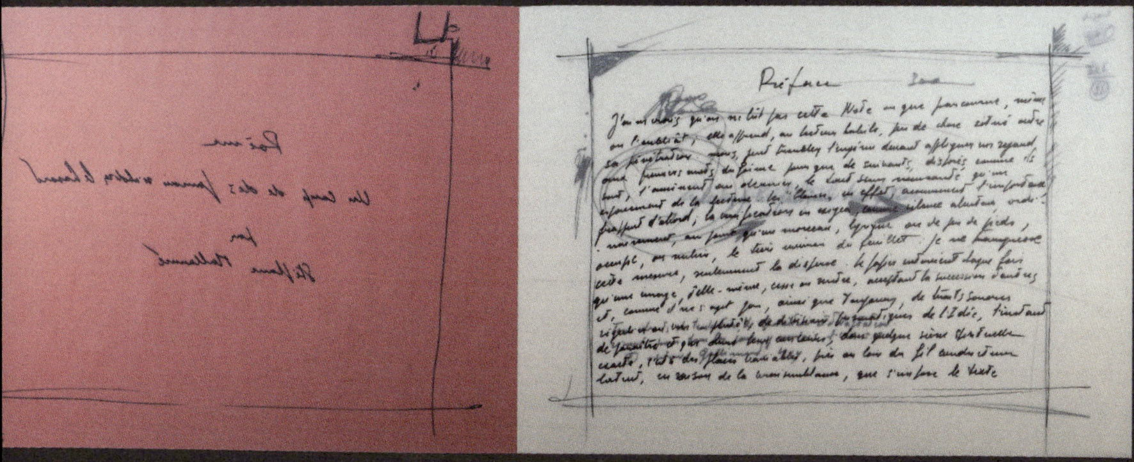

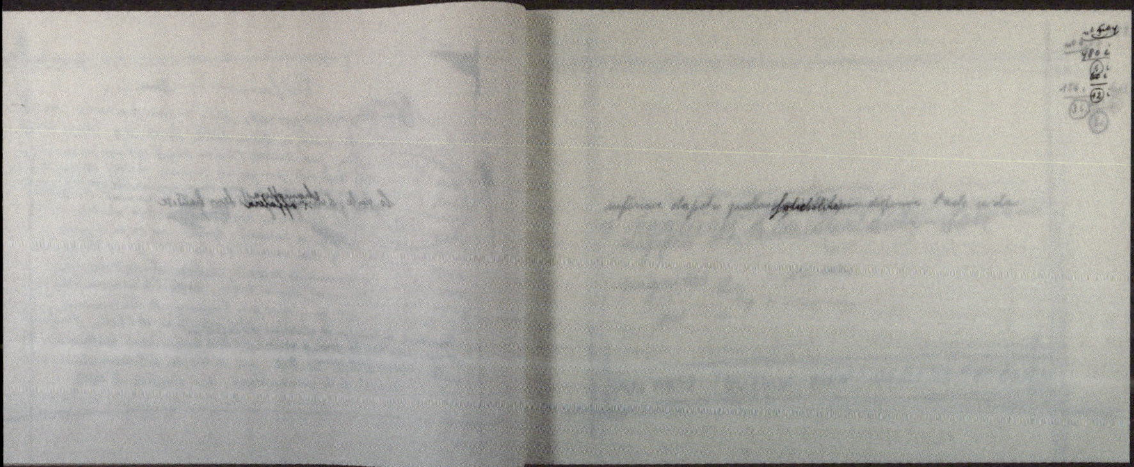

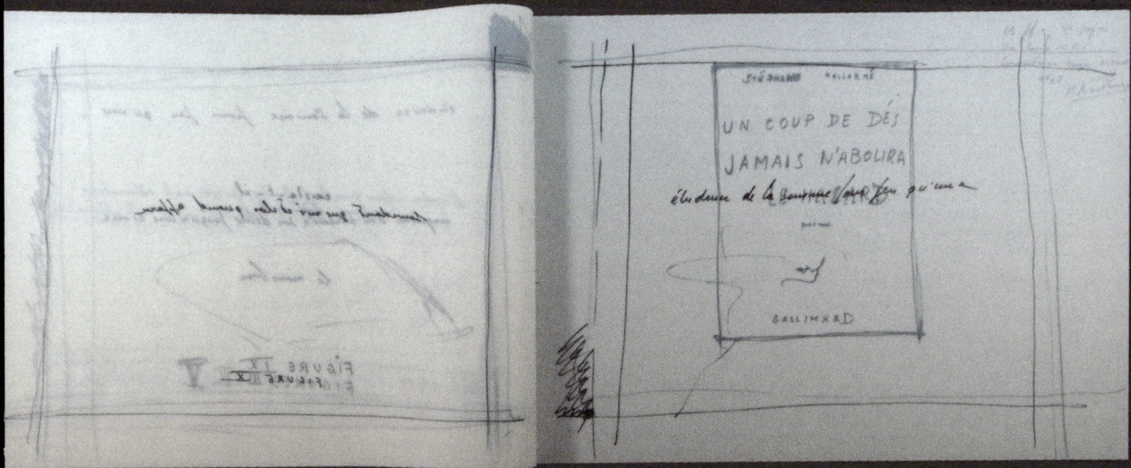
UN COUP DE DÉS
JAMAIS N'ABOLIRA
GALLIMARD

Here, for his homage in book form, Hurtig displays his originality by avoiding the red-bordered NRF cover and collapsing all of the text into a single-page text block for his cover. In addition to his freely downloadable version of the poem, Hurtig insightfully provides side-by-side views of different versions of Bodoni and views of a page of the poem set in three different typefaces that he considered as substitutes.

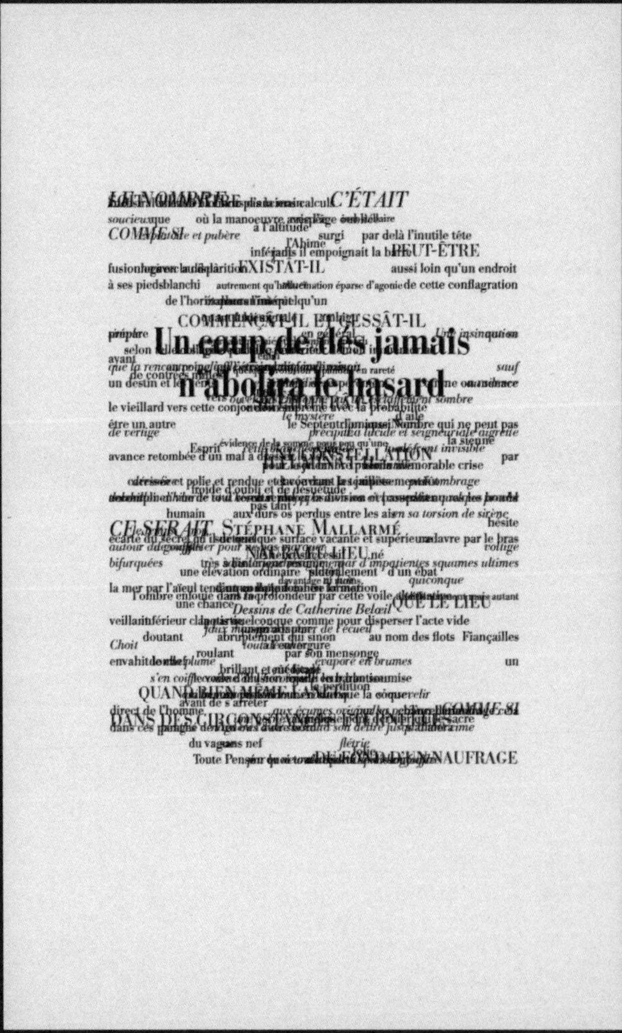

Jérémie Bennequin, ed. Éric Pesty
K.O.S.H.K.O.N.O.N.G., le hasard n'abolira jamais un coup de dés (omage) NUMÉRO 3 AUTOMNE 2013
Marseille: Éric Pesty Éditeur, 2013
240 x 155 mm, 20 pp.
Offset, stapled

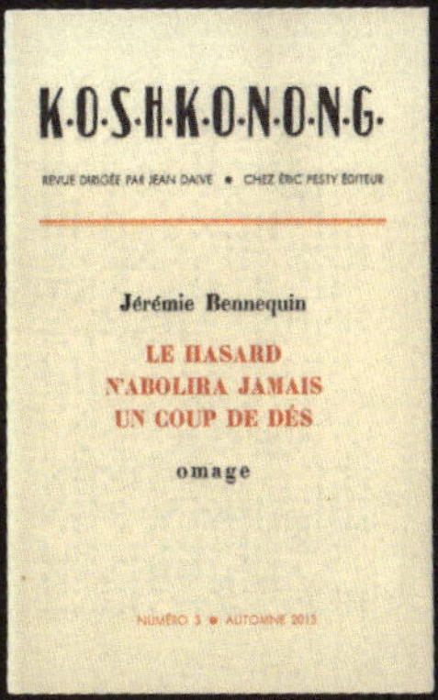

K.O.S.H.K.O.N.O.N.G. 3 is a graphic and literary work based on a fusion of the whole twenty booklets of my omage (LBF), that is why you can see the numbers (1.1, 1.2, 1.3, etc.) of each Dé-composition inside the pages, next to the fragmented verses. The reversed title (and order of the main pages) anticipates the YL édition, as does the *Cosmopolis* version (1897) regarding the Gallimard version (1914).

Jérèmie Bennequin

Image on following spread: scale 1:1

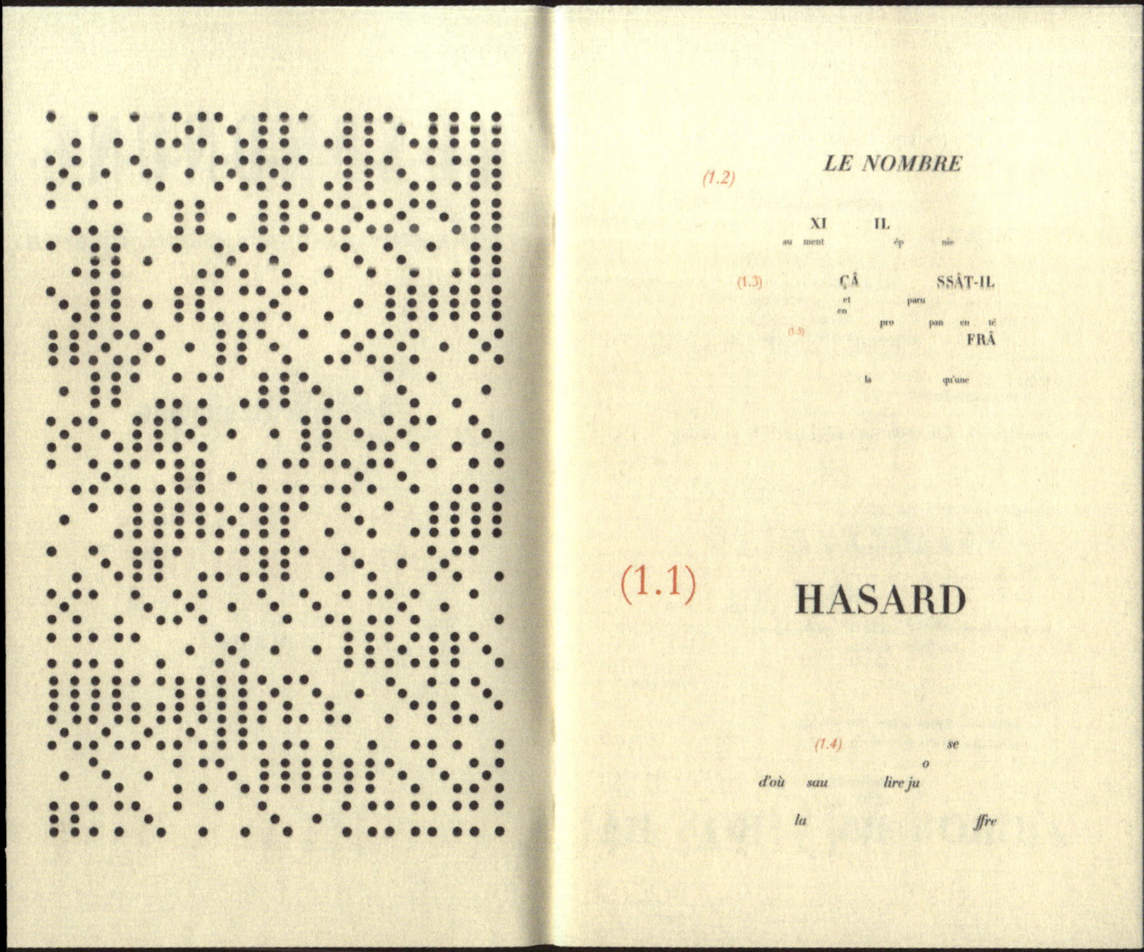

1:2

ancestra à n'ouvrir pas la
spée
là nutile

legs dis tion

à quelqu'un
gu

l'ultérieur mmé ial

a
de contrées
induit
le cette ction suprême probabilité

ce
é
caressée et lie ren et vée
ssou par la gue
aux durs os dus entre les ais

né
ébat
la mer par l'aïeul ou l'a contre la mer
une oiseuse

çailles

le le llu reja tise
ainsi que le geste

chancelle
s'a ra

BO RA BO RA

HA HA HA

main lement

BIEN MÊME LANCÉ DANS CONSTANCES

tête l'i par de

TERNELLES 1.1

MÊME LANCÉ DANS pari angla STANCES

ÉTERNELLES FOND D'UN FRAGE 1.2

amdi

MÊME LANCÉ STANCES

NELLES amor D'UN démon i FRAGE 1.3

a

CÉ STANCES

nulles

NELLES D'UN 1.4

avec la conjon vieillard vers

D'UN lui

son ombre pu rile

la due et po

JAMAIS et soustraite va JAMAIS plis a per *quelque*

vol

d'un LE BO

ïeul tentant

chance

Fian

dont

illi leur han sion d'i voi

fantôme d'un

ra

fiale

N'A BO ile N'A BOLIRA

Jérémie Bennequin
LE HASARD N'ABOLIRA JAMAIS UN COUP DE DÉS (OMAGE)
Paris: Éditions de la Librairie Yvon Lambert, 2014
330 x 250 mm, 32 pp.
Printed on Olin regular paper, thread binding
ed. 10 numbered I to X on Vellum, 90 numbered 1 to 90 on Olin regular paper

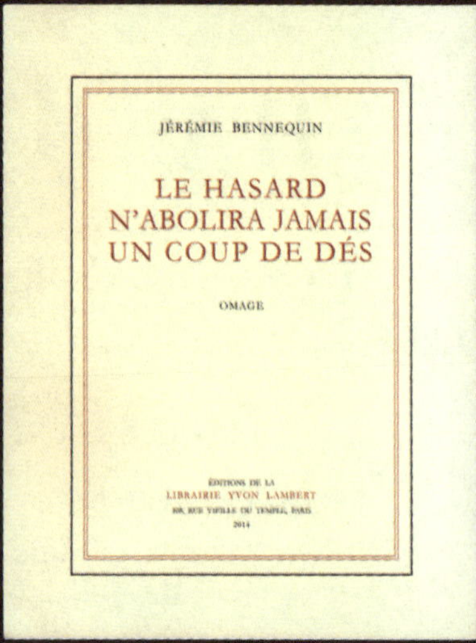

It is indeed possible to read *UN COUP DE DÉS* in one direction then in the other, backwards... A stroke of poetic genius to which the work of Jérémie Bennequin testifies, where each line is found strangely reversed in the pages, inviting the reader to turn the book over to gain possession of an unprecedented meaning, a fundamental gesture through which the artist himself discovered the extraordinary *mallarméénne* reversibility, by inadvertently consulting one day upside down, the famous iconoclastic reappropriation of Marcel Broodthaers (book cult shot in 1969 in Antwerp). Hence the black rectangles within which the fragments of the poem now reappear and, on the cover, the subtitle "OMAGE."

Éditions de la Librairie Yvon Lambert

The parts enclosed in square brackets correspond to the phonetic transcription of the verses of the Poem by Stéphane Mallarmé (original edition of La Nouvelle Revue Française dated July 10, 1914) thus grouped end to end, such as in the Préface to the iconoclastic book by Marcel Broodthaers (printed in 1969 in Antwerp) with the difference that the order of the fragments is reversed here. This introduction establishes a link between the essentially sonorous dimension of the poetic score according to Mallarmé and the world of visual abstraction in Broodthaers while resolving the rare grammatical contradictions which may appear when reading *UN COUP DE DÉS JAMAIS N'ABOLIRA LE HASARD* in reverse. The main innovation of this new "état" ("state") of the work therefore consists in the fact that there exists a reversibility of meaning—revealed, one day, by the fortuitous reversal of Broodthaers' "approximate" image and probably premeditated by Mallarmé—hence the reading, which is always done on both pages at the same time, simply taking into account the ordinary descent of the lines, thus operates perfectly backwards.

Author's note below the "PREFACE"

The "PREFACE" features a phonetic transcription of the Mallarmé poem, in reverse order. Line breaks are indicated by /.

The main body of the book features all lines in order of appearance as drafted by Mallarmé; within each line, the text is placed in the inverse (in white) on black bars rotated by 180 degrees and are readable upside down.

According the the imprint, the book was printed on July 10, 1914, exactly one hundred years after the printing of Mallarmé's NRF edition.

Jérémie Bennequin
LE HASARD N'ABOLIRA JAMAIS UN COUP DE DÉS (OMAGE)
Berlin: Literaturwerkstatt Berlin, 2014
210 x 145 mm, 32 pp.
Xeroxed, stapled

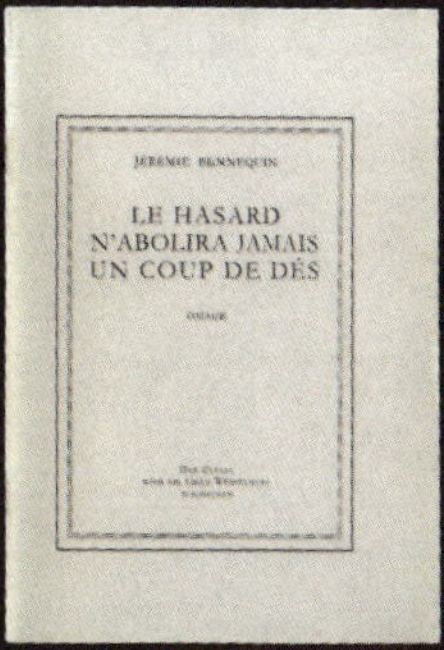

The book is a German translation of Bennequin's Librarie Yvon Lambert edition of the same year and was given out on occasion of a reading at Literaturwerkstatt Berlin on December 6, 2014, as is indicated at the end of the book.

Produced as a stapled zine in DIN A5, the main body of text features a facsimile of the French edition from July 2014. The Preface features Gerhard Goebel's German translation of the poem, with all text blocks separated by a slash and appearing in reverse order.

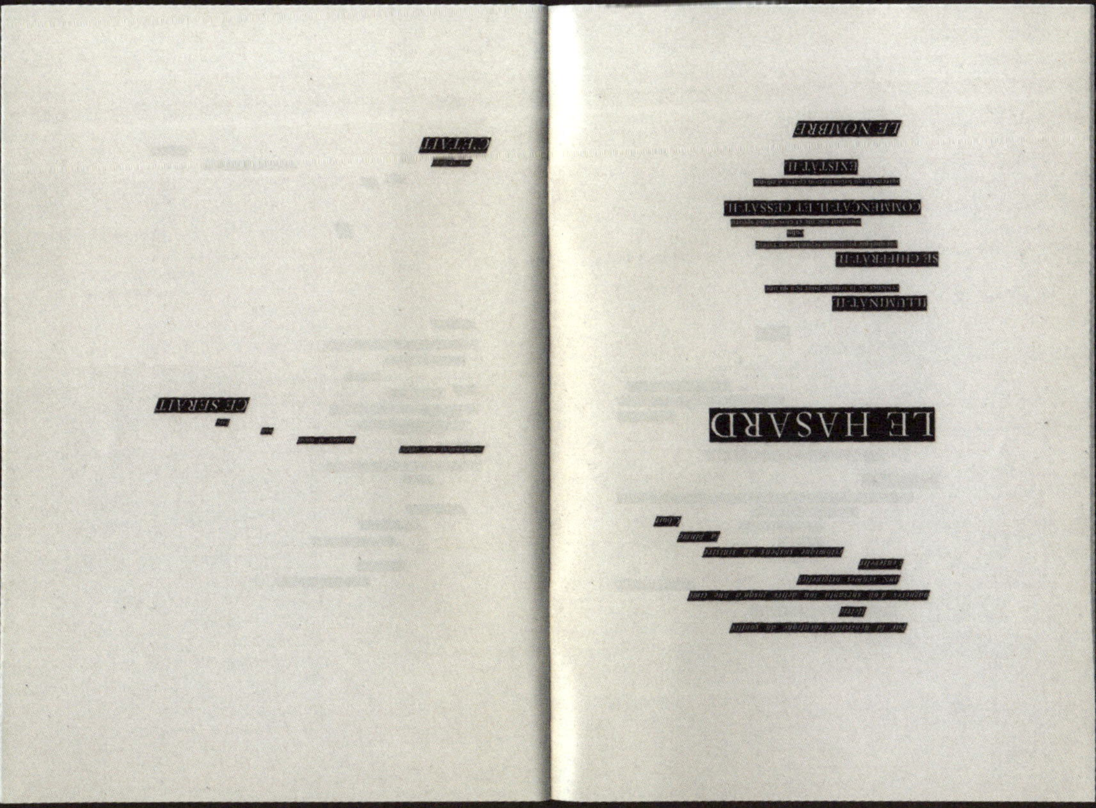

1:2

Angela Grasser
GRAND BAU 3
Berlin: KronosWerke GmbH, 2015
270 x 210 mm, 60 pp.
Offset, perfect binding

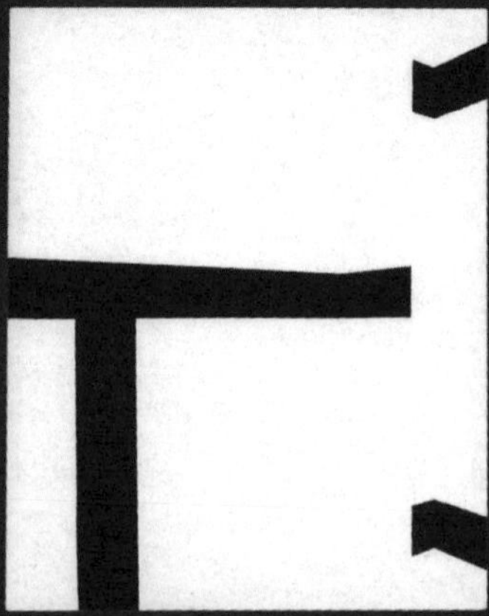

Angela Grasser
GRAND BAU 2
Berlin: KronosWerke GmbH, 2015
270 x 210 mm
Offset, perfect binding

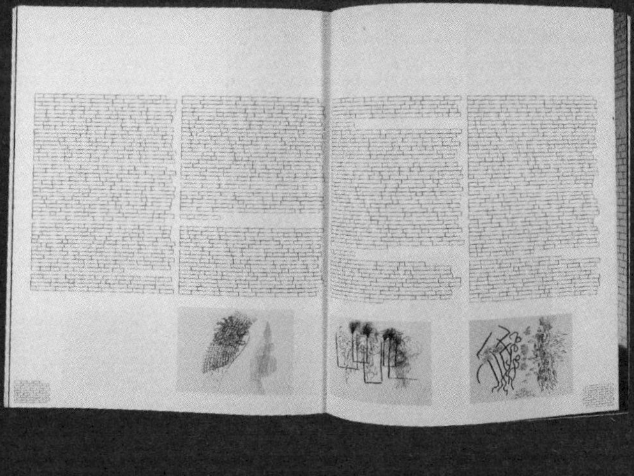

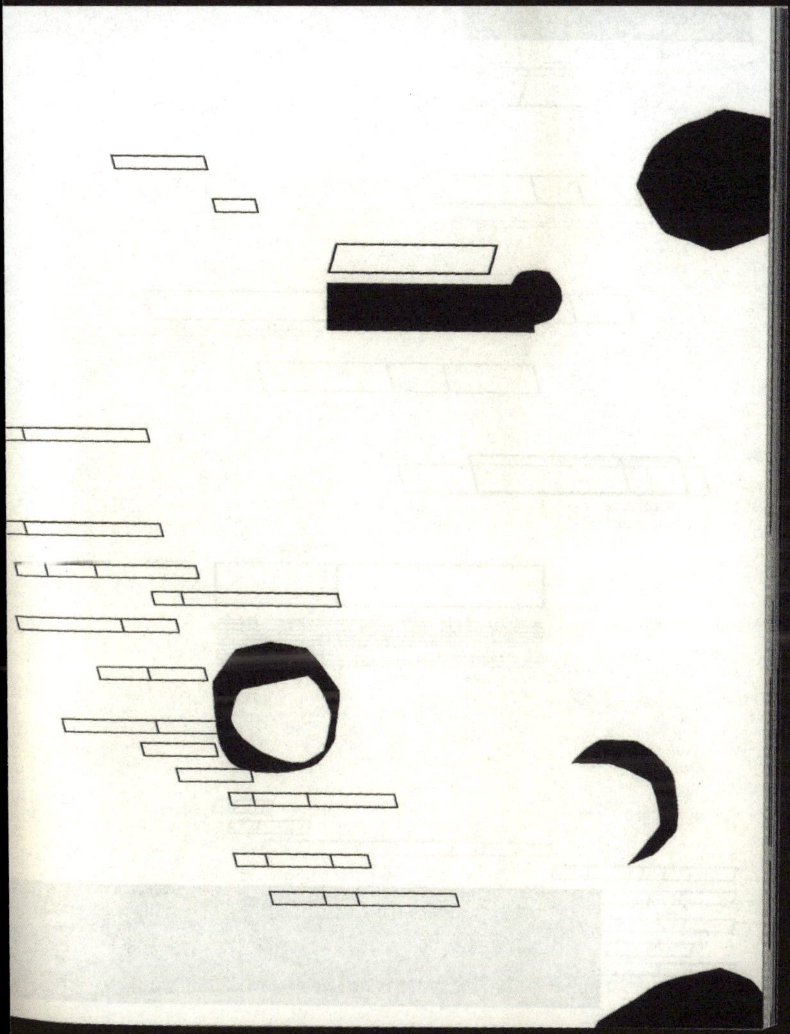

1:2

Felix Philipp Ingold
Fortschriift
Klagenfurt and Graz: Ritter Verlag, 2016
220 x 220 mm, 80 pp.
Offset, perfect binding, paperback

The motto—*quel*—of "Fortschrift," which was created between 2013 and 2015, goes back to a forgotten anecdote reported by André Rolland de Renéville about Stéphane Mallarmé's paperwork; Here is the wording: "Mallarmé had compiled a large number of small pieces of paper, the contents of which aroused the greatest curiosity among his contemporaries. He maintained absolute silence when asked questions about the matter and ordered that the papers be burned after his death. All I can say is that at a time in my life when I was working with Mallarmé on translating Whistler's *Ten o'clock*, I came to his house one day and found him in his study with one of those tiny ones Paper in hand. He remained silent for a few moments and then murmured as if speaking to himself: 'I'm probably not even allowed to write this for you because I'm still giving too much away.' As I stood next to him, I read this single word on the piece of paper: *quel* (which). He put it back with his papers and I didn't have a chance to find out more about it." To find out more? That's not the point; it's about doing something with it. The poem presented here in fifteen "rolls" is the result of multiple intensive readings and associative continuations of Mallarmé's late poem *UN COUP DE DÉS JAMAIS N'ABOLIRA LE HASARD*.

Felix Philipp Ingold

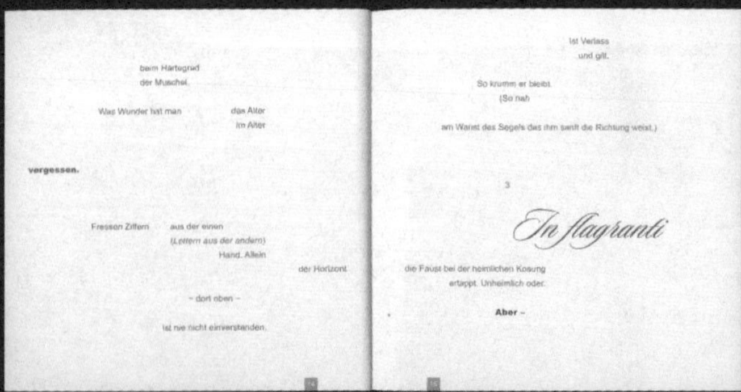

Klara Vith
UN COUP DE DÉS JAMAIS N'ABOLIRA LE HASARD (DISCOURS I–III)
with contributions by Donald J. Trump
160 x 120 mm, 24 pp.
Letraset, thread binding
ed. 20

In her 2017 three-volume work *UN COUP DE DÉS JAMAIS N'ABOLIRA LE HASARD*, Klara Vith uses the typographical layout of Mallarmé's 1914 edition as a blueprint for publishing speeches by Donald J. Trump. What is astonishing is how the free layout corresponds to the nature of public and political speeches. The work highlights certain topoi and buzzwords of hate speech that occur in Trump's speeches, such as POTENTIAL, AMERICA'S INTERESTS, as well as RAPISTS, TWO TRILLION, and AMERICA FIRST AMERICA FIRST. The beautifully executed, tiny edition, printed using a letterpress, somehow counteracts its semantic content. On the cover, the artist attributes the authorship to Donald J. Trump.

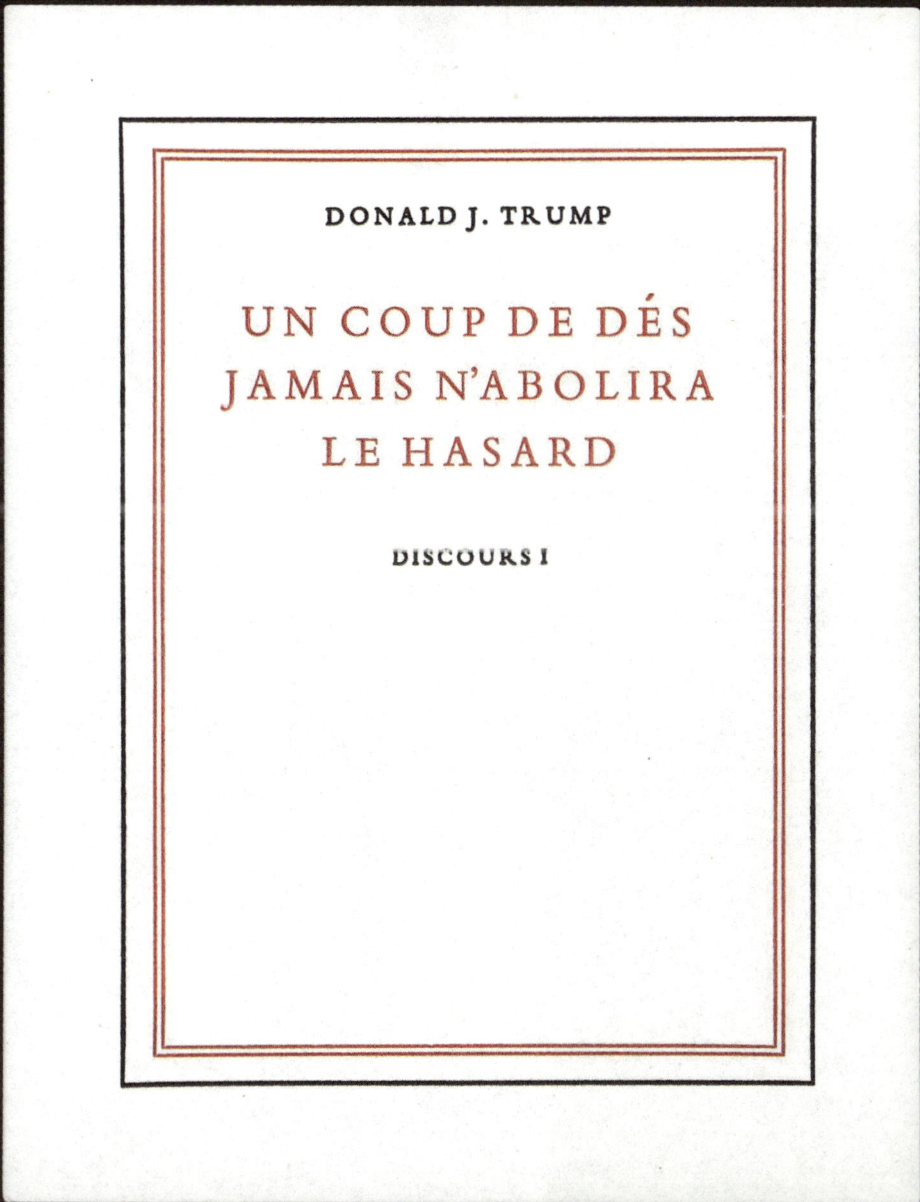

1:1

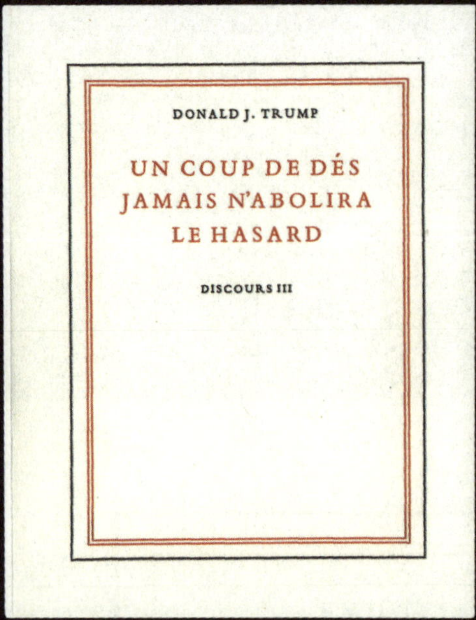
DONALD J. TRUMP
UN COUP DE DÉS JAMAIS N'ABOLIRA LE HASARD
DISCOURS III

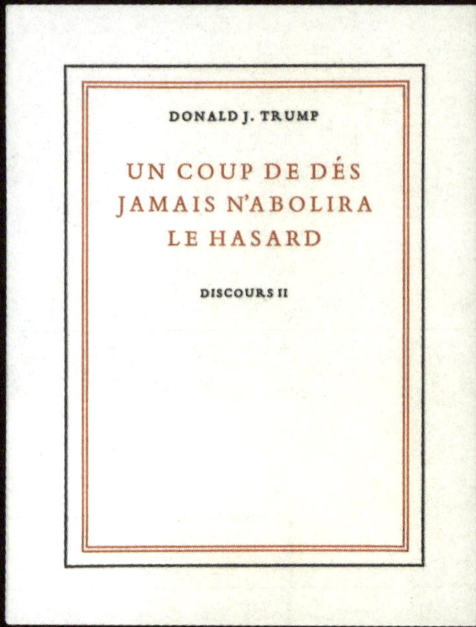
DONALD J. TRUMP
UN COUP DE DÉS JAMAIS N'ABOLIRA LE HASARD
DISCOURS II

1:2

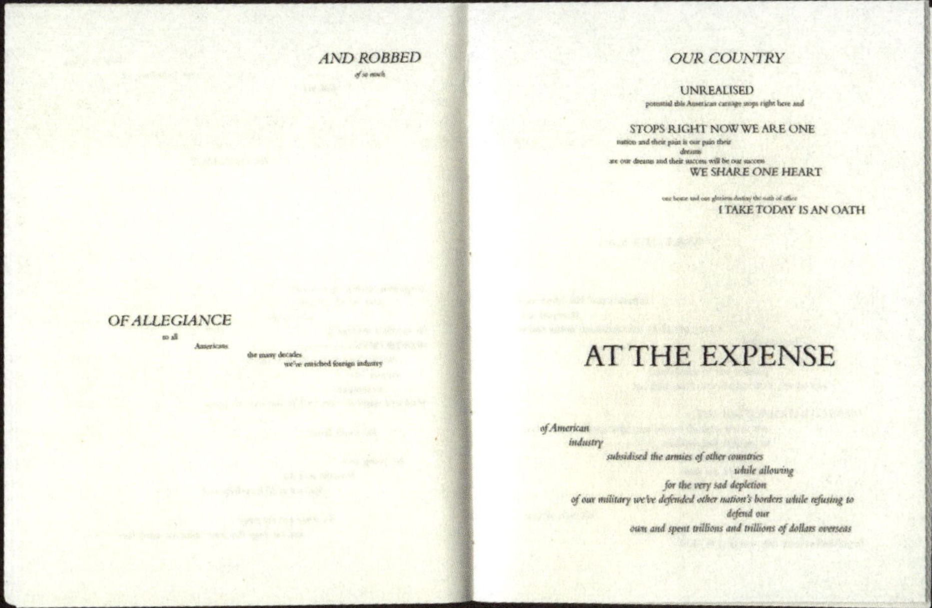

AND ROBBED

of so much

OF ALLEGIANCE

to all

Americans

the many decades

we've enriched foreign industry

OUR COUNTRY

UNREALISED

potential this American carnage stops right here and

STOPS RIGHT NOW WE ARE ONE

nation and their pain is our pain their

dreams

are our dreams and their success will be our success

WE SHARE ONE HEART

one home and one glorious destiny the oath of office

I TAKE TODAY IS AN OATH

AT THE EXPENSE

of American

industry

subsidised the armies of other countries

while allowing

for the very sad depletion

of our military we've defended other nation's borders while refusing to

defend our

own and spent trillions and trillions of dollars overseas

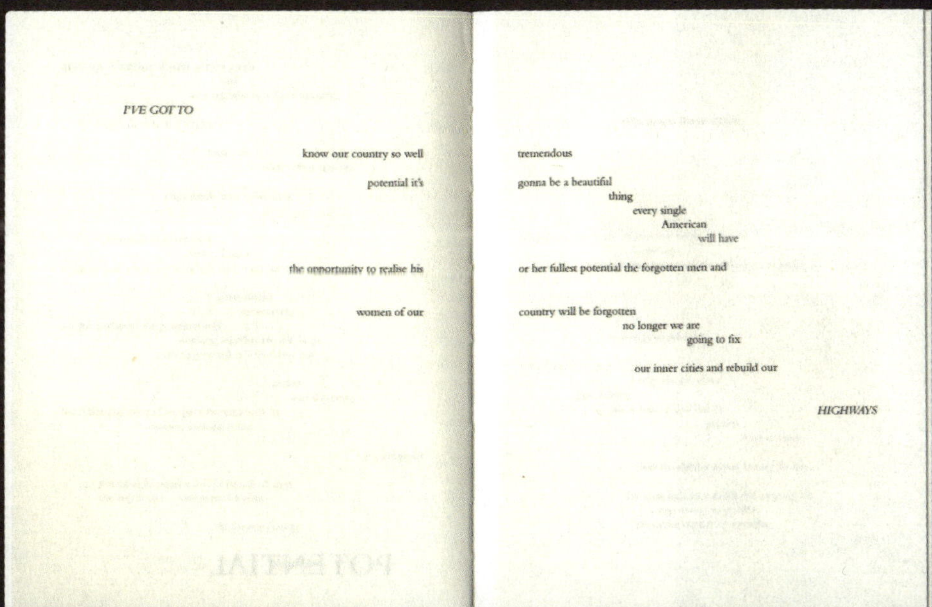

I'VE GOT TO

know our country so well

potential it's

the opportunity to realise his

women of our

tremendous

gonna be a beautiful

thing

every single

American

will have

or her fullest potential the forgotten men and

country will be forgotten

no longer we are

going to fix

our inner cities and rebuild our

HIGHWAYS

1:2

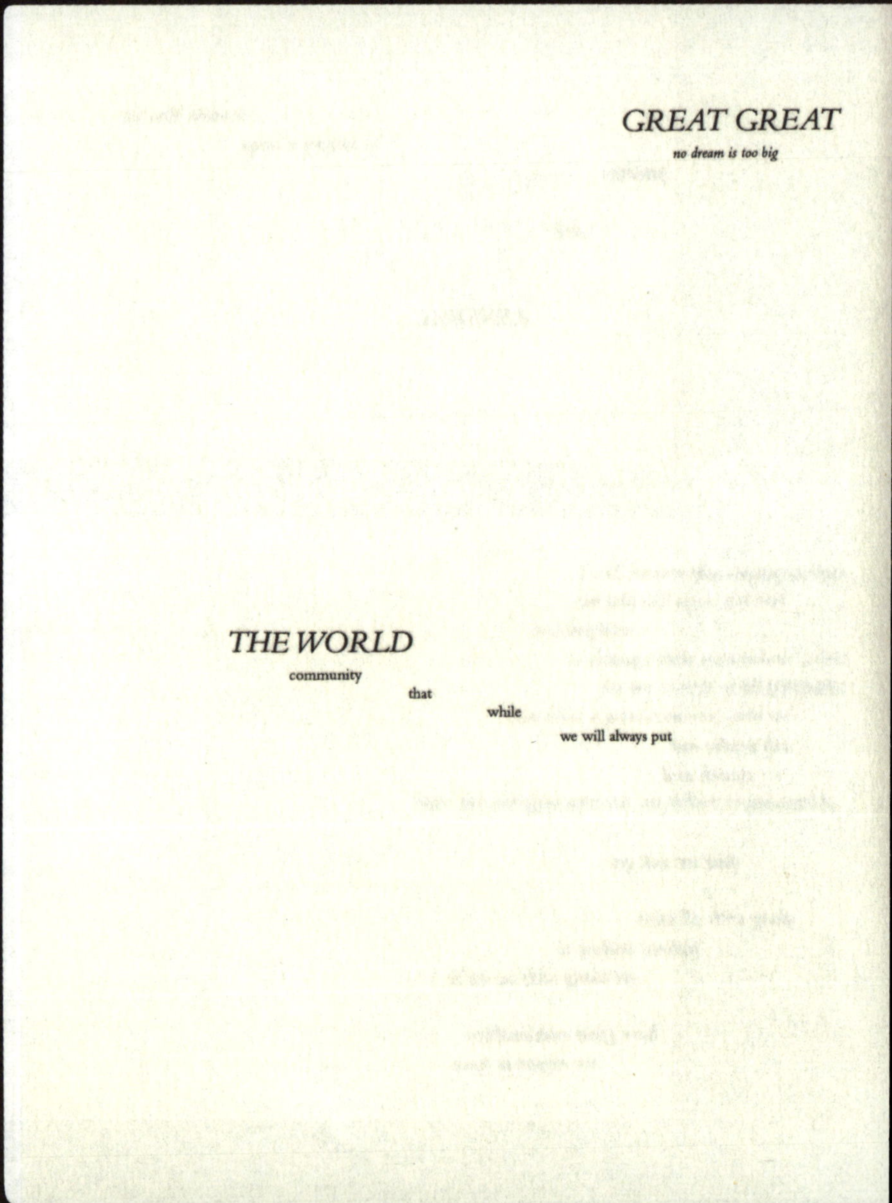
GREAT GREAT
no dream is too big
THE WORLD
community
that
while
we will always put

Klara Vith

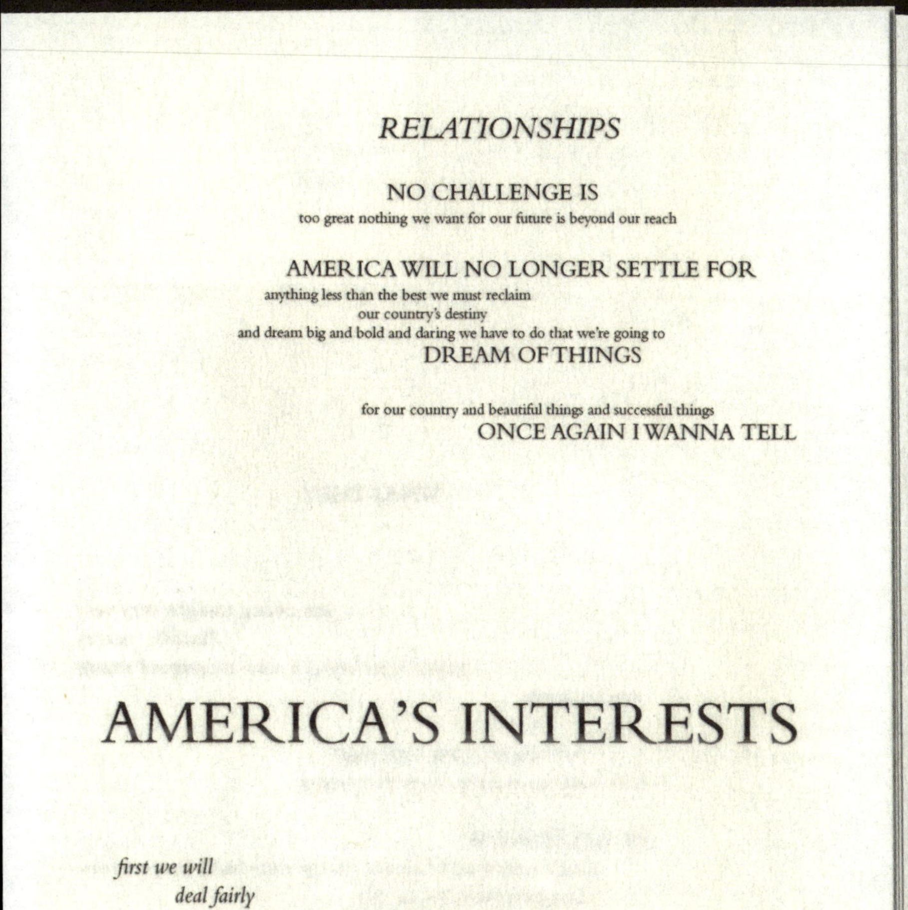

RELATIONSHIPS

NO CHALLENGE IS
too great nothing we want for our future is beyond our reach

AMERICA WILL NO LONGER SETTLE FOR
anything less than the best we must reclaim
our country's destiny
and dream big and bold and daring we have to do that we're going to
DREAM OF THINGS

for our country and beautiful things and successful things
ONCE AGAIN I WANNA TELL

AMERICA'S INTERESTS

first we will
deal fairly
with everyone with everyone all people
and all other
nations we will seek
common ground not hostility partnership not conflict and now I'd like to
take this
moment to thank some of the people who really helped me with this

1:1

Eric Zboya
UN COUP DE DÉS JAMAIS N'ABOLIRA LE HASARD: TRANSLATIONS
with contributions by Christian Bök
Manchester: Apple Pie Editions, 2018
280 x 204 mm, 60 pp.
ed. 120

Critical theorist Virginia A. La Charité writes that Stéphane Mallarmé's Un Coup de dés exemplifies a primary field [of space] against which form, shape, color, [and] dimensions gain delineation and definition—a space that expresses a cartesian geometric continuum rather than a state of static linearity. In the past 50 years, many artists have produced exquisite dialogical renditions of Mallarmé's vanguard text that explore the higher-dimensional characteristics of the poem (artists that include, but are not limited to, Marcel Broodthaers, Guido Molinari, and Michalis Pichler). In his debut book of poetry, un coup de dés jamais n'abolira le hasard: translations, artist Eric Zboya continues this dialogical exploration by further showcasing the "dimensional potentiality" in Mallarmé's text through a computer-generated process he calls Algorithmic Translation. With the aid of graphic imaging software, this highly unique process transforms each letter, each mark of punctuation, each individual pixel into big bang bursts of frozen sound that propagate like cosmic sculptures through the space of the page. This new visual rendition acts as a Mallarméan companion guide for both the poetically-minded scholar and conceptually-minded artist in today's avant-garde community.

From Eric Zboya's website

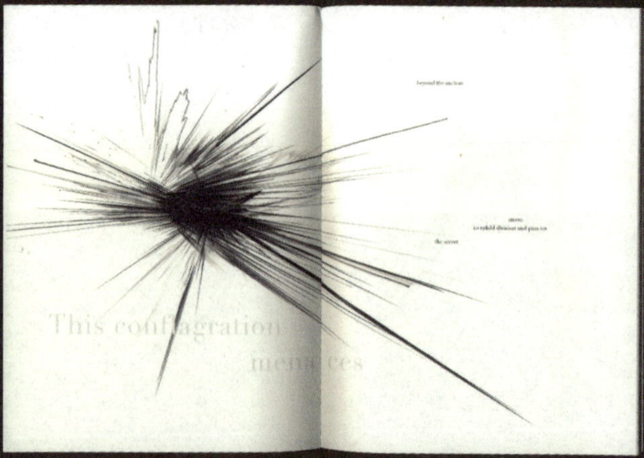

Derek Beaulieu
tattered sails (after un coup de dés)
Ottawa: above/ground press, 2018
215 x 140 mm, 12 pp.
Inkjet, stapled

Broodthaers's version of *UN COUP DE DÉS* elevates layout and structure to the level of writing itself; content becomes secondary to decisions of the tactile treatment of text. With Tattered Sails, I have continued the tactile treatment of this poem by folding the double-sized pages of Broodthaers's poem (suggesting the hang and fold of sails on the mast), shifting Broodthaers's bars in to the heaving beams and broken masts of a ship-wreck of meaning.

Derek Beaulieu

1:2

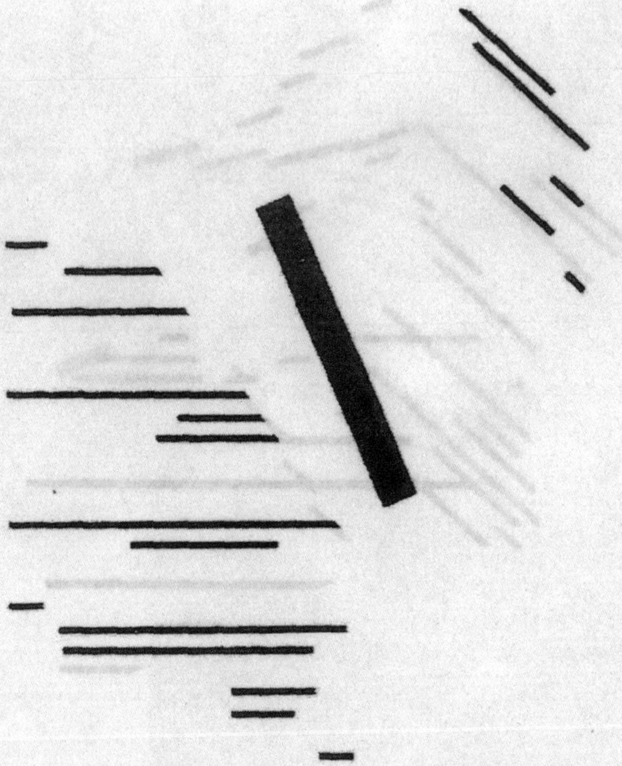

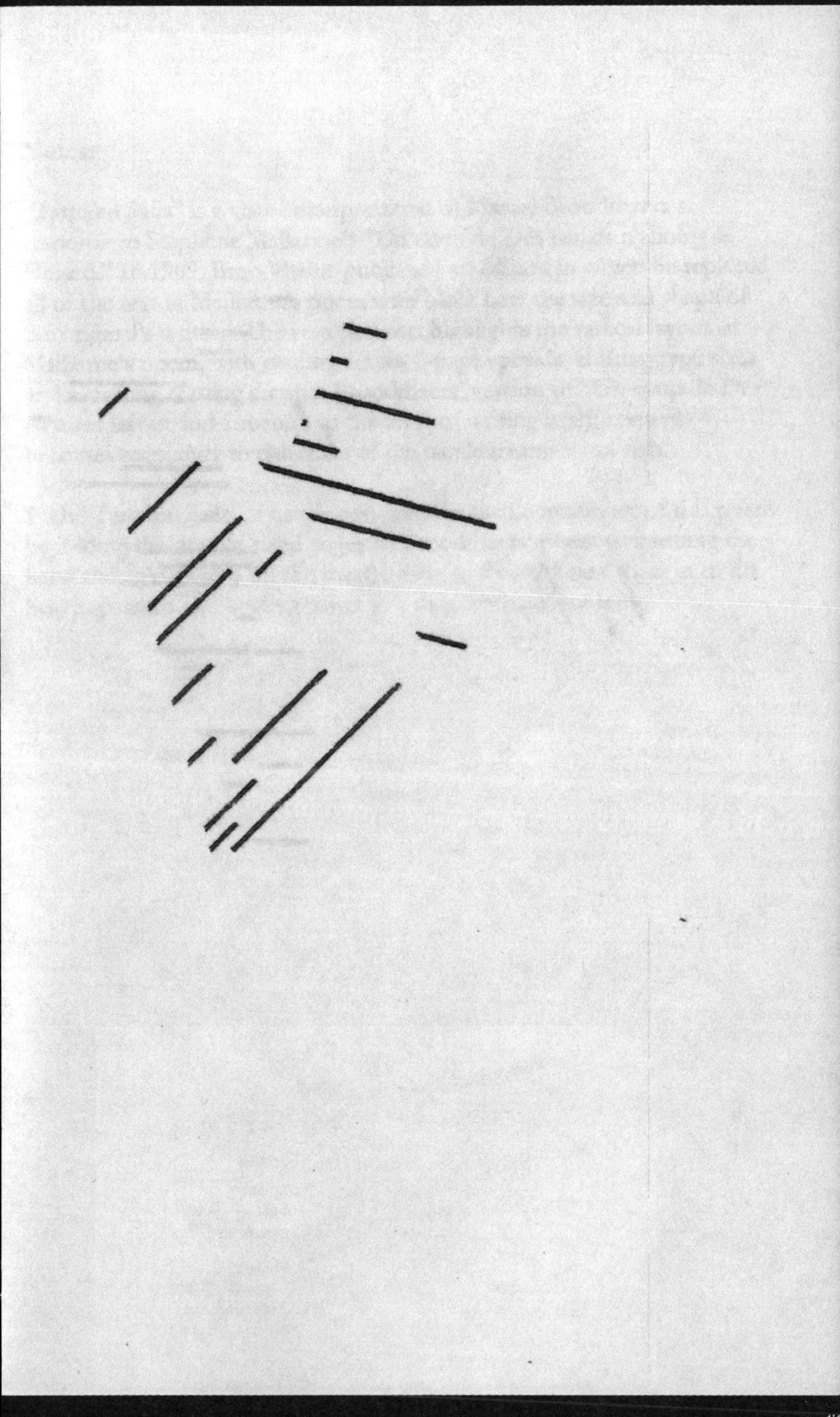

Benjamin Lord
THE ABOLITION OF CHANCE
Los Angeles: Benjamin Lord, 2019
280 x 210 mm, 70 pp.
Printed on translucent cellulosa paper, perfect binding with inlaid red linen thread, hand-assembled
ed. 50

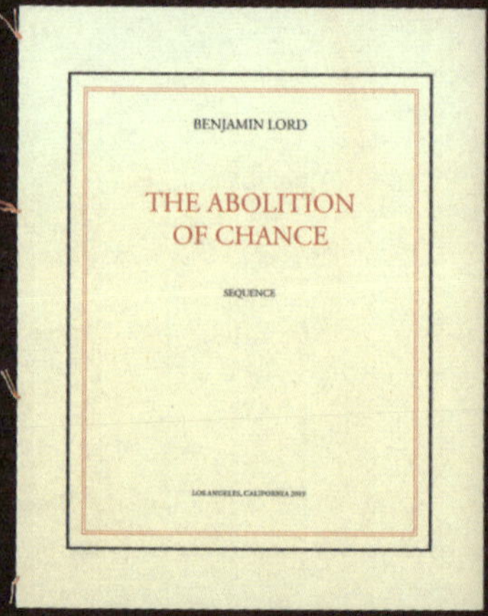

THE ABOLITION OF CHANCE is a book about the relationship between poetry and logic.

The first spread of the book copies the last spread of Marcel Broodthaer's book UN COUP DE DÉS JAMAIS N'ABOLIRA LE HASARD (A throw of the dice will never abolish chance), made in 1969. Broodthaers's book reproduced the 1887 modernist poem of the same name by the French poet Stéphane Mallarmé. In Broodthaers's edition, he blocked out the words with black bars of varying sizes corresponding to the typographic layout of the poem, turning it into an abstract image.

The subsequent spreads of *THE ABOLITION OF CHANCE* are successively generated using a simple mathematical formula known as the Game of Life, originally devised by the mathematician John Conway, also in the year 1969. (The Game of Life is a significant precursor to modern chaos theory. It vividly demonstrates how radical complexity can emerge from the repeated application of very simple rules.) Each pixel in the image evolves based on the color of its neighbors. Each spread in the book deterministically generates the subsequent spread. The lines of Mallarmé's poem inflate into balloons which expand and then pop into nothingness, or collide with each other to generate debris, or collapse into thicker bars. The image fragments into a vibratory bitmap constellation of expansions and contractions, in which interactions between forms continuously generate new forms, in a way that is neither random nor intuitive.

Benjamin Lord

Sam Sampson
UN COUP DE DÉS JAMAIS N'ABOLIRA LE HASARD (((SUN–O)))
Calgary: No Press, 2020
250 x 190 mm, 24 pp.
Offset, handsewn binding
ed. 60

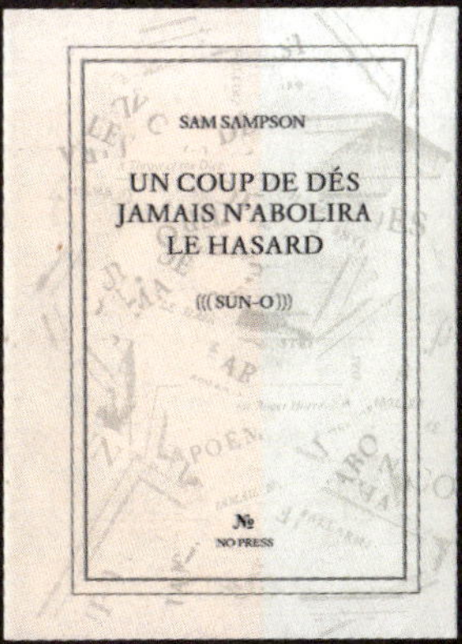

My response takes the form (scaffolding) of measuring each Mallarmé line on the page and approximating the font size. Each of my bullet pointed lines is an approximation of his line and the spatial dimension of the page represents the flow of his work. As Mallarmé's poem is a form of metaphysical gambling, his sentences reproduce the sensation of being both in and outside time, a type of prismatic subdivision, and I wanted to respond to this rhythm and arrangement of the poem by using the original text such that each of my pages reproduces collaged text from the exact same page of Mallarmé's poem. The Gallimard manuscript is the source, but it also brings into context a voice, a conversation from 1962 onwards where Roger's inscription (his name) leaves a mark in time. As with Mallarmé, I wanted the fungibility of time—the timeliness of a toss of the dice and the timelessness of chance. I wanted the poem to somehow capture, as Mallarmé had described it, 'the invitation of the great white space', and the successive, incessant, back-and-forth motions of our eyes travelling from one line to the next, and beginning all over again.

Sam Sampson

The superimposed text is further fragmented by cutting out circular pieces, which get rotated and superimposed on the plane of the page.

Image on following spread: scale 1:1

Sam Sampson
UN COUP DE DÉS JAMAIS N'ABOLIRA LE HASARD (((SUN–O)))
New Zealand: Waitakere Ranges, 2022
300 x 225 mm, 28 pp.
Digital Indigo, handsewn binding
ed. 20

speech

bubbles

silent

storied

slow

scenes

measured

the molecular

rise

&

fall

a throw of the dice

bless

the frame

of the same name

CE

CO

extinct personnel

breaking waves

ionised

word-hoards

wavelets

mouth

the spoken

imminent threat

Nontsikelelo Mutiti
BOX BRAID COLOR STUDY orange, green, purple
BOX BRAID COLOR STUDY fresh pink, blue, red
BOX BRAID COLOR STUDY fresh pink, orange, red
BOX BRAID COLOR STUDY purple, fresh pink, orange
BOX BRAID COLOR STUDY purple, green, blue
BOX BRAID COLOR STUDY orange, purple, green
Berlin: Miss Read/Conceptual Poetics Day, 2022
420 x 297 mm
Risography by we-make.it
ed. 10 of each color combination
ed. 500 monochromatic

These were created by Nontsikelelo Mutiti as a fundraising edition for Conceptual Poetics Day 2022, which had *UN COUP DE DÉS* as a tentative theme.

A monochromatic version featured the program on its verso side and was distributed as a giveaway during Miss Read 2022 at HKW.

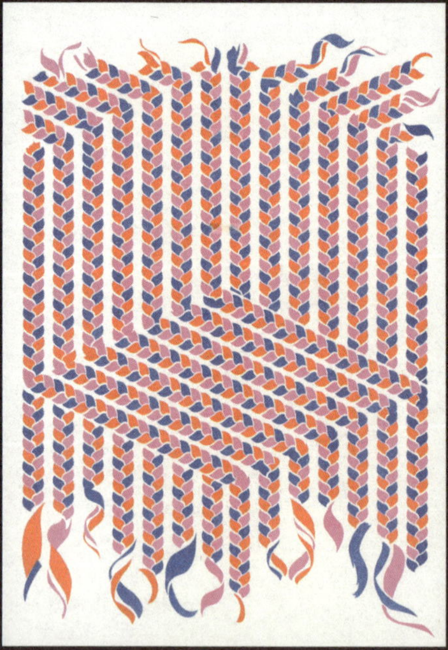

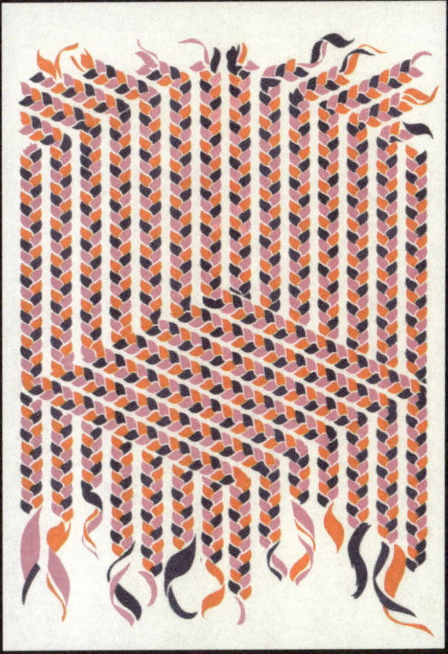

Nontsikelelo Mutiti

1:2

Nicolas Richard
COMMENTAIRES UN COUP DE TÊTE JAMAIS N'ABOLIRA LE HASARD
Rennes: Édition VROUM, 2022
280 x 195 mm, 46 pp.
Offset, perfect binding
ed. 400

To compose the score for this sound and visual event, part of the text comes from the transcribed, adapted, rewritten comments of Thierry Gilardi, Jean-Michel Larqué, Arsène Wenger and David Aiello during the broadcast of the 2006 World Cup final match live on the French television channel TF1. A short passage comes from the comments of Fabio Caressa and Beppe Bergomi during the broadcast of this final at the same time on the Italian channel Sky Sports 1. Excerpts from the poem by Stéphane Mallarmé, *UN COUP DE DÉS JAMAIS N'ABOLIRA LE HASARD* were used. Quotations are italicized in the text.

We will never really know if Mallarmé played football. On the other hand, we know that he was an English teacher.

Nicolas Richard

A "foot-oratorio" replaying the 2006 World Cup final match between France and Italy.

Nicolas Richard composes a score of sound poetry based on Zinedine Zidane's header. This now-famous gesture, which marked the end of the footballer's career, is multiplied by live accounts and deferred words. The author collects and combines a wide range of voices, from sports commentators to Hegel, Guy-Ernest Debord and Shakira. The page, transformed into a playground, is then made up of a variety of writings that Nicolas Richard brings together and puts into dialogue across the centuries.

Les Presses Du Reel

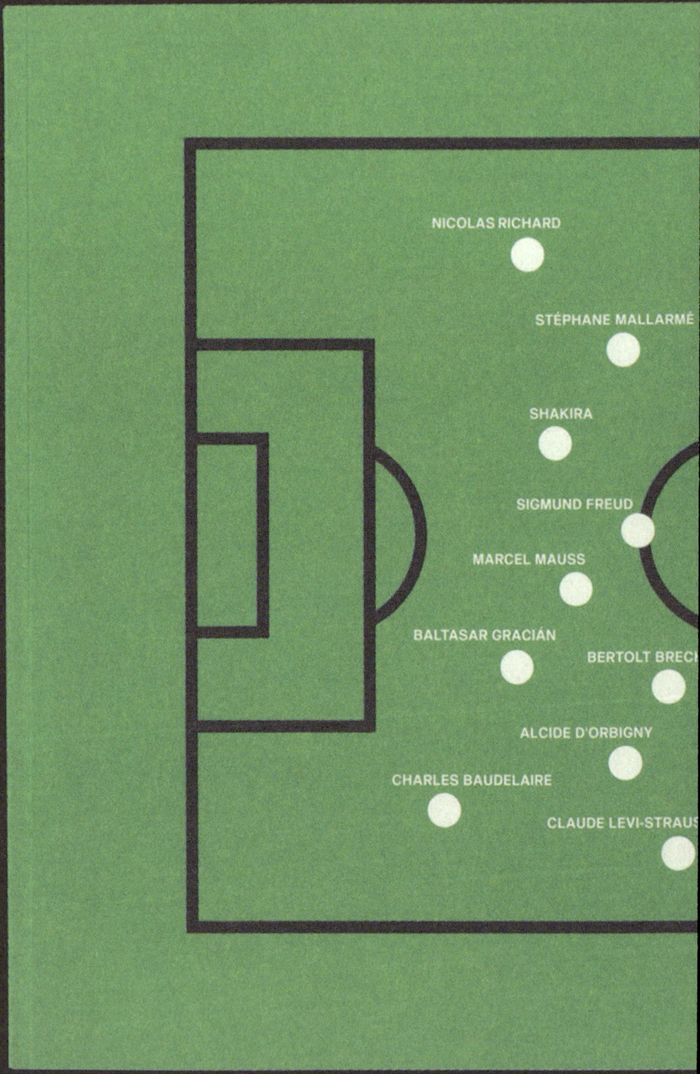
NICOLAS RICHARD
STÉPHANE MALLARMÉ
SHAKIRA
SIGMUND FREUD
MARCEL MAUSS
BALTASAR GRACIÁN
BERTOLT BREC
ALCIDE D'ORBIGNY
CHARLES BAUDELAIRE
CLAUDE LEVI-STRAUS

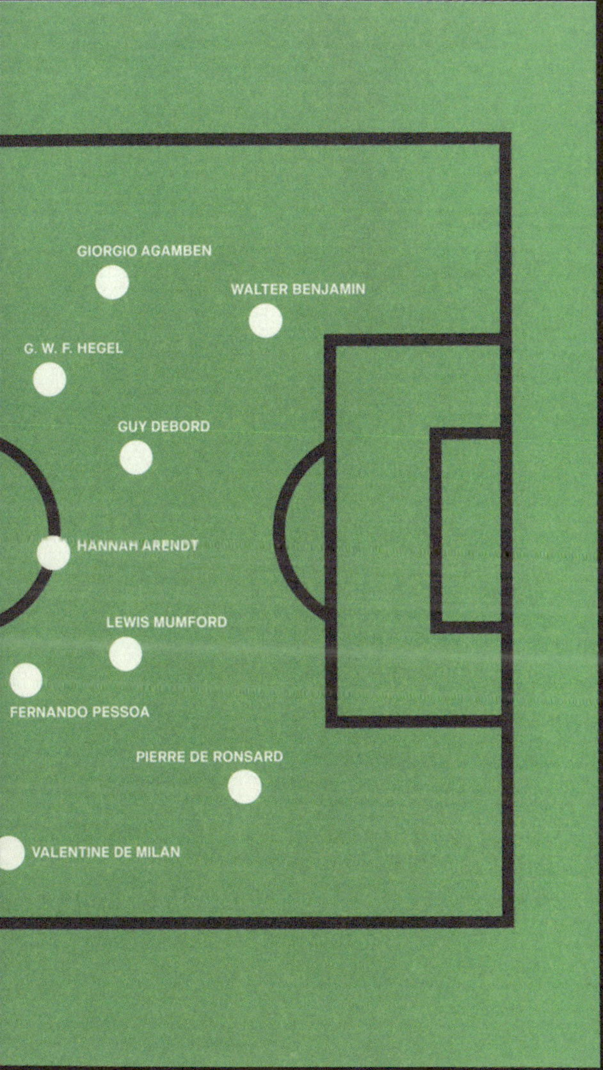

GIORGIO AGAMBEN
WALTER BENJAMIN
G. W. F. HEGEL
GUY DEBORD
HANNAH ARENDT
LEWIS MUMFORD
FERNANDO PESSOA
PIERRE DE RONSARD
VALENTINE DE MILAN

1:2

Chapter Three
Books that feature the phrase *COUP DE DÉS* on their covers

Colonel J. Argueyrolles
LE DERNIER COUP DE DÉS DE TANNENBERG
Paris: ÉDITIONS DE LA NOUVELLE REVUE CRITIQUE, 1937
225 x 140 mm, 224 pp.
Offset, thread binding

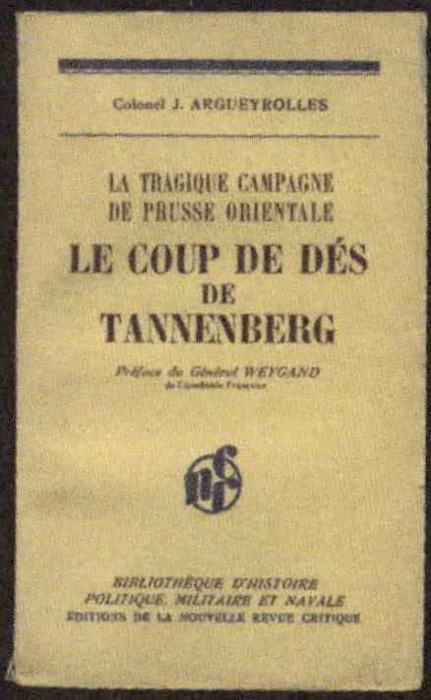

The Battle of Tannenberg was fought between Russia and Germany between August 23 and 30, 1914, the first month of World War I. The battle resulted in the almost complete destruction of the Russian Second Army. Although the battle actually took place near Allenstein, Hindenburg renamed it after Tannenberg, thirty kilometers to the west, in order to overshadow the Teutonic Kinght's defeat at the First Battle of Tannenberg five hundred years earlier.

The battle is particularly notable for fast rail movements by the German Eighth Army, which are referred here to as *COUP DE DÉS*.

Walter Nauman
Mallarmé's UN COUP DE DÉS JAMAIS N'ABOLIRA LE HASARD
Erlangen: Verlag Junge & Sohn, 1938
235 x 160 mm, 40 pp.
Offset, thread binding

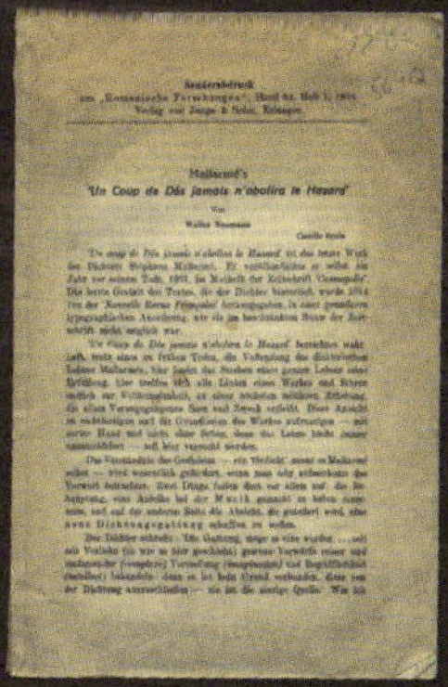

Monographic *Sonderabdruck* (special print) of a scholarly essay on *UN COUP DE DÉS* by Walter Naumann, who had submitted his PhD on Mallarmé's *Sprachgebrauch* in 1936 under the supervision of Ernst Robert Curtius Marburg. At the time this booklet was published, Naumann already had fled Nazi Germany.

Claude Roulet
ÉLÉMENTS DE POÉTIQUE MALLARMÉENNE D'APRÈS LE POÈME UN COUP DE DÉS JAMAIS N'ABOLIRA LE HASARD
Neuchâtel: Ides et Calendes Editions du Griffon, 1943
231 x 162 mm, 163 pp.
Offset, thread binding

In writing this work, I set out to answer this question: How, in the name of what conceptions, according to what method, by what means, if we can know,—was the UN COUP DE DÉS made? In the interest of my business, I have submitted to observing several rules, which I believe I can formulate as follows: Group and compare analogous facts and find out if a guiding idea emerges from their comparison. Group and compare these guiding ideas and investigate whether from their comparison emerges a central aesthetic conception, capable of claiming the primitive conception and allowing the poem to be enclosed in a higher synthesis.

Claude Roulet

Gardner Davies
VERS UNE EXPLICATION RATIONELLE DU COUP DE DÉS
Paris: LIBRAIRIE JOSÉ CORTI, 1953
230 x 150 mm, 208 pp.
Offset, softcover

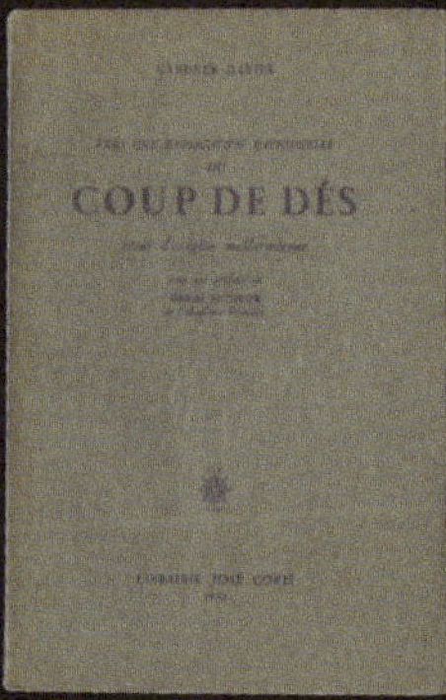

In this scholarly monograph, Gardner Davies (pen name of Bill Davies) condemns critics for their failure to render Mallarmé's texts comprehensible to the reader and for the obscurity of their own analyses, claiming that ""“a rational approach” is necessary to address the enigmatic nature of the poem.

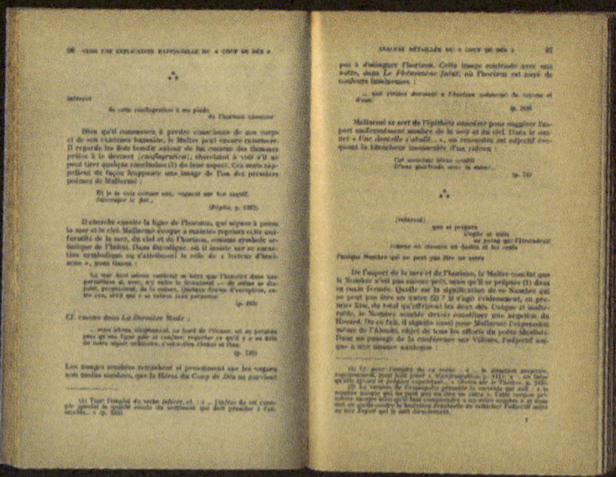

Monchas
Les 2 Risque-tout COUP DE DÉS
Paris: ÉDITIONS RAY-FLO, 1951
320 x 240 mm, 12 pp.
Offset, paperback

MENSUEL N°12
25fr BELGIQUE 5 SUISSE 0.50
LES 2 RISQUE-TOUT
COUP DE DÉS
MONCHAS
EDITIONS RAY-FLO

1:2

Annie Hot, Pierre Hot
COUP DE DÉS
Paris: Éditions Ferenczi, 1954
160 x 111 mm, 96 pp.
Rotation offset, thread binding

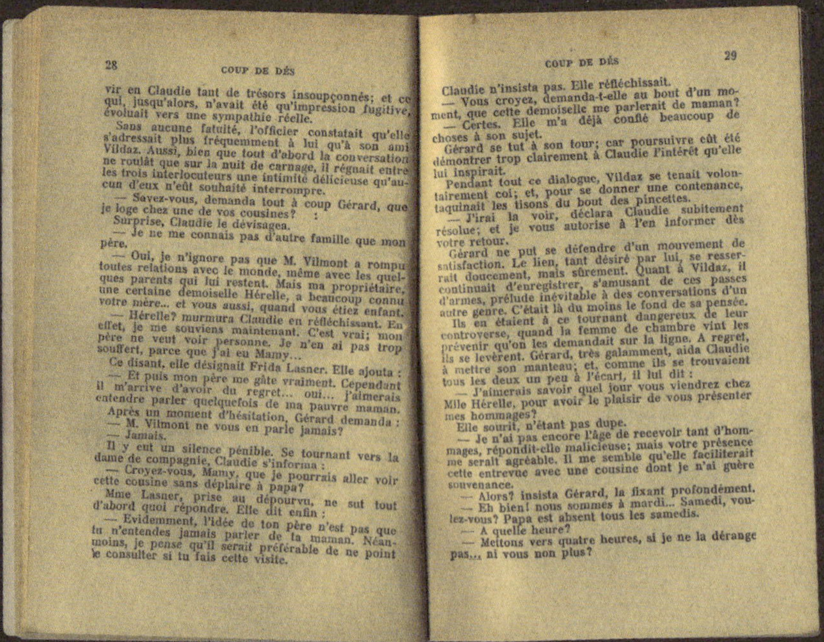

28 COUP DE DÉS

vir en Claudie tant de trésors insoupçonnés; et ce qui, jusqu'alors, n'avait été qu'impression fugitive, évoluait vers une sympathie réelle.

Sans aucune fatuité, l'officier constatait qu'elle s'adressait plus fréquemment à lui qu'à son ami Vildaz. Aussi, bien que tout d'abord la conversation ne roulât que sur la nuit de carnage, il régnait entre les trois interlocuteurs une intimité délicieuse qu'aucun d'eux n'eût souhaité interrompre.

— Savez-vous, demanda tout à coup Gérard, que je loge chez une de vos cousines?

Surprise, Claudie le dévisagea.

— Je ne me connais pas d'autre famille que mon père.

— Oui, je n'ignore pas que M. Vilmont a rompu toutes relations avec le monde, même avec les quelques parents qui lui restent. Mais ma propriétaire, une certaine demoiselle Hérelle, a beaucoup connu votre mère... et vous aussi, quand vous étiez enfant.

— Hérelle? murmura Claudie en réfléchissant. En effet, je me souviens maintenant. C'est vrai; mon père ne veut voir personne. Je n'en ai pas trop souffert, parce que j'ai eu Mamy...

Ce disant, elle désignait Frida Lasner. Elle ajouta :

— Et puis mon père me gâte vraiment. Cependant il m'arrive d'avoir du regret... oui... j'aimerais entendre parler quelquefois de ma pauvre maman.

Après un moment d'hésitation, Gérard demanda :

— M. Vilmont ne vous en parle jamais?

— Jamais.

Il y eut un silence pénible. Se tournant vers la dame de compagnie, Claudie s'informa :

— Croyez-vous, Mamy, que je pourrais aller voir cette cousine sans déplaire à papa?

Mme Lasner, prise au dépourvu, ne sut tout d'abord quoi répondre. Elle dit enfin :

— Evidemment, l'idée de ton père n'est pas que tu n'entendes jamais parler de ta maman. Néanmoins, je pense qu'il serait préférable de ne point le consulter si tu fais cette visite.

COUP DE DÉS 29

Claudie n'insista pas. Elle réfléchissait.

— Vous croyez, demanda-t-elle au bout d'un moment, que cette demoiselle me parlerait de maman?

— Certes. Elle m'a déjà confié beaucoup de choses à son sujet.

Gérard se tut à son tour; car poursuivre eût été démontrer trop clairement à Claudie l'intérêt qu'elle lui inspirait.

Pendant tout ce dialogue, Vildaz se tenait volontairement coi; et, pour se donner une contenance, taquinait les tisons du bout des pincettes.

— J'irai la voir, déclara Claudie subitement résolue; et je vous autorise à l'en informer dès votre retour.

Gérard ne put se défendre d'un mouvement de satisfaction. Le lien, tant désiré par lui, se resserrait doucement, mais sûrement. Quant à Vildaz, il continuait d'enregistrer, s'amusant de ces passes d'armes, prélude inévitable à des conversations d'un autre genre. C'était là du moins le fond de sa pensée.

Ils en étaient à ce tournant dangereux de leur controverse, quand la femme de chambre vint les prévenir qu'on les demandait sur la ligne. A regret, ils se levèrent. Gérard, très galamment, aida Claudie à mettre son manteau; et, comme ils se trouvaient tous les deux un peu à l'écart, il lui dit :

— J'aimerais savoir quel jour vous viendrez chez Mlle Hérelle, pour avoir le plaisir de vous présenter mes hommages?

Elle sourit, n'étant pas dupe.

— Je n'ai pas encore l'âge de recevoir tant d'hommages, répondit-elle malicieuse; mais votre présence me serait agréable. Il me semble qu'elle faciliterait cette entrevue avec une cousine dont je n'ai guère souvenance.

— Alors? insista Gérard, la fixant profondément.

— Eh bien! nous sommes à mardi... Samedi, voulez-vous? Papa est absent tous les samedis.

— A quelle heure?

— Mettons vers quatre heures, si je ne la dérange pas... ni vous non plus?

1:2

Heinz Risse
UN COUP DE DÉS (GROSSE FAHRT UND FALSCHES SPIEL)
Paris: Éditions Albin Michel, 1959
200 x 113 mm, 258 pp.
Offset, thread binding

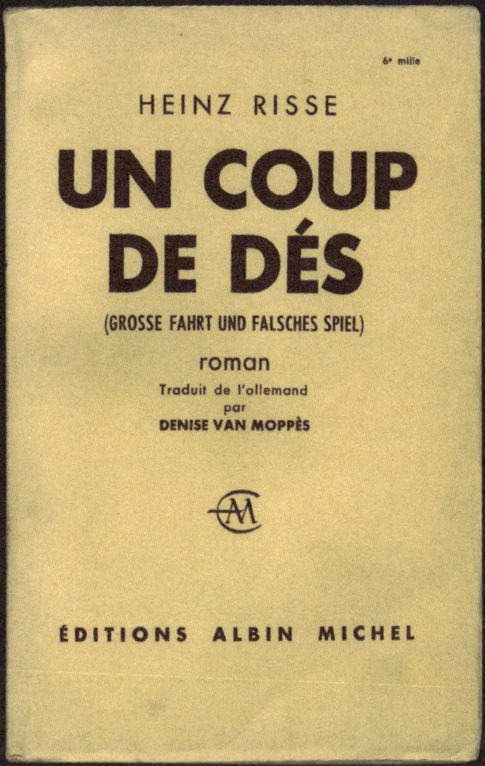

1:2

Florent Manuel
Mon Roman Policier EN TROIS COUPS DE DÉS
Paris: Éditions Ferenczi, 1964
160 x 110 mm, 32 pp.
Rotation offset, stapled

Éditions Ferenczi was one of the major players in the three-penny-novel genre during the first half of the 20th century. The present story is part of the "Mon Roman Policier" series.

1:2

Jaques Nobécourt
LE DERNIER COUP DE DÉS DE HITLER
Paris: ROBERT LAFFONT, 1962
220 x 140 mm, 440 pp.
Offset, thread binding

1:2

Jaques Nobécourt
Le dernier coup de dé de Hitler
Paris: ÉDITIONS J'AI-LU LAFFONT, 1964
165 x 115 mm, 448 pp.
Offset, perfect binding

1:2

Joseph Guglielmi, ed. Jean Todrani
"Comme un Lecture d'Un Coup de Dés..." in *Manteia* 1 (1967)
Marseille: Éditions Manteia, 1967
210 x 130 mm, 72 pp.
Offset, thread binding

Featuring the table of contents on its cover, this issue of *Manteia* 1 includes Joseph Guglielmi's "Comme un Lecture d'Un Coup de Dés..."

A year later, *Manteia* 5 (1968) published the first French version of Roland Barthes's "The Death of the Author."

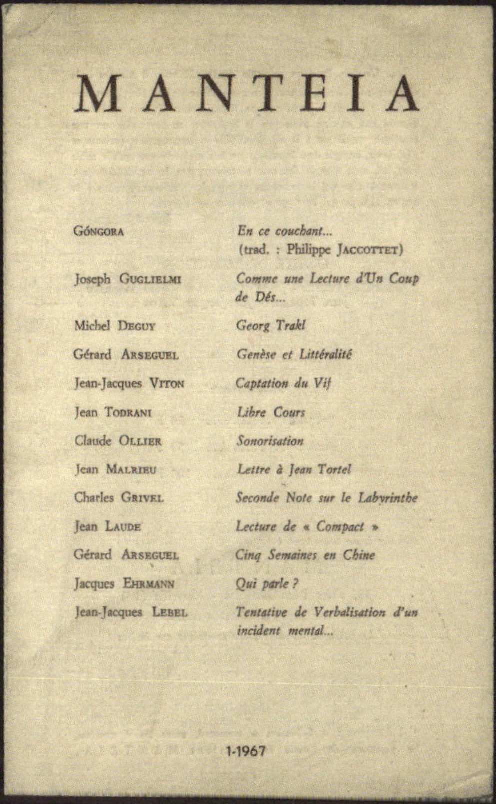

MANTEIA

GÓNGORA	*En ce couchant...* (trad. : Philippe JACCOTTET)
Joseph GUGLIELMI	*Comme une Lecture d'Un Coup de Dés...*
Michel DEGUY	*Georg Trakl*
Gérard ARSEGUEL	*Genèse et Littéralité*
Jean-Jacques VITON	*Captation du Vif*
Jean TODRANI	*Libre Cours*
Claude OLLIER	*Sonorisation*
Jean MALRIEU	*Lettre à Jean Tortel*
Charles GRIVEL	*Seconde Note sur le Labyrinthe*
Jean LAUDE	*Lecture de « Compact »*
Gérard ARSEGUEL	*Cinq Semaines en Chine*
Jacques EHRMANN	*Qui parle ?*
Jean-Jacques LEBEL	*Tentative de Verbalisation d'un incident mental...*

1-1967

1:2

Jean De Meur
THEATRE
Gand: EDITIONS UN COUP DE DÉS, 1967
210 x 140 mm
Offset, thread binding

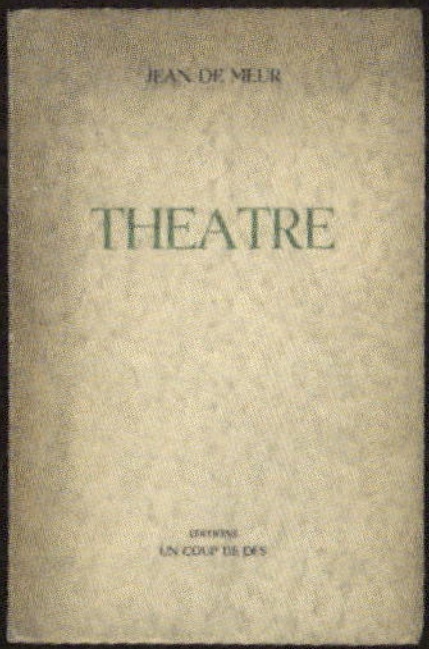

FRANCE FOOTBALL

LA PLUS FORTE VENTE DES HEBDOMADAIRES SPORTIFS

N° 1206 ● 24° ANNEE ● 13 MAI 1969 ● 1,50 F

Algérie : 1,30 Din. ● Maroc : 1,30 Dir. ● Tunisie : 125 Mil. ● Belgique : 20 FB ● Espagne : 17,50 Pes. ● Suisse : 2,10 FS

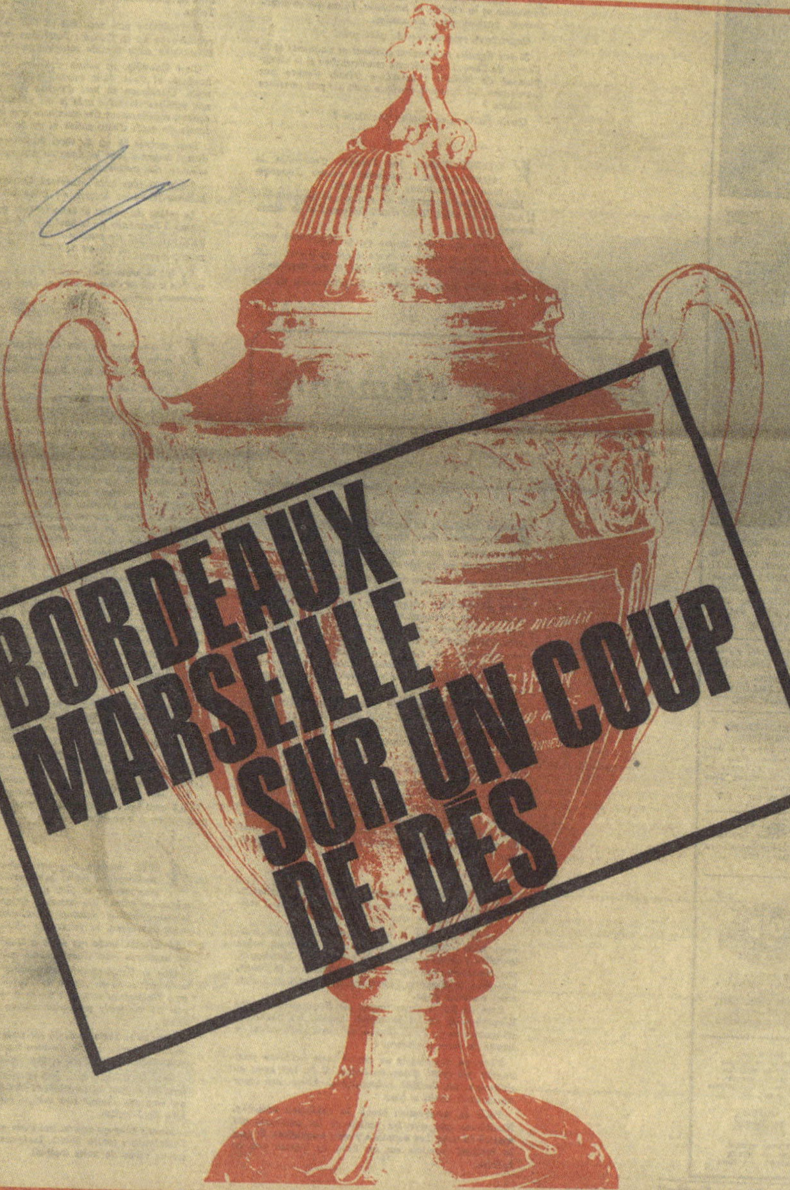

BORDEAUX MARSEILLE SUR UN COUP DE DÉS

FRANCE FOOTBALL NO 1206 BORDEAUX MARSEILLE SUR UN COUP DE DÉS
1969
420 x 300 mm, 36 pp.
Rotation offset, loose

Georges Bielec
LE DESTIN SUR UN COUP DE DÉS
Paris: Éditions EVILFRANCE, 1982
175 x 130 mm, 195 pp.

1:2

Monique Tornay
LE LIVRE D'HEURES
Lausanne: Éditions l'Aire. Le Coup de Dés, 1982
210 x 140 mm, 230 pp.
Offset, perfect binding, paperback

Nicolas Kolly
LE TEMPS IMPARTI
Lausanne: Éditions l'Aire. Le Coup de Dés, 1986
210 x 140 mm, 182 pp.
Offset, perfect binding, paperback

Loretta Verna
LE FOURBI
Lausanne: Éditions l'Aire. Le Coup de Dés, 1986
210 x 140 mm, 110 pp.
Offset, perfect binding, paperback

David Moginier
LE ROI DES NOCTAMBULES
Lausanne: Éditions l'Aire. Le Coup de Dés, 1988
210 x 140 mm, 110 pp.
Offset, perfect binding, paperback

The L'Aire collection was directed by Michel Dentan and later by Jean Pache. Its main income came from trading Rencontre SA shares listed on the stock exchange. The Cooperative's sales were symbolic.

May 68 and its aftermath (strike at Imprimerie Rencontre in Mulhouse, devaluation of the French franc, postal strikes) dealt a terrible blow to Éditions Rencontre. The title lost 90% of its value overnight. In the years that followed, the Cooperative reduced its activity and suspended it. In 1974, Rencontre SA, a victim of the stock market, announced that the coexistence of the two companies had become impossible, as in the meantime the S.A. had changed owners twice and modified its articles of association.

In May 1978, after four years of inactivity, the Cooperative changed its name, modified its articles of association and became Éditions de l'Aire. The first book published was Requiem pour une révolution perdue by Claude Jaquillard. Since 1978, around a thousand titles have appeared under the L'Aire name.

Éditions de l'Aire

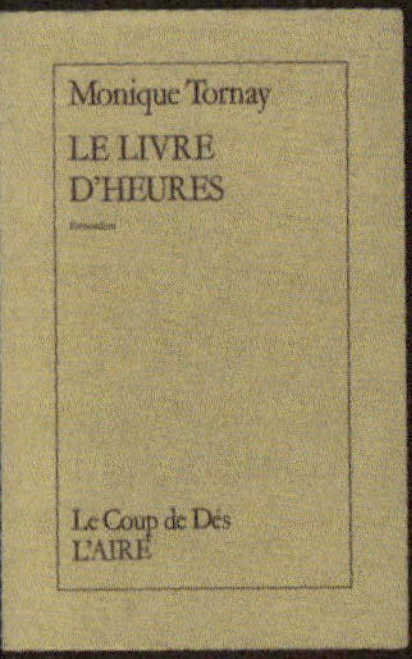

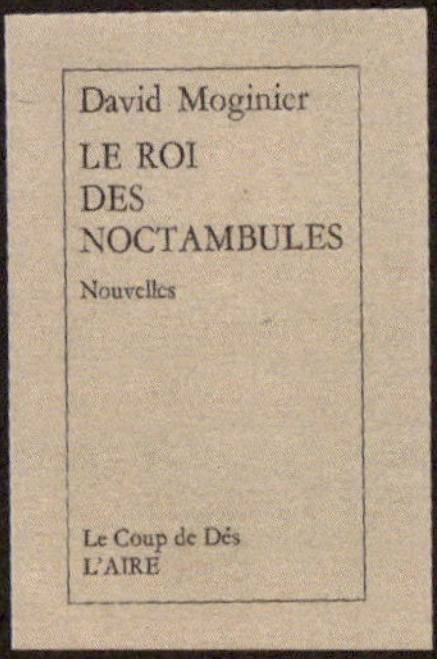

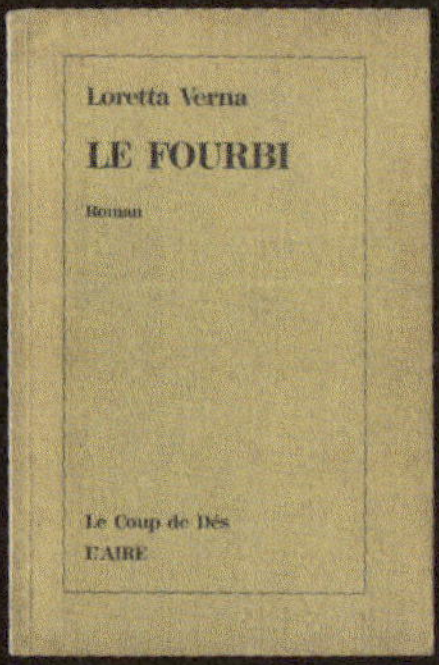

Marie-Francoise Hans
COUP DE DÉS
Paris: ÉDITIONS DU SEUIL, 1982
200 x 140 mm, 282 pp.
Offset, thread binding

Sophie inhaled sharply, started to bite a nail, stopped.
—Since he is incapable of deciding, since he is a gambler, since this woman believes in destiny, since you are ready to do anything to get out of it, play him at the dice.
—What are you talking about... You're laughing.
—Do I look like one?
—No. But, with you, I never know. Playing dice, you say... He won't want to.
—You will not ask his opinion. You will present this part to him as a test. And it will work. No, he's not the obstacle. As I know him, the idea of being played by two women will rather excite him. The important thing is to convince her.

Backcover text

Nicole Serge-Rainer
LE HASARD ET LE COUP DE DÉS
Marsat: Éditions Henri Veyrier, 1984
230 x 150 mm, 119 pp.
Offset, perfect binding

Nicole Serge-Rainer's anti-hero, "good man and poor guy," as he defines himself, makes the front page of a bloody news story. Taken hostage by Sermine, public enemy number one—barely disguised pseudonym of Mesrine, whose story appears implicitly throughout the story—he miraculously escapes the shooting. Lying on a hospital bed, this paranoid taciturn has a secret; it is this secret that he tells. Disdained by his wife, despised by his children, ridiculed by his bistro companions, without a future because without a present and without a past, his life oscillates between resignation and revolt. One day, however, things get better. He reads a facsimile of a letter from Sermine in a newspaper and discovers that they have the same handwriting. Fascinated by the coincidence, he decides to take on the personality of the gangster and send press releases—which he signs Sermine. While the latter continues to hit the headlines, he shapes a new face—immediately conveyed by the media.

He is Sermine much more than Sermine himself... until the day when, ironically, "chance, which a throw of the dice will never abolish", according to Mallarmé's famous formula, brings them together for the first and last last time in the back room of a cafe. A novel of despair and refusal, N. Serge-Rainer's book is also a political fable in which the State, the family, work, religion and morality are undermined in turn, without forgetting the values refuge that is love and friendship.

Backcover text

Andrié Luc ed. Pierre-Alain Giesser
COUP DE DÉS CAHIER D'ART NO.1
Lausanne: COUP DE DÉS CAHIER D'ART, 1987
280 x 210 mm
Offset, perfect binding

Monographic catalog of artist Luc Andrié in the *COUP DE DÉS, cahier d'art* series. Other artists represented in the same series are Félix Plattner (1991), Anne Sauser-Hall (1993), and Janos Urban (1995).

ed. Benjamin H. D. Buchloh
OCTOBER 42 BROODTHAERS
with contributions by Rainer Borgemeister, Benjamin H. D. Buchloh, Joan Copjec, Douglas Crimp, Yves Gevaert, Rosalind Krauss, Annette Michelson, Michael Oppitz, Birgit Pelzer, Anne Rorimer, Dieter Schwarz, Dirk Snauwaert
Cambridge, MA: MIT Press, 1987
230 x 180 mm, 210 pp.
Offset, perfect binding

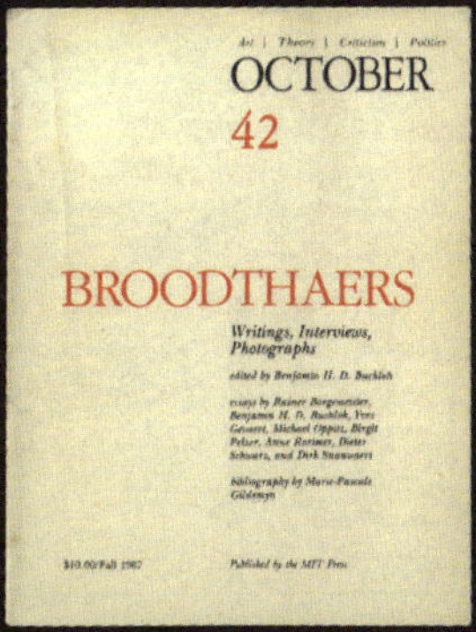

While the original impulse to edit this issue was occasioned in part by the tenth anniversary of Broodthaers's death, it also originated in the desire to counteract both the work's obscurity and the falsification inherent in its art historical institutionalization. Moreover, it was our desire to have Marcel Broodthaers's work reconsidered (or rather, since it is all but unknown in the United States, to suggest it for a first consideration) in relation to currently dominant cultural practices and their respective capacity and willingness to reflect upon their discursive, institutional, and economic status.

Benjamin H. D. Buchloh in the "Introductory Note"

The back cover features an untitled poem by Marcel Broodthaers from 1968. It includes the whole phrase UN COUP DE DÉS JAMAIS N'ABOLIRA LE HASARD and compares the alphabet to dice, referring to the twenty-six letters as sides of a die.

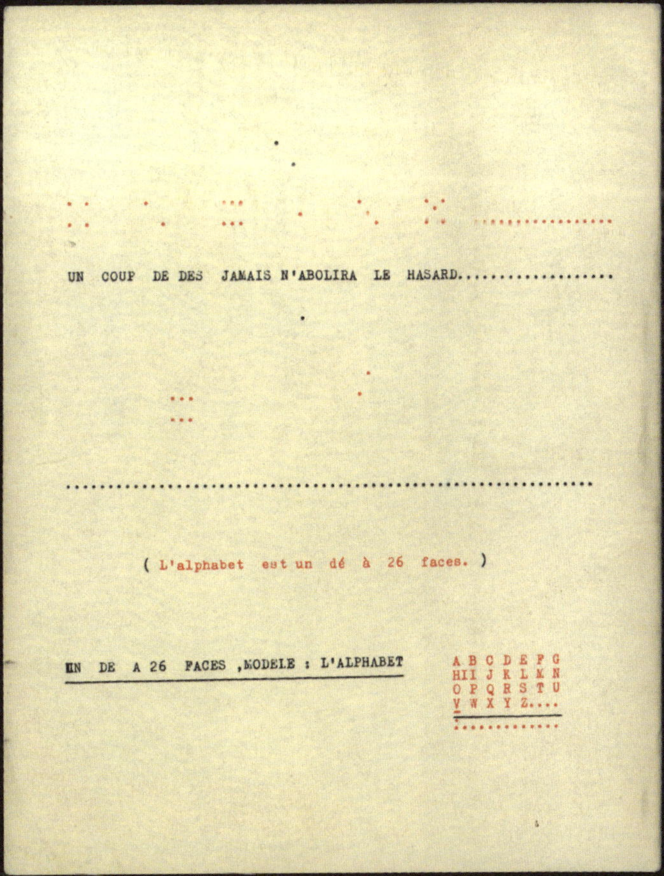

UN COUP DE DES JAMAIS N'ABOLIRA LE HASARD..................

....

(L'alphabet est un dé à 26 faces.)

UN DE A 26 FACES ,MODELE : L'ALPHABET

A B C D E F G
HII J K L K N
O P Q R S T U
V W X Y Z....

1:2

Jacques Jourquin
Revue du Souvenir Napoléonien N° 418
Paris: BUREAU DE LA REVUE, 1998
270 x 210 mm, 80 pp.
Offset, thread binding

The Souvenir Napoléonien, founded in 1937, is an association which promotes the historical study of what they conceive of as "the Napoleonic Era." The cover of this issue sports the phrase "Le coup de dés de Bonaparte."

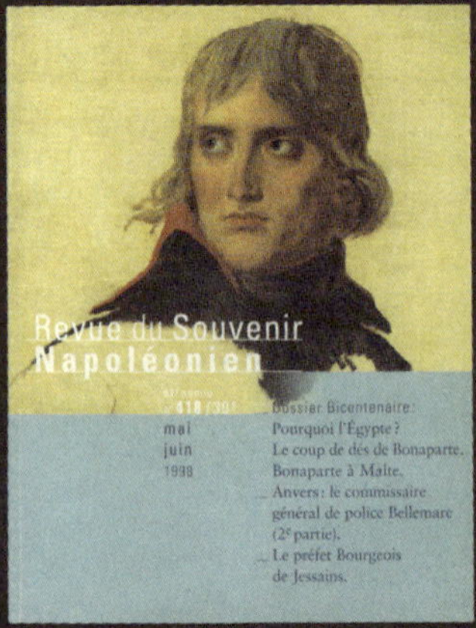

Christine Givry, Raoul Fabrègues
Les Échos de Mallarmé, Du Coup de Dés...
à l'INFORMATIQUE
Sens: MUSÉES DE SENS, 1998
250 x 220 mm, 110 pp.

An exhibition catalog that presents a variety of visual artists and poets who work on both sides of the imaginary border between visual art and literature.

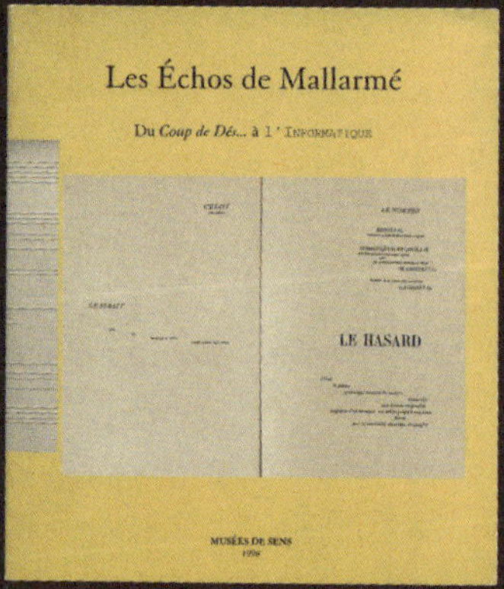

Jean-Paul Michel ed. Tristan Hordé
Bonté seconde. "Coup de dés"
Nantes: ÉDITIONS JOSEPH K, 2002
240 x 160 mm, 256 pp.
Offset, thread binding

ed. Judd D. Hubert and Renée Riese Hubert
A Throw of the Dice: Artists Inspired by a Visual Text,
UN COUP DE DÉS JAMAIS N'ABOLIRA LE HASARD
Irvine, CA: UCI Libraries, 2003
215 x 140 mm, 20 pp.
Offset, stapled

Booklet published on occasion of the exhibition *A Throw of the Dice*, curated by Professors Emeriti Renée Riese Hubert and Judd D. Hubert, who previously published extensively on both artists' books and Mallarmé. The show featured fifteen exhibits.

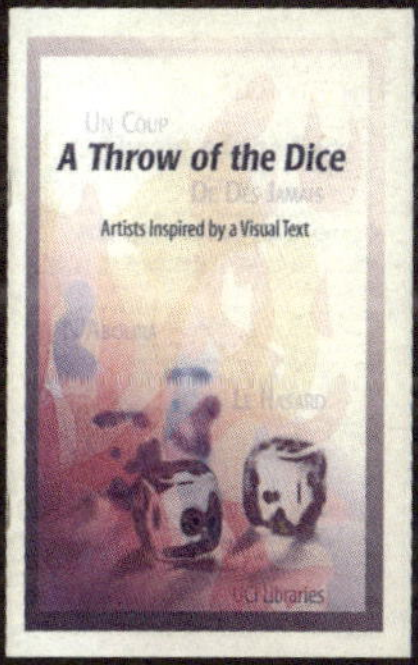

Michel Murat
LE COUP DE DÉS de Mallarmé
Paris: Belin Éditeur, 2005
350 x 215 mm, 208 pp.
Offset, paperback

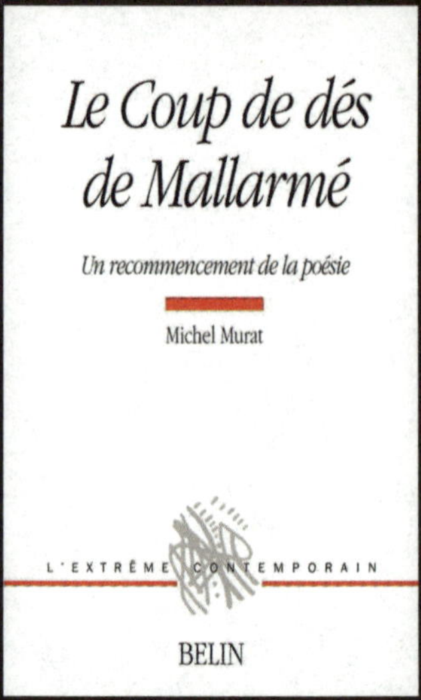

Patrick Cintas
D'un coup de dés ... l'espace du poème depuis *Mallarmé*
with contributions by Ann-Sarah Delaroche
Toulouse: Bibliothèque d'étude et du patrimoine, 2007

Anna Sigrídur Arnar, Jacques Rancière, Gabriele Mackert, Michael Newman, ed. Sabine Folie
UN COUP DE DÉS, Bild gewordene Schrift. Ein ABC der nachdenklichen Sprache Writing Turned Image. An Alphabet of Pensive Language
Vienna: Generali Foundation, 2008
270 x 213 mm, 250 pp.
Offset, softcover

What Stéphane Mallarmé envisioned in *UN COUP DE DÉS* (A throw of the dice), 1897, became an integral part of avant-garde practice in the twentieth century: To expose language as a convention that is there to discipline individuals and subject them to a regulated system of capitalist exploitability. In contrast, language should be subjected to a revision and reclaim its imaginative freedom by wresting it from its purposive purpose. In this comprehensive publication, art theorists and artists reflect on the poetic and subversive potential of language.

Verlag der Buchhandlung Walther König

Philippe Lemaire
DEBUTEZ AU BACKGAMMON
Du premier coup de dés à la stratégie gagnante!
Paris: Micro Application, 2008
210 x 150 mm, 146 pp.
Offset, perfect binding

1:2

ed. Diane Grey
Coup de Dés Issue 1: Housing and Public Space
Barcelona: Fundacio Mies van der Rohe, 2010
200 x 135 mm, 96 pp.
Offset, thread binding

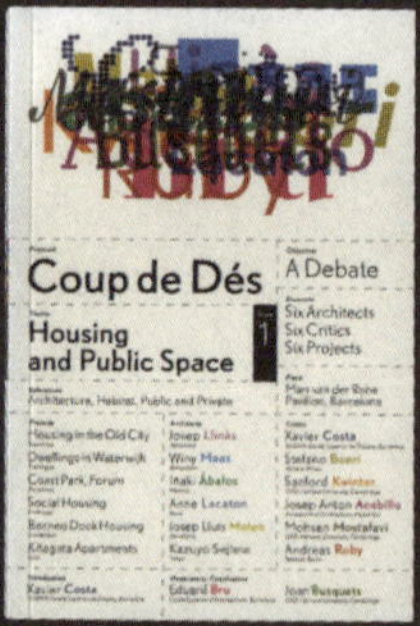

ed. Diane Grey
Coup de Dés Issue 2: Emerging European Architects
Barcelona: Fundacio Mies van der Rohe, 2008
135 x 200 mm, 96 pp.
Offset, thread binding

ed. Diane Grey
Coup de Dés Issue 3: New Ideas, New Experiences in the European Context
Barcelona: Fundacio Mies van der Rohe, 2009
200 x 135 mm, 96 pp.
Offset, thread binding

ed. Diane Grey
Coup de Dés Issue 4: What's New? Searching for Clues
Barcelona: Fundacio Mies van der Rohe, 2010
200 x 135 mm, 96 pp.
Offset, thread binding

ed. Diane Grey
Coup de Dés Issue 5: Mediterranean Cities
Barcelona: Fundacio Mies van der Rohe, 2012
200 x 135 mm, 96 pp.
Offset, thread binding

The Fundació Mies van der Rohe organises a series of debates and lectures entitled "Coup de Dés" that provide an opportunity to discuss some of the most significant architecture being produced today, with the objective of offering a wide panorama of current architectural practice. The debates are generated by the presentation of various projects. Each presentation is followed by a dialogue between the architect and a critic who proposes an interpretation of the project and raises related questions.

Fundació Mies van der Rohe

Ángel Marcos
UN COUP DE DÉS
Madrid: Galería Soledad Lorenzo, 2008
220 x 275 mm, 40 pp.
Offset, perfect binding

"Euro Disney, the troubled theme park near Paris, was described by a disgruntled French critic as a cultural Chernobyl, though perhaps a cultural Stalingrad would be close to the truth: the battleground where the relentless advance of American popular culture was at last stopped and turned. I suspect that Mickey Mouse and Donald Duck no longer satisfy today's children, whose retinas flicker with the electronic phantoms of the arcade video games. Super Nintendo rules, and the Disney empire now merchandizes nostalgia" (Ballard). It is clear to us that Disneylandization which is now the most important of the urban development projects, a model for even contemporary artistic experiences, is the logic that prevails in Las Vegas now. Whilst the persuasive neon signs continue with their nasal cacophony, the tourists hooked on the show, live a dream that is, in reality, a nightmare in disguise. "Behind the city the only transition between the Strip and the Mojave desert is a dump covered with rusty beer cans" (Venturi).

Fernando Castro Flóres, quoting J. G. Ballard
and Venturi/Izenour/Brown in the introductory essay.

Monographic catalog of Ángel Marcos, featuring photographs taken by the artist in and around Las Vegas, comprising his *UN COUP DE DÉS* series.

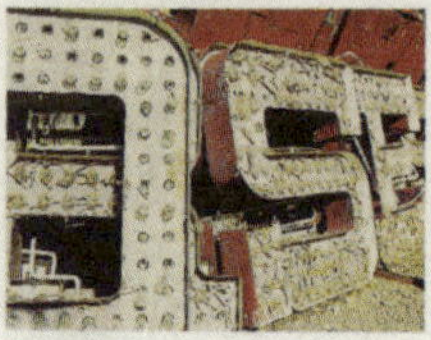

16 17 18
22 23 24
28 29 30
34 35 36

19 20 21
25 26 27
31 32 33
37

Un coup de dés, 2008
cajas de luz. 34 x 45 x 12 cm. c/u

29

1:2

Thierry Roger
L'Archive du Coup de dés Étude critique de la réception d'Un coup de dés jamais n'abolira le hasard de Stéphane Mallarmé (1897-2007)
Paris: ÉDITIONS CLASSIQUES GARNIER, 2010
240 X 160 mm, 1060 pp.
Offset, paperback

We must break with an overly intuitive vision of the effect of COUP DE DÉS in the twentieth century and undertake the genealogy of a doxa which made this Mallarmean writing the prototype of the avant-garde poem. The text appeared in 1897 to indifference By what mediations was it transmitted to us? This book reconstructs the stages of a reception 'in discourse' which made an incredible poetic object more readable. But this posterity was also theoretical, philosophical and artistic through a reception 'in action', properly creative: image, staging, concept or layout. This archive of COUP DE DÉS then reveals the archeology of a certain modern tradition, captured through the manifestations of the polymorphic productivity of a literary work.

Thierry Roger

The book features Thierry Roger's a doctoral thesis, submitted at Paris-Sorbonne under the supervision of Betrand Marchal.

creativecommons.org
Belgian Art: Le Genie Du Mal, Un Coup de Des Jamais N'abolira le Hasard, Hisk, Jozef Peeters, Marcel Lempereur-Haut, Art La Rue, Luminism
Memphis: Books LLC, 2010
230 x 155 mm, 31 pp.
POD, offset, perfect binding

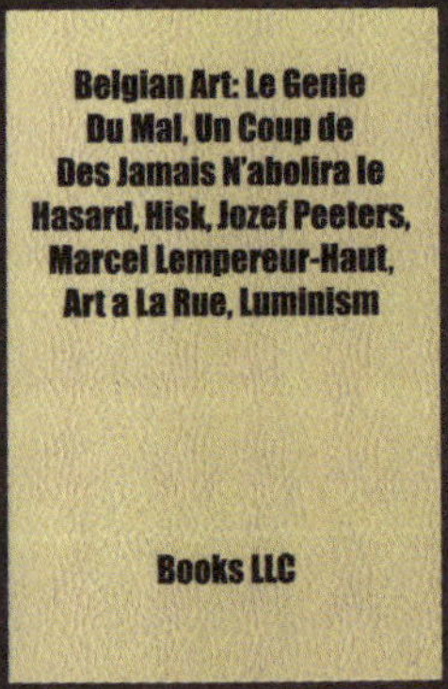

Riccardo Boglione
Riscrivendo l'illegibile. Quattro cancellature del Coup de Dés.
Genova: Liberodiscrivere, 2011
150 x 100 mm, 46 pp.
Offset, stapled

Texts are assaulted: partially erased, shredded and re-pasted, superimposed on other texts. Outlines vanish, letters are screened with other letters or slashes, scratches, abrasions. One has to wait until the late 1960s, however, for a work as capital for visual writing as Mallarmé's *COUP DE DÉS* (1897) to be directly put back into play.

Ocra Press

In *Re-writing the illegible. Four erasures of Coup de Dés.*, Boglione analyzes erasure strategies in the books of Mario Diacono, Marcel Broodthaers, Michael Maranda, and Michalis Pichler. Besides his scholarly work, Boglione is also known for editing and publishing *Crux Desperationis*, a magazine of conceptual writing from Montevideo. The cover features an image from Mario Diacono's *JCT1*.

1:1

Les Amis du Foot
LE COUP DE DES CHAMPIONS RENCONTRES SPORTIVES À BUT CARITATIF
297 x 210 mm, 10 pp.
Digital, stapled

ed. Joost Baars
De Fraktie "Un coup de dés — poéme, image of sculpture"
Amsterdam: Stichting Perdu, 2009
150 x 150 mm
Offset, stapled

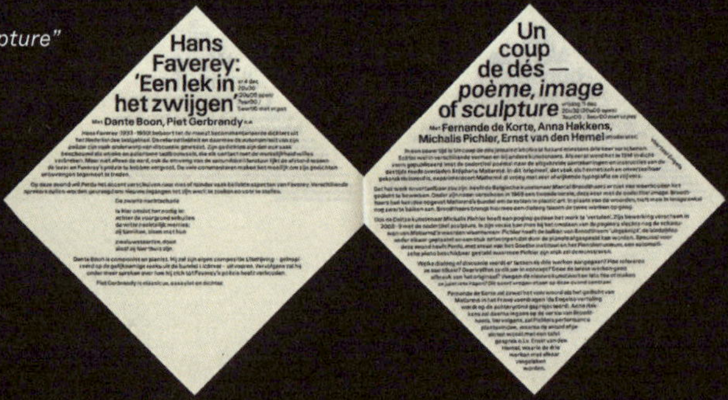

Malcom Green
UN COUP DE DORIS DAY
Berlin: Red Sphinx, 2012
140 x 105 mm
Offset

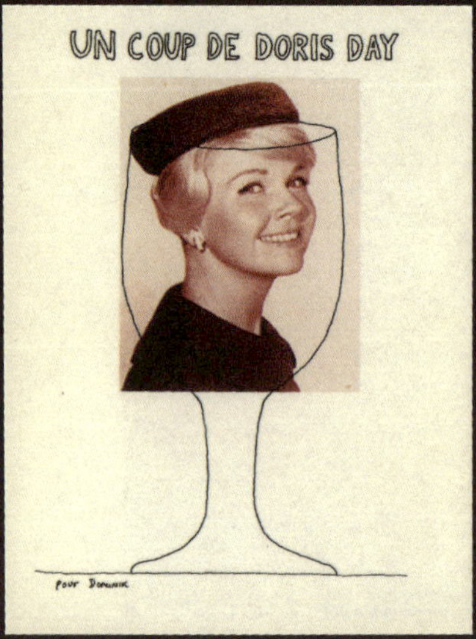

Anonymous
Memory of Present
Berlin: coup de dés art series, 2012
140 x 105 mm
Offset

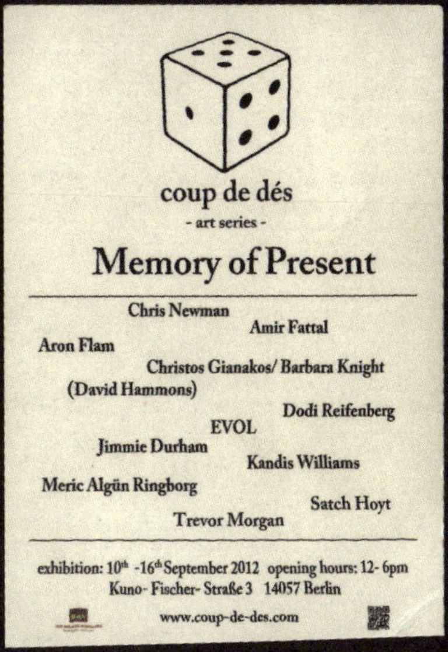

1:2

Fredéric Teschner Studio
UN COUP DE DÉS.NET
Paris: Association française de développement des centres d'art, 2013

1:2

Jean-Jacques Birgé, Médéric Collignon, Julien Desprez
Un coup de dés jamais n'abolira le hasard

Jean-Jacques Birgé is an independent French musician and filmmaker, at once music composer (co-founder of Un Drame Musical Instantané), sound designer, multimedia artist, writer and blogger. (Mediapart)... Specialist of the relations between sound and pictures, he has been one of the early synthesizer players in France in 1973, the initiator of the return of silent movies with music in 1976.

Improvisations recorded live at Le Triton, Les Lilas, by Florian Tirot, November 28, 2014

The audience chose the theme of each piece from the Oblique Strategies cards conceived by Brian Eno and Peter Schmidt.

Sérgio Bento
O co-relato Mallarmé-Haroldo: O mito moderno em Un coup de dés
Riga: Novas Edições Acadêmicas, 2015
220 x 50 mm, 120 pp.
Offset, paperback

In its modern concept, myth is a behavioral paradigm, a semiological system of some external referent. Based on this, this paper argues that Stéphane Mallarmé's poem acquires mythical status, both because of its cosmogonic character—commonly ignored by critics—and because of its formal innovation—a fact that consecrated it, and from which perspective it is only remembered. As a result, throughout the twentieth century he underwent a process of mythification, being promoted to the status of one of the most important sources of inspiration for recent and contemporary poetry. In order to make this approach possible, we sought to delimit the study of the proposed text in correlation with its recreation in Portuguese by Haroldo de Campos.

Novas Edições Acadêmicas

Saggiomo Carmen, Denis Fadda
UN COUP DE DÉS Cahier du culture française, francophone et maghrébine 5
Napoli: Edizione Scientifiche Italiane, 2017
230 x 160 mm, 272 pp.
Offset, perfect binding

Claude Minière
UN COUP DE DÉS
Paris: Tinbad, 2019
188 x 115 mm, 57 pp.
Offset, thread binding

"Chacune des *Pensées* émet un coup de dés" writes Minière of Blaise Pascal, echoing and paraphrasing the last line of Mallarmé's poem: every thought emits a throw of the dice.

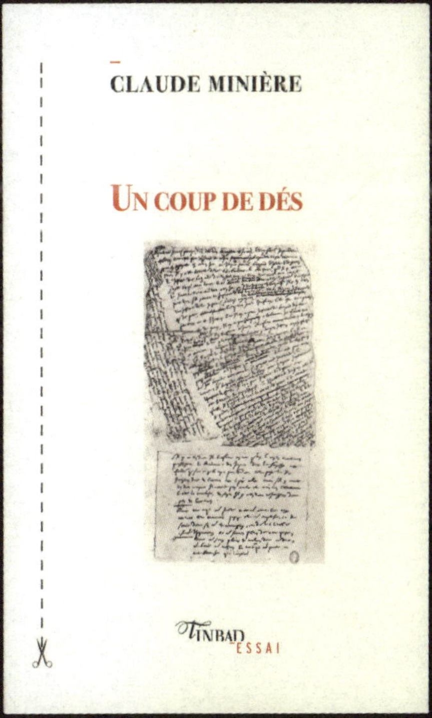

1:2

Bibliography

Bibliography of Books about After-Mallarmé

A Throw of the Dice. Edited by Judd D. Hubert and Renée Riese Hubert. Irvine, CA: UCI Libraries, 2003.

Arnar, Anna Sigrídur. *The Book As Instrument: Stéphane Mallarmé, The Artist's Book, and the Transformation of Print culture.* Chicago: University of Chicago Press, 2011.

Boglione, Riccardo. *Riscrivendo l'illigibile: Quattro cancellature del Coup de Dés.* Genova: Ocra Press, 2011.

Bolick, Robert. "Bookmarking Book Art: 'Un Coup de Dés Jamais N'Abolira l'Appropriation'—An Online Exhibition." Accessed 2022. https://books-on-books.com/2022/05/01/bookmarking-book-art-un-coup-de-des-jamais-nabolira-lappropriation-an-online-exhibition/.

Bourchenin, Barbara. "From text to texture in Marcel Broodthaers, Michalis Pichler, and Jérémie Bennequin: A rereading of Stéphane Mallarmé in the era of the glitch." *Études Stéphane Mallarmé* 6 (2018): 23–45.

Charité, Virginia. *The Dynamics of Space: Mallarmé's Un Coup De Dés Jamais N'abolira Le Hazard.* Lexington, KY: French Forum, 1987.

Cintas, Patrick, and Ann-Sarah Delaroche. *D'un coup de dés ... l'espace du poème depuis Mallarmé.* Toulouse: La Bibliothèque d'Étude et du Patrimoine: 2007.

Drucker, Johanna, "Artists' Books and Conceptualism(s)." In *MULTIPLE, LIMITED, UNIQUE: Selections from the permanent Collection of the Center for Book Arts.* Edited by Alexander Campos. New York: The Center for Book Arts, 2011, 17–25.

Gualdoni, Flaminio, and Giorgio Maffei. *Il Caso Stephane.* Milano: Galleria l'Affiche, 2010.

Illouz, Jean-Nicolas. "*Noli me legere:* Stéphane Mallarmé, Marcel Broodthaers, Michalis Pichler, *Un coup de dés jamais n'abolira le hasard.*" *Poésie* 172–73, no. 2–3 (2020): 211–22.

MALLARMÉ BROODTHAERS ET LES AUTRES. Edited by Reiner Speck. Cologne: Galerie Michael Werner, 2022.

Mallarmé's Coup d'État: Un coup de dés. Claremont, CA: Clark Humanities Museum, Ella Strong Denison Library, 2007.

O'Toole, Mary-Bernadette. *beyond the space of painting and poetry: mallarmé and the embodied gesture.* PhD thesis, Sheffield Hallam University, 2020.

Rancière, Jacques. *L'espace Des Mots: De Mallarmé À Broodthaers.* Paris: Musée des Beaux-arts: 2005.

Roger, Thierry. *L'Archive du Coup de Dés: Étude critique de la réception d'Un coup de dés jamais n'abolira le hasard de Stéphane Mallarmé (1897–2007).* Paris: Éditions Classiques Garnier, 2010.

Roger, Thierry. "Sur le genre du Coup de dés." in *Poétique*, vol. 4, no. 160 (2009): 443–70.

Schraenen, Guy. *HOMMAGE AN MALLARMÉS WÜRFELWURF.* Bremen: Neues Museum Weserburg, 1998.

Schwabsky, Barry. "MALLARMÉ, OUR CONTEMPORARY." *caesura.* Last modified February 18, 2021. https://caesuramag.org/posts/barry-schwabsky-mallarme-our-contemporary.

Stark, Trevor. *Total Expansion of the Letter: Avant-Garde Art and Language after Mallarmé.* Cambridge, MA: MIT Press, 2020.

UN COUP DE DÉS Bild gewordene Schrift. Ein ABC der nachdenklichen Sprache Writing Turned Image. An Alphabet of Pensive Language. Edited by Sabine Folie. Vienna: Generali Foundation, 2008.

Wieland, Magnus. "about blank: Appropriationen des Leerraums seit Mallarmé." In *Wiederaufgelegt. Zur Appropriation von Texten und Büchern in Büchern.* Edited by Annette Gilbert. Bielefeld: transcript, 2012, 193–216.

Wieland, Magnus. "SCULPTURE LECTURE Reading Un coup de dés." In *Michalis Pichler—Thirteen Years: The materialization of ideas from 2002 to 2015.* Edited by Annette Gilbert and Clemens Krümmel. New York: Printed Matter, Inc. and Leipzig: Spector Books, 2015.

Zboya, Eric. *Dimensional Translations: A Topological Journey Beyond the Two-Dimensional Space of the Page in Stephane Mallarmé´s Un Coup de dés.* Honors thesis, University of Calgary, 2010.

Zboya, Eric. "Übersetzungen in höhere Dimensionen. Eine topologische Reise über den zweidimensionalen Raum der Buchseite in Stéphane Mallarmés Un Coup de Dés hinaus." In *Wiederaufgelegt. Zur Appropriation von Texten und Büchern in Büchern.* Edited by Annette Gilbert (Bielefeld: transcript, 2012), 193–216.

Bibliography of After-*COUP* Artworks (unique or small editions)

Odilon Redon, *Un coup de dés*, 1897–98. Lithograph, 45 x 38 cm, ed. 4

Pablo Picasso, *Bouteille, verre et journal sur une table*, 1912. Gouache, collage (includes truncated newspaper headline "UN COUP DE THÉ"), 48 × 62 cm

Art et Action Laboratoire de Théâtre (Édouard Autant, Louise Lara and Claude Autant-Lara), *Un Coup de Dé [sic] Jamais N'Abolira le Hasard* (1919/1942). Polyphonic vocal performance of the poem planned as early as 1919, realized in 1942

Hella Guth, *Un Coup de dés jamais n'abolira le hasard: poème/par Stéphane Mallarmé.* Collages, 1952

Marcel Broodthaers, *Exposition Littéraire autour de Mallarmé* at the Wide White Space Gallery, Antwerp, December 1969

Marcel Broodthaers, *JAMAIS*, 1968. Ink on paper, 21 x 29.5 cm. MZB 76, Collection Speck

Marcel Broodthaers, *Le Dé*, 1968–69. Wood, paint and handwritten inscription, 51 x 51 x 51 cm

Marcel Broodthaers, *Untitled*, 1969. Felt tip pen on paper, 36 x 27 cm

Marcel Broodthaers, *Garniture Symbolique*, 1975. Blue tinted glossy photo strip with 9 photos on glossy paper, 12.9 x 125.5 cm

Marcel Broodthaers, *Un coup de dés jamais quand bien même...*, 1969. Oil, gold paint, felt tip pen on canvas, 165 x 122 cm

Ian Wallace, *Image/Text*, 1979. Hand-coloured sliver gelatine print, 276 x 549 cm

Eugenio Miccini, *Un colpo di dadi*, 1980. Mixed media and collage of wood on wooden board, 50 x 70 cm

Robert Filliou, *Eins. Un. One.*, 1984. Composed of 16,000 dice of different colors and size

Geraldo de Barros, *Jogos de Dados*, 1986. 55 geometric sculptural forms mounted on wires stretched from ceiling to floor

Reinhold Nasshan, *Würfelwurf: fragmentarische Annäherung an Stéphan Mallarmé* (Landau: Einhand Press, 1992). 30 x 25.5 cm
Reinhold Nasshan, *Un Coup: Stéphane Mallarmé*, 1997. "Letter-sculpture" (folding design, paper binding), 9 x 9 cm
Ian Wallace, *In the Studio (Le Livre)*, 1993. 81 x 71 cm
Alastair Noble, *As if / As if*, 1997. Steel frames with screen mesh and cable
Kathy Bruce, *Valise for Mallarmé*, 1997. Valise, altered book, X-ray film, wood, glass, die, collage, 22 x 27 x 13 cm
Kathy Bruce, *Solitary Plume Lost*, 1998 or 2000. Small cigar box, feather, pine wood, collage, cloth. 4 x 16,5 x 9cm
Kathy Bruce, *Comocíon, Contucíon, y Compresíon Cerebrales*, 1998. Framed, altered book, surrounded by white cloth and containing an embedded box containing another box with dice and collage, 38 x 30,5 x 7,5cm
Kathy Bruce and Alastair R. Noble, *Foldings*, 1998. Wearable art, performance, see https://www.kathybruceartist.com/wearable-art
Michael Graeve, *Hexagram 12. Obstruction. Earth Below, Heaven Above. Heaven and Earth Do Not Commune.*, 1998. Twelve canvas panels
Alastair Noble, *Mallarmé 2000*, 2000. Glass and steel brackets
Alain Satié, *poéme: un coup de dés, bien ou mal armé, jamais n'abolira le hasard*, 2001.
Small paintings, collages, and book-like objects placed into clear plastic sheet pockets
Didier Mutel, *Four Speeches by George Walker Bush [together with] Four Speeches by Tony Blair [together with] Un Coup de Dés Jamais N'Abolira Le Hasard*, 2003
Joëlle Tuerlinckx, *3 Dés 'j.t.'*, 1994
Joëlle Tuerlinckx, *3 Dés 'j.t.'*, 2008
Joëlle Tuerlinckx, *3 Dés 'j.t.'*, 2013
Marine Hugonnier, *The Bedside Book Project: La forme du mystère (Odillon Redon)*, 2006–07. Collage, 11 elements, 32.4 x 50 cm
Marine Hugonnier, *The Bedside Book Project: Altération (Kurt Schwitters)*, 2006–07. Collage, 11 elements, 32.4 x 50 cm
Marine Hugonnier, *The Bedside Book Project: L'espace social No. 2 (Richard Hamilton)*, 2006–07.
Collage, 11 elements, 32.4 x 50 cm
Michalis Pichler, *UN COUP DE DÉS JAMAIS N'ABOLIRA LE HASARD (SCULPTURE)*, 2008. 12 loose sheets of paper with laser cut-outs, 25 x 32.5cm each, ed. 3
Kathy Bruce, *Navigating the Abyss*, 2008. 54 hardwood blocks
Cerith Wyn Evans, *'... après Stéphane Mallarmé'*, 2008. Text in neon
Cerith Wyn Evans, *Un coup de dés jamais n'abolira le hazard*, 2009. 22 perforated book pages, each 32.5 x 24.7 cm (54 x 45.3 cm framed)
Rainier Lericolais, *Carton Perforé*, 2009. 35 pages, each 16 x 32.5cm, glued together with Scotch tape as a leporello
Raffaella della Olga, *Un Coup De Dés Jamais N'abolira Le Hasard—Constellation*, 2009. White acrylic paint, phosphorescent powder, glue, 32 x 50 cm
Raffaella della Olga, *Jamais Le Hasard N'abolira Un Coup De Dés – Permutation*, 2010. See https://raffaelladellaolga.com/works/jamais-un-coup/
Cerith Wyn Evans, *Elective Affinity*, 2010. Neon, 28.1 x 343.9 cm. Courtesy of the artist and White Cube, London
Sammy Engramer, *JAMAIS, eighteen 3D PVC renderings*, 2010
Ian Wallace, *Table with Un Coup de Dés I, II, III*, 2011. 3 photo laminates with acrylic on canvas, each 183 x 152 cm
Jorge Méndez Blake, *Toute Pensée Émet un Coup de Dés*, 2013. Colored pencil, paper, 150 x 120 cm
Estelle J., *STÉPHANE MALLARMÉ: Un coup de dés jamais n'abolira le hasard*, n.d. Self-covering accordion format with three tipped-in pages. 245 x 185 mm closed, 2,100 mm open. 24 panels and flap-insert for closing. Ed. of 6 variations
Stéphane Mallarmé [Roland Vachez], *Un coup de dés jamais n'abolira le hasard*, 2013. Letterpress with two original engravings by Roland Vachez, Conflans, L'atelier, each 32.5 x 25.2 cm, ed. 5
Kathy Bruce, *Navigating the Abyss*, 2014
Michel Lorand, *Après Un Coup de Dés*, 2015. Cover and gatherings, untrimmed and unbound, in glassine envelope, 36.2 x 26 cm
Michalis Pichler, *Exposition Littéraire autour de Mallarmé* at Kunstverein Milano, December 2016
Serge Chamchinov, *Le Hasard à l'Infini*, 2016
Olivier Foulon, *Untitled [3 Bücher – Vortrag in Bilbao #1–#3]*, 2016. Photo on Bristol paper, each 65 x 50 cm
Dolores Zinny and Juan Maidagan, *Un Coup de Dés/Una Tirada de Dados*, 2017. Permanent sidewalk, cement bricks of different colors, Fundación Proa Buenos Aires. See https://zinny-maidagan.com/public-art/un-coup-de-des-una-tirada-de-dados.html
Raffaella della Olga, *Un Coup de Dès-Trame*, 2018. Typewritten on tracing paper with fabric and carbon paper, 32 x 50 cm
Bernadette O'Toole, *Variant Sail*, 2015. Reproductions of 12 digital prints, 38 x 57 cm
Bernadette O'Toole, *As If*, 2016. The prints inspired paintings (same dimensions) that are reproduced in a second book, *As If*
Serge Chamchinov, *Le Hasard à l'Infini*, 2016
Bernadette O'Toole, *A Rare State*, 2018. 12 booklets, 38 x 57 cm each
Guillaume Theulière, *Par Hasard/By Chance*, October 18, 2019–February 23, 2020

Bibliography of After-*COUP* Film/Video

Man Ray, *Les Mystères du château du dé*, 1929
Chenal, P. *Un Coup de dés*, 1929
Danièle Huillet and Jean-Marie Straub, *Toute révolution est un coup de dés*, 1976
Carol Rudyard, *Salt Cellar and Glass*, 1988. Video installation, dimensions variable
Bill Seaman, *Red Dice / Dés Chiffres*, 2000. https://vimeo.com/404676389
Kathy Bruce, James Cook, and Alastair Noble, *Digital Mallarmé*, 2008. https://www.youtube.com/watch?v=onnMOXRcGgQ
John King, *Dice Thrown*, 2010. https://www.youtube.com/watch?v=YeiMp1UzmBE
Ruth Loos and Frouke Hermens, *"Eye Drawings,"* 2011. https://www.youtube.com/watch?v=5ZiwWcuBpMk
William G. Franklin, *Toute Pensée émet un Coup de Dés*, 2014. https://www.youtube.com/watch?v=BAIRxP_8IKQ
Jean-Jacques Birgé, *Un Coup de Dés à l'Atelier du Plateau*, 2014. https://www.youtube.com/watch?v=JgdIOUHYiWs

Tayyib Yavuz, *Experiment Book*, 2015. https://www.tayyibyavuz.com/portfolio/experimentbook/.
James Reynolds, *A Throw of the dice will never abolish chance*, 2015. https://www.youtube.com/watch?v=veEeqbEQlsw
Giulio Maffei, *Le Vite dei Libri 26 – Un coup de dés jamais n'abolira le hasard*, 2016. https://www.youtube.com/watch?v=LxZoysYSLVQ
Derek Beaulieu, *UnCoupDeDes*, 2017. https://www.youtube.com/watch?v=n6eWscswC4c&feature=youtu.be
Sylvain Moore, *Troisième Coup de Dés*, 2019. https://www.youtube.com/watch?v=eFP1OQglKu8&feature=youtu.be
Jérémie Bennequin, *LE HASARD N'ABOLIRA JAMAIS UN COUP DE DÉS (Changes of Music): FILM*, 2020. https://jeremiebennequin.com/reversibilite-23

Imprint

COUP DE DÉS (COLLECTION)
Books and Ideas after Mallarmé

Editor: Michalis Pichler
Copy editing support: Jayne Wilkinson, Mark Soo / linguistic.services
Archivists: Julia Gwendolyn Schneider, Concetta Luise
Art direction: Michalis Pichler, Maira Fragoso Peña
Design: Maira Fragoso Peña, Ott Kagovere
Printed in the EU: Baltoprint, Vilnius
Paper: Munken Print white 90g
Typefaces: ITC Century Std and ABC Whyte
First edition: January 2024, 800 copies
Special edition: 50 copies with white cover

Copublished by: The Center For Book Arts, Spector Books

Spector Books
Harkortstraße 10
04107 Leipzig
www.spectorbooks.com

Center for Book Arts
28 West 27th St, 3rd Fl
New York, NY 10001
www.centerforbookarts.org

Distribution
Germany, Austria: GVA, Gemeinsame Verlagsauslieferung Göttingen GmbH&Co. KG, www.gva-verlage.de
Switzerland: AVA Verlagsauslieferung AG, www.ava.ch
France, Belgium: Interart Paris, www.interart.fr
UK: Central Books Ltd, www.centralbooks.com
USA, Canada, Central and South America, Africa: ARTBOOK/D.A.P., www.artbook.com
South Korea: The Book Society, www.thebooksociety.org
Japan: twelvebooks, www.twelve-books.com
Australia, New Zealand: Perimeter Distribution, www.perimeterdistribution.com

Photographs are reproduced courtesy of the creators and lenders of the material depicted. Every reasonable attempt has been made to identify the owners of copyright. Errors and omissions will be corrected in the subsequent editions.

Published on the occasion of the exhibition *Exposition littéraire autour de Mallarmé* at Center for Book Arts, January 18–May 1, 2024

ISBN: 978-1-951163-17-4
ISBN: 978-3-95905-817-9

About CBA
Center for Book Arts promotes active explorations of both contemporary and traditional artistic practices related to the book as art. CBA seeks to facilitate communication between the book arts community and the larger spheres of contemporary visual and literary arts, while being a model organization locally, nationally, and internationally within the field. We achieve this by presenting exhibitions, workshops, public programming, literary presentations, opportunities for artists and writers, publishing, and sharing our collections.

Support for the exhibition *Exposition littéraire autour de Mallarmé* and this catalog is provided in part by the National Endowment for the Arts; the New York State Council on the Arts with the support of Governor Kathy Hochul and the New York State Legislature, and by public funds from the New York City Department of Cultural Affairs, in partnership with the City Council.

Center for Book Arts SPECTOR BOOKS